QUAKERISM;

OR

THE STORY OF MY LIFE.

BY A LADY,

WHO FOR FORTY YEARS WAS A MEMBER OF THE SOCIETY

OF FRIENDS.

PHILADELPHIA.

J. W. MOORE, 193 CHESTNUT STREET.

1852.

PRINTED BY I. ASHMEAD.

CONTENTS.

CHAPTER I.

CHAPTER II.

CHAPTER III.

CHAPTER IV.

CHAPTER V.

CHAPTER VI.

CHAPTER VII.

CHAPTER VIII.

CHAPTER IX.

CHAPTER X.

CHAPTER XI.

CHAPTER XII.

CHAPTER XIII.

1*

PREFACE.

It is with a humiliating feeling of my own incompetence for the task I have undertaken, that I presume to offer these pages to the public eye. Circumstances over which I have had no control, have occurred to liberate me from the painful feelings which might deter others from speaking of the system in which they are incorporated. No desire to place myself ostentatiously before the public has influenced me; indeed I would have shrunk from revealing my personal experience, but that anxious to do good to the Society to which I once belonged, I could not hope to succeed in that effort without a simple detail; and therefore, I resolved to narrate what has come under my own observation, and that which I know to be authentic. Every scene I have delineated is drawn from nature; every circumstance I have related is substantially true. I have carefully abstained from exaggeration, and repeatedly thrown the veil of obscurity over the record of scenes which too strongly developed the subject I was treating.

So very little is known of the mystery of Quakerism, and so established is the character of the Society for respectability and morality, that I am quite prepared to find myself accused of ungenerous and malicious motives for writing; but persuaded that truth is after all the most powerful weapon which can be employed to accomplish any purpose, I have endeavoured to place it conspicuously forward, and on it alone I rely.

I have found it impossible to compose my sentences, so as to make my meaning intelligible to Quaker minds, without using the phraseology of the Society; and this I hope will be accepted as an apology for what might otherwise be considered as quaint and inelegant.

As a fire which has not been stirred, will burn away, and become so choked up with ashes as to be incapable of yielding warmth or light, and requires not merely a gentle application of the poker, but a strong and vigorous stirring up, to dislodge the burnt out, and rekindle the good coals, so I conceive the Society of Friends now needs a thorough good rousing; for the ashes have accumulated, and well nigh put out the fire. "The Beacon," a few years ago, gave a very decided stir, and there was a little corner brightened up by it. "Holy Scripture, the test of truth," stirred it again; but all too gently; and now my rough hand attempts to scatter the ashes, and rekindle the spark of life-giving heat.

My chief motive for writing is, because I see the precious souls of so many Friends perishing for lack of knowledge; the blind leaders have led and are leading the people astray; and I would hope, that by reading the nonsense, which when heard is generally allowed to pass away from the memory without leaving any impression, and by permitting common sense to assume its due empire, some at least may be ashamed any longer to submit to so degenerate, and may I not add, so demoralizing a creed.

The Society of Friends profess to be a religious and a Christian corporation; can they then object to come to the light that their deeds may be made manifest? And if they do object, is it not conclusive that they are conscious their deeds will not bear to be investigated, either by common sense or Scripture? Hitherto, Quakerism has enjoyed an immunity which no other public body in the land has claimed or sought for. The public press has not been allowed to bear upon it. Amongst themselves, the censorship of the press is actually tyrannical. The Quaker purse has so often been lavishly poured out to punish, by the heavy costs of a lawsuit, every person or newspaper that dared to publish anything derogatory of their wealthy and commercial fraternity, that now no one thinks it worth the risk of offending such implacable adversaries.

To consider the Society of Friends as a religious body, is a monstrous stretch of imagination. Respectable, active, intelligent, benevolent, useful, wealthy and influential, they undoubtedly are; but a man may be all this, and yet devoid of that religion, without which, he can never hope for life eternal.

The ridiculous nonsense of many of the scenes I have related will, doubtless, annoy the Friends; and those who have not attended the Meetings, or previously known the curious discipline of the Society, may perhaps imagine, that the men's Meetings are more sensible than the women's; they will be greatly mistaken who do so; the women are infinitely the most religious portion of the community. There are twenty women preachers or more, to one man. But when the Bible is superseded, the commandments neglected, and man's imaginings allowed to assume the place of the law of the Lord, what can the Christian expect to meet but error and folly, delusion, and alas! a soul-destroying system of self-deception.

Should Friends venture to intimate that as an anonymous writer I have presumed to step beyond the line of truth, or even to colour my pictures too highly, I am ready to meet them in a second edition, which cannot be called for too soon, and in it to give not only my own name, but also the true name of every single actor in my drama, the place and time of each circumstance, and the original documents from which my story is condensed.

In performing a task—which may be considered an invidious one, and will no doubt be reprobated by Friends, as it is designed to strip the Society of the flimsy covering which has so long shrouded its workkings—I am cheered with the hope, that the souls now perilled by the false and specious system may be roused, ere too late, and that a determination may spring up to refuse the silly babblings of those incapable preachers who now infest the Society, and to insist on the Bible being read, and its truths preached. The Apostle Paul commands, that if even an angel from heaven should attempt to preach any other doctrine than that revealed in Holy Writ, he should not be received, as all other is counterfeit—is base coin, which will not pass current in that day when the secrets of all hearts shall be revealed, and judged according to the glorious Gospel of our Lord and Saviour Jesus Christ. Eternity is not a fable, neither is the judgment day an hypothesis; therefore it behooves Friends, as well as all other men, to make their calling and election sure. Many and many a Quaker has sunk into the sleep of endless death, lulled into a false security by these blind guides. How can an unconverted, an unregenerate, an unenlightened mortal point a fellow-sinner to the Christian's rock of safety? They know it not themselves; and the slang language they adopt to disguise their ignorance, is ruining their own souls, as well as those who depend upon them. "Faith cometh by hearing, and hearing by the Word of God." Let then the Word, the written Word, the Holy Scriptures, be taken for a guide, as they are indeed the only safe guide to steer a mortal man through the perils of time, the temptations of the devil, and the snares of the world, in safety to the grave, and to the judgment which must follow it.

Dublin, April, 1851.

QUAKERISM.

CHAPTER I.

Reasons for writing—Ancestry—Emigration to Ireland—My home—Orangewoman's ideas of dress—First school—Knee Worship—Mental occupation in Meetings.

I HAVE often asked myself, Can it be, that the story of the life of an obscure Quakeress would interest the public?

It is said, that every page of social life has already been unfolded, that every phrase of domestic manners has been portrayed; but, as I have never met any thing in print, that was at all like the life I so long led, I am tempted to hope, that these pages may have the charm of novelty, if nothing better, to recommend them.

It is true that Friends' libraries, contain many volumes of memoirs. The lives of many Friends have been written; but as these books must, before they are published, be subjected to the severe censorship of the "Morning Meeting," by which they are unsparingly curtailed of all matter, which it is thought desirable to conceal from public view, they are but partial records. Besides, it is only the lives of persons who have been prominent in the Society, and who have reflected credit on it, by their public preaching, or eminent situation, that it has been thought worth while to commemorate.

I hope I am not mistaken in imagining that the true and simple record of what passed before my eyes, may prove both instructive and interesting.

In the reign of Charles II., when religious persecution assailed the Quakers on every side, several families of them banded together, resigned both titles and estates, and emigrated to Ireland. Amongst these men was one, who, though he had lost an Earldom, had retained much wealth. He was my father's ancestor; and a portion of the lands he purchased, are in my brother's possession to this day. My mother's family came from England also, but at a much later period. They came to Ireland likewise, to obtain freedom to worship God according to the mode their own conscience or feelings demanded. We were often taunted, and called a proud family; and if it is good to confess one's faults, I may as well own that we quite deserved the name, for we were, aye, and are, proud of our descent from the noble and the good; and the moral excellence of one ancestor, and the intellectual superiority of the other, have been as magnets to attract us on the road to virtue. And perhaps the sacrifices they made, to obtain mental freedom, have influenced their descendants, in these degenerate days, to assert that right to liberty of thought and action, which the Society of Friends now, forbids its members to exercise.

My father was a wealthy merchant, and an extensive landed proprietor. Our dwelling, a short distance from the town, stood in a lawn of about ten acres. The garden was large, and as well as the conservatories and shrubberies, was always kept in the most complete and elegant order. My mother had her chariot; we, girls, had a handsome open barouche, for my father's own use was a stanhope; and there was the jaunting car for every body. There were seldom less than six horses in the stable, and often more; for my brothers were fond of riding, and were first-rate horsemen.

My father bore a more than unblemished character. There was not a man in the city who stood higher in general estimation. Our Bishop, Dean, and the noble and learned representatives of both county and city, greeted him with a cordial shake of the hand when they met. He was a learned man; had graduated at Trinity College; and could speak and write both the French, Spanish, Portuguese and Dutch languages; in addition to an accurate acquaintance with Greek and Latin. Besides all this, he was conscientiously, and scrupulously, a plain Quaker. Having passed through all the minor gradations in the Society, such as clerk and overseer, he was at last appointed an Elder; after having for five years, at each succeeding Quarterly Meeting, when the office was pressed upon him, declined it. And when at length he yielded to the desire of the Meeting, and suffered his name to be enrolled amongst the Elders of the Society, it was in very great humility of mind, and fearfulness of heart, lest he should prove unworthy of so high a nomination.

My father's lofty descent, his wealth, liberality, education, his character as a citizen, and his ardent attachment to the principles of the Society, caused his family to rank high, and gave them pre-eminence in all the Meetings. The best and foremost seats were offered them in Meetings; and out of it, their society was courted.

My childhood was a very happy one. Six brothers and sisters of us, sporting about our beautiful lawns; and surrounded with every conceivable comfort and luxury, with which my mother's care, and exquisite taste, had embellished our home; we were all happy; I well remember how often I thought myself supremely so.

The first time that I became aware of our Quakerism, was when I was very young. My sister Ellen and I, were standing at the hall-door, watching some baskets of oranges, which two old fruit women had brought for sale. One of them was an old acquaintance, the other a stranger. I suppose they thought us too young to mind speaking before us, for one said—"I thought you told me that Mrs. Peregine was very rich, and just look at them children, how ugly they are dressed?" "Oh! no," said the other, "it is not ugly they are, but she is a Quaker, so she dresses them pretty and plain, for that is her notion of duty, the cratur." The oranges were bought, and the fruit women went away. But the mysterious connection between my mother's duty, and our ugly dresses, puzzled me. I did not know before, that they were so ugly. As I had then no intercourse whatever with the "people of the world," I had no idea how other children were attired; and we were undoubtedly the best dressed in our own Meeting. Our first day frocks were made of beautifully fine cambric, with rows of herringbone, exquisitely worked, over each of the six tucks. Our Friends' bonnets were of the richest and most delicate drab silk; and our silk tippets, to match, had a row of stitching over the broad hem, instead of the plain running. I could not understand why our dress was called ugly by these poor, shabby, barefooted women; and after keeping the matter in my mind for weeks, at last I summoned courage, and asked my father himself to explain it. A smile spread itself over his dear grave face, as he said, it was quite time for me to understand, that it was a rule of our Society, that we should dress plain. "But," he added, "do not think it ugly, and what matter what those poor women think or say." He then explained to me, that "plainness of speech, behaviour and apparel," was a cross which Friends were given to bear in the sight of the world, as a testimony against the vain fashions and vanities of life, by which others were ensnared and led away.

The matter ended there, though I was not satisfied,

nor could I understand it. But it was a great comfort to know, that my father did not think it ugly; and I felt, as if rather elevated, at the idea of superiority over the rest of the world, and proud of having a cross to bear.

Soon after this I was sent to a day school, kept by a lady, in the outskirts of the city. She was not a Friend, and the greater number of her pupils were not neither. Some few were. I was very strictly charged to remember that I was a Friend—not to say *you* to any one; and not to pick up any unfriendly habits or words.

It was a great event to me, and I felt quite elated when mounted on a well appointed donkey, and attended by the old coachman, carrying my books, I set off for school for the first time. But before I reached the house, I had to endure a great mortification. The rude boys, out of the cabins, stared at me, shouted, and I distinctly heard them saying—"Oh! look! there is a little 'thee and thou' on a donkey!" And "oh! what a bonnet!" And some of them ran after me the whole way, singing out, "Thee and Thou the Quaker's cow."

The mistress received me very kindly, but she too vexed me; for I saw her smile at my bonnet as she untied, and placed it on a table among all the other children's straw bonnets. I saw that it was, indeed, a very ugly thing, but there was no time to think about it then; I was hurried into the school-room, and formally introduced to my twenty-three fellow-pupils. Oh! how they all looked at me! They did not say so, but I felt satisfied that they thought me very ugly; and I almost hated myself for my odious Quaker dress. But this was only the beginning of my troubles. After a little time, I was desired to learn a task, which seemed to me, unreasonably difficult. It was twelve words of two syllable spelling. I looked at it in despair, and then said, "I tell thee Charlotte, I never could learn such a long lesson." She smiled, and the girls all tittered. I saw they were laughing at me; and, vexed, mortified, and puzzled to know the cause of my annoyance, I looked about, and seeing the sash of a low window up, which opened into the garden, I sprang out, and ran down the walk; and when quite out of sight, sat down on the grass, and indulged myself with a good hearty fit of crying.

I was just beginning to get tired of that amusement, when one of the girls, a little older than myself, came and sat down beside me. She looked so pretty, and was so kind and gentle, that she soon wiled me out of my bad temper, and then I asked her why they all laughed at me?

"Why," said she, "it was so funny to hear you say Charlotte to Miss Vivier, and you said, 'I tell *thee*'—we never heard any one say such a thing before. You may call me Sophy, and you may call all the girls by their names, if you like it, but you must never be so rude as to call Miss Vivier, anything but Miss Vivier."

"But," said I, "I did not mean to be rude, only I am a Friend, and Friends are not allowed to say *Miss* to any one. And sure thee would not have me be so wicked as to say *you* to any one."

"Well, no matter now," said Sophy, "but come back to school, or Miss Vivier will be angry with us —you will be wiser in a few days."

We returned together, and as we entered the room I observed that Sophy made a slight but very graceful curtsey. I was very sorry to see her do so bad a thing; for not long before, I had heard a plain Friend speaking about the "people of the world" curtseying, and she called it "knee worship;" so that I was quite horrified when Miss Vivier called me over, and said—"Miss Peregrine, do not leave the room again, without asking permission, and then go out by the door, not by the window; and when you come into the room, make a curtsey, as all well taught young ladies do. Go back now, and come in as you saw Miss Sophy, just now."

I was afraid to speak, lest they should laugh at me again. So I obeyed with a very bad grace, for it was against my conscience, and made a very awkward kind of a full stop at the door, which was allowed to pass for that day. I was very glad when the time came to go home; and as the car had been sent for me, I had no more annoyance from the rude boys.

Mamma met me at the door. She saw the traces of tears, and asked the cause. I told her all. She smiled and kissed me, and told me not to fret about such things, that it was no sin at all, to say *Miss* or *you*, either, or to curtsey. That as papa liked us to be Friends, and use the plain language, we must do so among Friends, but that there was not one word about such things in the Bible.

"Well then, Mamma, said I, if it is no sin to say Miss, because it is not forbid in the Bible, it would be no sin to give me a straw bonnet, for that is not in the Bible either, I am sure." Oh! how fondly I loved her; when I saw her dear face smiling again, and she desired me to go call back the car, and she would take me to town and buy me a straw bonnet. She did so, and all my vexations ceased. The girls congratulated me next day on my pretty bonnet; and though my attempted curtsey was still only a full stop; and though I sometimes forgot myself, and said *thee*, yet I felt as if a mountain had fallen off me, and to my great surprise I had no pricking of conscience, which I was fearful would have tormented me, as it always did when I told a lie, or stole anything nice out of the closet at home.

I continued at that school for three years. My companions there, are all scattered over the face of the earth, or lie hid beneath its bosom. I soon lost sight of them; but Miss Vivier, my clever, sweet-tempered, affectionate teacher, continued to be my friend until a very short time since, when it pleased the Almighty to recall her to himself, from the fond husband and cherished family to whom she was most dear. She was married to a most estimable gentleman, soon after I left her school.

I was always afterwards allowed to wear my straw bonnet in summer, and a drab beaver in winter, every where except at Meeting. Going there, I had to put on the cold stiff badge of the Society.

Oh! what a weariness those long formal first-day Morning Meetings were to me! Sometimes I would resolve to be good, and try to think holy things. It was impossible. I could not keep on for two hours at a time, thinking religion, without getting any external help. Our meeting was a very large one. We had five women ministers, and one man. He was then only just "acknowledged," and seldom spoke; and when he did, he shook so much, and his voice trembled so greatly, his eyes were shut very tight, and his two large hands spread out on the gallery railing, that it was quite an awful thing to me, to hear him, though indeed I never then thought of attending to the purport of his sermons. They were not intended for the comprehension of a child.

There was one of the women ministers who seldom spoke, but I liked to see her stand up. I could understand her. She would say something like this:—"Since I took my seat in this Meeting, these few words have been greatly impressed on my mind. Oh! that my people were wise, that they would consider their latter end!" She rarely gave utterance to a longer sentence, and though she did jerk it out in a very extraordinary manner, still it was pleasant to hear her.

Then there was Mary Dalton; she was, as our Friends used to say, "very large in the ministry."

She could keep on for an hour and more at a time. I have by me a book, containing some dozens of her sermons, taken down by my dear mother; and they are such long rambling discourses, that it would be a wonder if any child attended to them.

The way I tried to get over the time generally, was saying over in my mind all my hymns, verses, and songs; I had a good large stock of all these in my memory. Then I would reckon first the women, and then the men; then the men who wore broad brims, and then those who wore churn hats; then the plain women who had their bonnets plaited, and then the gay young Friends who had gathers and frills behind. This was, no doubt, all very silly and very childish, but I was very young then. When I grew older, I had other kinds of ideas, more sensible and more amusing, but quite as far off from religion, or even the most distant approach to worship.

We always drove to Meeting in the carriage, and I used to feel very well satisfied at stepping in before so many watchers, to the best appointed of all the equipages that waited at the gate. The men leaving the Meeting first, would cluster round the hall and gate to wait for the women, or it might be to gaze at them. Every Friend who owned a car or carriage, was sure to have it there on first days, even those who lived in the next street, would drive to Meeting. My dear father highly disapproved of this custom; he always walked, whether wet or fine; and I have often heard him say, he never took cold from sitting in Meeting in damp clothes or wet shoes.

CHAPTER II.

Visit to Cork—Immigration of souls from Purgatory—Bible reading —Old Dolly—Chapel of the Presentation Convent—Church—Quaker servant—Novels—Pious roguery—Teachers.

My first excursion from home, was a visit to Cork, with my mother, and an uncle, who lived with us. We travelled with our own carriage and horses, and were four days on the road. I enjoyed greatly the journey; the inns seemed to me such wonderful places; and the strange beds, and the people talking Irish; and some of them looked so wretched, and some so savage, and my uncle told me delightful stories; and one about robbers, just as we were driving over Watergrass Hill, which was then notorious for its lawless and brutal inhabitants.

We were going to visit a lady, not a Friend, an old acquaintance of my mother's; and the idea of going among "the people of the world," was a delightful idea to me, although I more than half thought I was going into a den of wickedness; for a firm conviction had been very early implanted in my mind, that whatever was not quakerish, was wicked. How I had imbibed the notion I cannot tell, certainly, it was not from my mother. She was no bigot, and it was only to please my father, that she either wore the dress of the Society herself, or put it on her daughters.

Cork was my mother's native-place; and as most of her relations lived there, we had many visitors. We went to several large dinner parties; our conveyance was a sedan chair. I had several nice dresses, and was taken much notice of; and as my dear mother was in the habit every night of requiring me to give her a kind of resume of all that passed in the day, before I repeated the Lord's prayer on my knees, as usual, it all made a great impression on my memory.

It is a most advantageous habit to acquire, that of rehearsing to one's-self, nightly, the events of the day. Though many, or most of them, may appear too trifling to be worth impressing so firmly on the mind; yet, as every trifle, as well as every passing word, will undoubtedly be revived in our memory at the day of judgment, it is well to ponder over them beforehand. We have a sure promise, that all things shall work together for good to those who love God. I am sure, there is not one of those most trifling circumstances which I am now recording, that has not exercised a great influence over me, and that has not eventually conduced very greatly to my happiness.

We were in Cork on All Souls' Day; and my mother, accompanied by some of her friends, went in the evening to the Roman Catholic Cathedral, having heard that there would be there a curious exhibition of the efficacy of prayers for the dead. She told me that on going in, the Chapel was dazzlingly light.

Wax candles three feet high, blazed upon the altar; and every one of the numerous priests in attendance carried in his hand a lighted taper. One of them gave an oration, or sermon, on the inestimable value of masses for the souls in purgatory; and assured his hearers, that that very evening, they should behold the souls of their own dead ancestors; who, having spent years in torment, were now, thanks to the masses offered up in that Chapel, emancipated from their misery, and going to enter into the regions of glory. When he ceased speaking, the prayers for the dead were chanted. The lights gradually went out, until the whole chapel and its vast congregation were in total darkness; then, a sickly glare was visible around the altar; and in that dim light, was distinctly seen a number of small, bright-red, queer looking objects, passing over it. One of the priests, as if in an ecstasy, then gave thanks for the answer to his prayers; and called on the people to be no longer faithless, but believing, as they now saw with their own eyes, that souls were indeed released from purgatory by the prayers of the Church.

This curious exhibition interested me greatly; and we were all guessing and puzzling ourselves to understand it, but in vain. However, before leaving Cork, my mother went to pay a visit to her old nurse, and took me with her. The old woman was delighted to see her foster child; and called her as of old, "my own dear Miss Mary." They chatted together for a long time, giving each other intelligence of their different families. At last my mother asked for James, her own foster brother. Nurse said, he was well, and had now got a fine situation. He was clerk to the priest. Whilst speaking of him, James came in. A nice looking man, with an eye beaming with fun and good humour. He was most cordial in his welcome; and my mother, with her usual tact, set him at his ease. In a few moments he joined in the conversation, but I forget all they said, except one part, that no one could ever forget that heard it. My mother told them of her visit to the chapel, and of the queer things she had seen crawling over the altar; and she asked James what they were? "The souls, to be sure, ma'am," said James. But my mother laughed, and said, surely he knew she was only a heretic; and he might gratify her, by telling what they really were. "Indeed then," said James, "when you were a child, like myself, I never could refuse you any thing; and I am sure I wont begin to deny you now; and besides, as you say, you are a heretic; and I wish I had half as good a chance of heaven, for all that, as you have; but at any rate, there is no chance of the priest ever knowing that I told you; so you may as well hear it. It was I, myself, that got them for him; I got all the crabs I could lay my hands on, for love or money; and Father Kelly and I put the little red cloth jackets on them; and we had a thread fastened to every one of them; if they did not chose to walk right, to make them. And, you know, it was so dark, you could not see much about it; and now, ma'am dear, was in not a capital clever delusion for the poor ignorant creatures that believe every thing?"

Soon after our return home, we received a visit from two men Friends, who had been appointed by the Monthly Meeting, in accordance with directions from the Dublin Yearly Meeting, to go about to each family, and to admonish them, that the Yearly Meeting deemed it advisable they should read the Holy Scriptures daily aloud in their families. The Friends were received most respectfully; they performed their task very seriously, and were then regaled with cake, fruit, and wine. We had been in the habit of reading the Bible after breakfast every morning, as long as ever I could remember; but previous to this visitation, I believe it was not the habit of Friends generally to do so.

I was very fond of reading; Bibles were not then as easily to be had as they are now. I greatly desired to have one of my own; but it was many years before I accomplished my wish. At last, however, I succeeded, and I still possess the remains of the precious treasure, for which I paid eleven shillings; I could now purchase as good for two.

In addition to my father's daily readings, and to his repeated verbal instruction, I had another opportunity of acquiring spiritual knowledge. Our old housekeeper, Dolly, had been married to a Roman Catholic, and by him, forced to unite herself to his Church. He was captain of a band in the rebellion of 1798; and whilst in the thick of the battle which was fought on the bridge of Ross, was, with many other rebels, thrown over the bridge, and perished in the waters. He had left a will; and in it directed his widow to pay two shillings and six-pence monthly to the priest for masses for his soul. This Dolly regularly paid. We found after her death a pile of receipts amounting to over £50. Out of what she deemed respect to his memory, she continued to go to Chapel regularly; but she was too much enlightened to yield herself entirely to the teaching of the priest, and read her Bible indefatigably. About the time I now allude to, her sight was very defective; and knowing how fond I was of reading, she proposed to me to read for her; and as doing so, might involve some personal sacrifice, she promised to give me a fresh egg for my breakfast every morning. I greatly disliked my usual bread and milk fare, and she knew I did so. I accepted the terms, and night after night, when my mother imagined me to be in bed, I was in Dolly's own little parlour, reading the Bible, the Douay version, whilst she darned her black stockings. I used to wonder they were never mended; for month after month, it was the same pair she worked away at; but at last I found out it was only doll idle stitch she did, for the poor woman could not see to do better; and she fancied that I would read more willingly, if she were employed.

When I was about ten years old, I had a great desire to go see the celebration of mass at a Chapel; and as I well knew there would be no use in asking leave to go, and unwilling to disobey, I coaxed our maid, Jenny Freeman, to take me with her, early one Good Friday morning, before the family were up, or aware of our departure.

We went to the Chapel attached to the Presentation Convent. I was indeed delighted, the altar was so beautifully ornamented; beside it was a wax doll, exquisitely dressed, to represent the Virgin Mary;—there was a real cradle, and a little wax doll in it, with the prettiest lace cap on its little head;—the quilt was white satin, embroidered with gold, to represent a lamb with a cross, as if held in its fore feet; and the flowers which were strewn so profusely around. I never before saw such elegant artificial flowers; and they were all highly perfumed. I pressed as close as possible to get a good view, and quite forgot to pay attention to all that was going on, until I was recalled to it, by feeling a great pull to my frock; I then looked round, and saw that all the people were kneeling; and the old woman who had pulled my dress whispered very loudly—"Go down on your knees, you heretic." I looked down, rather bewildered, and seeing the floor was very dirty, I said—"Oh! no, it would soil my frock, and mamma would be angry with me for it." An old soldier was near; I believe he knew who I was; he grinned, and made a face at the woman, and said—"Whist you; 'tis too dirty for you, Miss; so go over to the wall there, and may be his reverence wont pretend to see you." It was a very pretty show altogether; there were about a dozen priests, and they went in and out, always returning in a different dress; and two pretty little boys dressed in white, tossed the silver censers of incense about; and the nuns peeped out now and then from behind their screen. I thought it the prettiest piece of raree show I had ever seen, and well worth the reprimand I expected to receive on returning home. However, it was poor Jenny got all the blame; and I was so emboldened by my escape, that I resolved to watch for an opportunity to go see the Protestant Cathedral also. It was a long time before I attained my wish; and when I did, it was a great disappointment to me; for I had fancied there would be pretty things to see; and instead of that, it was only prayers that I could understand, and a sermon as long as one of those of our own Women Friends; besides, reading the Bible —which any one could do.

My father had a tolerably large and well selected library; there were several Spanish and Portuguese novels, but only two English in the whole collection. These two, Sir Charles Grandison, and the Modern Philosopher, he had purchased at an auction, and had never read them himself. I read them over and over again; partly because I liked them, and partly because I so often heard Friends preaching against reading novels; who, whilst they acknowledged generally having themselves been very fond of so doing, warned us of the danger, because they were so very fascinating. Therefore I craved after them, and in a way I little expected, my desire was gratified to its full extent.

Some of our overseers bethought them, that in a large family like ours, it would be well to have Friend-servants. They visited my mother on the subject; and as such visits are made professedly as being the result of a kind of inspiration, or as being the teaching of "best wisdom;" and are always commenced by sitting down in deep silence, with the visitee, in an awful solemn way, they were of course received with the greatest respect; and although, when these overseers had relieved their minds, as they said, of this burden laid upon them, and gone away, my mother candidly expressed her opinion, that they were a pair of busy bodies, meddling with what did not belong to them; yet she submitted, and received into the family an elderly Quaker, as head nurse-maid, Katey Rutter. She was fat, and fair, and very well looking. Her face was radiant with good humour and fun; her dress was orthodox; but she wore no stays, and was rather untidy. Her husband, a plain country Quaker, had turned out a vile scamp, and deserted her, leaving Katey and three children to be provided for by the Meeting to which they belonged. The children were placed at the provincial school, and Katey quartered on us. She proved an excellent servant, and most faithfully she performed her duty during the ten years she remained. But except in her dress, and her plain language, Katey was but little of a Quaker; and among others of her unquakerly propensities, was an ardent love of novel reading. It was by chance I discovered this; and when I did, I bargained with her, that I would not tell on her, provided she let me read them. She had an acquaintance in town, who kept a circulating library, and we had the full benefit of it, and all for nothing, but a basket of apples now and then, and a nosegay, which was never refused when Katey asked leave to have them, for her friend.

Katey's children being at the provincial school, led us often to visit it. They, as well as others of the children, were usually, about four at a time, invited to dine with us every first day. I did not then care anything about the system of education pursued there; but I remember being rather surprised, when Katey's daughter, after being seven years under what was called careful instruction, asked me one day to find out the story of Telemachus in the Bible for her.

There was also just then, a young man, who had been under the same careful teaching for seven years, the full time children are kept at that school, whose conduct had annoyed us exceedingly. He had been taken into the office of a most respectable merchant in Limerick; and on the strength of the good principles supposed to have been planted at the provincial school, he was placed in a situation of trust. He was no relative or connection of ours; but being a quiet, gentle lad, and but little noticed by others, my father had often taken him out of the ranks, as one of our first day dinner boys. He appreciated the kindly feeling, and turned it to value for himself.

At the time of our Quarterly Meeting, he told his employer that he felt a "drawing" to attend it; and asked permission, which was readily granted. He then wrote to my father, very humbly asking, would his ever kind and valued friend accommodate him with a bed, whilst the Meeting lasted, about three days. His request was thought presumptuous, but it was acceded to; and he arrived duly, as sanctified, and demure a looking youth, as ever wore knee breeches, standing collar, and broad brim. He attended both the first day Meetings; and looked so pious, that his former acquaintances concluded he was enduring "those turnings and over-turnings, and siftings," out of which, we are told, "the standard bearers of the Society come forth, purified for service." The next morning he received a letter, on reading which, he sighed, and told us, that he was obliged to leave immediately, that his master desired him to retnrn by the night's coach. Off he went, and we were all glad, for nobody liked him; though nobody could tell why. It was just a week after, when his master wrote to my father, to request we would not detain him any longer. Letters were exchanged; and then it came out, that this pious youth had levanted with £500—joined another dissolute young man, and sailed for South America, where he enrolled himself in a Portuguese regiment, and was killed in a drunken brawl.

As my mother was very anxious that we should be well educated, it was resolved in a family council, that we should have an English governess. Numerous applications were made for the situation, and one highly recommended was selected, at a salary of £100 per annum—Hannah Watthamstow. She was a native of Leeds, and had been educated at Ackworth School. She was a very nice lady-like Friend, about twenty-five years of age, fully competent to instruct us in the English language. As a good grammarian, a pleasing reader, and a beautiful writer, I have never met any one who excelled her. But we had commenced Latin and French, and it was quite a disappointment to find her totally ignorant of these branches, as well as of drawing. Indeed she thought it strange, that in a Friend's family such acquirements should be desired. So we had masters for these; a Friend for Latin—a churchman for drawing—and for French, Monsieur Tournay, the very model of a Frenchman; so small, so dapper, so polite, so exquisite in his finical proprieties, and withal so learned, that France his country, and Frenchmen his people, are ever since, for his sake, enveloped in an atmosphere of agreeability.

CHAPTER III.

Monthly Meeting—Contrast in character—Story of a robber—Executions—Archbishop of Tuam—Girl's school—Value of tears—Pious pockets—Preachings—Robbery—Visit to an elder—Novels—Return home.

I NOW began to attend the Monthly Meetings; and as I find among my papers, a relation of one of them, which I well remember, my governess giving me a good scolding for daring to write down, I will copy it here nearly verbatim.

Seventy women Friends, without counting the children, met in the Women's Monthly Meeting-Room, and took their seats in silence, showing, however, occasional acts of politeness to the elders, arranging comfortable cushions, and footstools. The silence continued unbroken for about ten minutes, when a minister arose, stood still for a couple of minutes, and then said—"Silence had been the covering of her mind, that she had desired to remain in silence; but felt that she could not have peace, and keep her peace; that she felt the language was going forth—Come out, come out, come out of her my people. Oh! that there might be a coming out; then peace would flow as a river, and righteousness as the waves of the sea." She resumed her seat, and a silence for about five minutes ensued. Then the clerk, a plain middle aged Friend—(our clerks and assistant clerks, were generally either widows or unmarried women)—rose up, and read from a large, heavy manuscript volume, the proceedings of the last Monthly Meeting; the appointments which had then been made, repeating the names, and calling for replies from those so appointed. She sat down, and after a short pause, up rose a dear sober-looking Friend, who said—she, and the other Friend named with her, (appointments are always made in couples,) had performed the service to which they had been nominated, and had found peace in so doing. The duty was to inform a young Friend, lately come to live in the city, of the receipt and acceptance of her certificate. A certificate of membership, and good conduct, and freedom from marriage engagement, had been received at the last meeting; as usual, when one Friend removes from the compass of one Meeting to reside within the compass of another. Then the assistant clerk rose, and read out of the Printed Book of Minutes the ten queries. The first, on attendance of Meetings, called forth a defective answer from the trembling overseer, to whom the duty appertained of replying; and as she had a very bad memory, and no one is allowed to give a written reply, she made many attempts to utter the few words required, before she succeeded. Then another pause of three minutes, and the second query, and so on all through the ten.

There are always some exceptions made in the answer to the query, as to Friends maintaining plain-

4

ness of speech, behaviour and apparel. It appears to be the most important of all the dogmas of our Society; at least there is always more preaching about it, and a stricter scrutiny into the answer given, than on any other point. On the present occasion, our minister, who had opened the Meeting, spoke on the subject in the most awfully solemn voice, (clutching a firm hold of the back of the seat near her) much as follows:—"If we were more careful to attend to the litle things—to give up the little things—to make the little sacrifices, oh! how different should we be! Oh, my dear friends!—my sisters! I did not wish to speak amongst you this day; but I feel that I am called on. Oh! dear friends, let us be faithful to those precious testimonies, which are given us to bear; let us be faithful. Now is the time; now is the acceptable time; the Lord's controversy is against those vanities and corruptions, with which so many amongst us are led away. Those Babylonish garments! Ah! my dear young Friends! you will not find a better way! Come now I entreat you in much love. I entreat you to cast away those outward adornings—those frills—those plaited frills—they are a snare unto you. Now, now is the time; cast those vanities hence, and ye shall find peace and joy. Yea, ye shall be as standard-bearers, raised up in the midst of a faithless and perverse generation, to uphold those precious testimonies, which our worthy predecessors were in best wisdom enabled to give forth."

This solemn address caused a feeling of deep awe,

and a prolonged silence, which was broken by a younger Friend. It was her first attempt, I believe, at preaching. (She has since joined the white Friends.) She was of a very plain countenance, and studiously plain in her dress. She rose slowly, grasped the back of the seat before her, and stood trembling, and greatly agitated. At last, in very broken accents she said—a concern had long rested on her mind, that Friends should "walk close;" that she was jealous for her dear sisters; that she wished they could see it right to wear plaits in their bonnets, instead of gathers; that she hoped no one would think this a trifle; it was by trifles people fell: and that it was under a feeling of great weight she was made willing to say those few words.

Then we had another long silence, during which glances were exchanged, which told plainly enough that some of the assembly did not quite relish this last address. However, nothing was said, and the clerk again went on with the queries. "Is there amongst you any growth in the truth?" The overseer made answer—"We believe there is amongst us a growth in the truth." She sat down, and soon a minister rose and said—she did fear it would hardly be right to use so strong a word as "believe;" she thought the word "trust" would be more suitable. An elder shortly after remarked, that she would be glad Friends could allow the word "believe" to remain; she did not think it was too strong. Another Friend, after two minutes' pause, thought "trust" would be preferable, on which the Friend who first suggested the alteration, rose again, and said—she was quite willing Friends should use the word "believe," if they thought it best. She then resumed her seat with rather an offended dignity air. A very long silence now came on, and then the clerk got up and said, she would be glad Friends would say, which word was to be inserted in the answer? She got no reply for a long time; at length a very intelligent nice looking Friend, who sat far away from the table, rose, and in a clear steady voice, said—"I would suggest the word 'hope,' perhaps it would meet the case." The moment she sat down—(for not being one of those accustomed to speak in Meetings, and having, morever, an unhemmed shawl on, with a collar of the most delicate fabric, no regard is ever paid to what such a one may say)—the first objector stood up, and ordered the clerk somewhat peremptorily to insert the very word at which she herself had first cavilled. And then after sitting down, whilst the clerk took up the pen to obey her, she again rose, and with an extra attempt at solemnity, spoke as follows:—"It is an awful thing for one, who is not of the called, to presume to touch the ark. For so doing Uzzah perished; and so let all thine enemies perish, oh, Lord! These are solemn Meetings, and my soul trembleth within me. Oh! it is a very solemn thing to speak in Meetings of discipline, to keep down the willings and the runnings. To be willing to sit still, this is what the Lord requires of us, this controversy is against the willings and the runnings. We must come down—come down. It is very painful for me to be called on to speak in this manner, but I dare not withhold; and I feel I am made willing to submit to the requirings of the life within."

She continued for a long time in the same strain and at last, to the great joy of every one, sat down. Whenever such a person as Betsey, who had suggested the word hope, presumes to speak in Meeting, though all have nominally the right equally to do so, they are invariably put down, snubbed as it were; and generally, or at least very often, a sermon preached, not to, but at them. A registry of birth was then read; also an Epistle from one of the American Meetings; and a message then sent to the Men's Meeting, sitting in another room, to ask, if they had any business to communicate to Women Friends. They kept us waiting a weary while; and then sent in a paper of disunion, testifying against a young man who had so far neglected the shinings of the light within, as to suffer himself to be joined in marriage with a person not of our society; thus ceasing to uphold our ancient and valuable testimony against a hireling ministry. After reading over the minutes of the whole, and a short silence, the ministers shook hands with each other, and all rose to depart.

Friends are frequently admonished not to speak out of doors of any thing that passes in the Monthly Meetings. Few of the advices there given have more wisdom in them than this. Often and often have I heard in them advices given, in a kind of half preaching way, which would redound but little to the common sense of the sisterhood. I have heard women Friends advised to burn all newspapers that came into their houses, to prevent their husbands, sons, and brothers from reading them. I could fill a volume, were I to write down all the advices I have heard given in those Meetings, about different articles of dress, curls, side-combs; every possible minutiæ has, from time to time, been expiated on, and censured ad nauseum. And, alas! these senseless ravings are given forth, as if the speakers were under the influence of immediate inspiration.

I attribute my mother's many unquakerly habits to the very superior education she had received at a first-rate Boarding-school, near London. There were several young Friends at it as well as herself, but the mistress was an Episcopalian. However it was, my mother had formed the opinion, that if a subject was of sufficient importance to be spoken of in our meetings, it was surely worth attention and reflection out of them. And also, that if it was not right to speak of such things out of Meetings, it was much less right to speak of them there.

We were early acustomed to discuss these things among ourselves, and anything very flagrant we told to our father; but being an elder, and in duty bound to take notice of them, he did not like to be told, lest it should bring him into collision with the women, about half a dozen of whom ruled the men as well as the women, with an arbitrary and tyrannical sway.

There was a little woman in our Meeting, whom no one seemed to think it worth while to speak to, or notice. She was so much accustomed to be thrust aside, that she was in the habit of running home before the crowd, which always loiters in the halls of our Meetings, to chat and exchange greetings, had come out. My father used to call her the Honourable Betty Green. He said if any one ever deserved that title, she did. Her husband, a dissolute, bad, old Quaker, died, and left her in poverty, and deeply in debt, with a family to provide for. Betty had a soul above dependence; and respectfully declined to receive assistance from the Meeting. She toiled on for years, and at last startled us all, by putting an advertisement in the Newspaper, inviting all her husband's creditors to furnish their accounts to her. She paid them every farthing due, and interest, and then relapsed into her old quiet way. And at her death, left her only surviving child a handsome independence. My father was her only confidant. He had lent her the fifty pounds she required for a commencement, and had cheered her on in her honourable course. Hers was the first funeral I attended. It was conducted all in silence, and few tears were shed for her. She died as she had lived, humbly, solitary, and neglected by the Friends. But who will say, that her happy and glorified spirit, does not now rank as high as the spirit of that self-righteous woman, who, because she was a minister, would sweep past poor Betty, nor deign to look a return to the timid salutation I have often seen given. That minister, was like Betty, left a widow, and her husband died in debt.

But no effort was made to pay his creditors. On the contrary, by the death of wealthy relatives, riches flowed in upon her. She lived in luxury, and died of over-eating. I was at her funeral also. It was very large, and Friend after Friend preached at the grave, or rather eulogized the departed, and spoke of her as one of the bright shining lights of our Society; calling on the young people to follow in the steps she had trod. And all this laudation—would it have been given had she not been rich, and gifted with effrontery to stand up, and with her bonnet off, her head merely covered with a little black silk skull cap, speak for an hour or more at a time? I trow not.

Our family was accustomed to spend a couple of months each summer, at the sea side. One evening when my father and uncle were driving there to meet us, they were attacked by three robbers. One seized the horse, and one at each side of the gig, with a loaded pistol, threateningly held up, demanded their money and watches. Of course there was nothing for it, but to obey. As my father gave his, he said to the robber—"If ever thou shouldst want a friend, remember and send for me."

Two years after this, a message was sent to my father, that a man under sentence of death in the county gaol wished to see him exceedingly. He obtained the necessary order for admission, and went without having any idea who it could be. On entering the condemned cell, he recognized the face of the person who had robbed him two years before. The man looked at him, and trembled violently. "Why," said he, "did you tell me, if I wanted a friend, to remember and send for you?" "Really," replied my father, "I hardly know why I said it; but if I can do anything for thee now, tell me, and if right to be done, I will do it." "Sir," said he, "I have never had a moment's peace since I robbed you. I knew I would be hanged for it, for no one can injure a Quaker, and not feel that vengeance will pursue them. Now, for stealing a horse, I am sentenced to death by the judge. But, sir, it is God has sentenced me for robbing you." He then told where the watch would be found, in a hole in a wall about four miles from the city, indicating the spot with minute accuracy. It was found there a few days afterwards, and had evidently lain there a long time.

My father spoke to him kindly; found that he was in some degree educated; he could read well, but was in the grossest ignorance of his duty either to God or man. He confessed freely, that he had lived a most wicked life; he was the leader or captain of a band of highwaymen; but strange to say, his conscience had never been silent. Its monitions had tormented him, and a fearful expectation of meeting the due reward of his crimes in this world, he had not been able to get rid of. He had never committed murder. Being free from that sin was his greatest and only comfort. He seemed to think it was almost a virtue. My father promised to make intercession for his life; but warned him of the improbability of his interference being successful—the law, then, was so severe, and the penalty of death so rigidly executed. "Sir," said he, "it is not that I want of you. I know I must die; but oh! sir, I am afraid to meet God. What shall I do?" And he wept abundantly. My father told him of the hope of the Gospel, of the free pardon given to all who believe in the Lord Jesus Christ. He listened with intense avidity, but was quite incredulous that such a glorious pardon would be given to him. The next day, my father again visited him, and brought him a Testament; marked the most suitable passages and desired him to believe in them, for that the promises there offered to him, were as true as they were simple. The poor fellow had been given what they called a long day; that was two weeks. During that time, my father had exerted himself in every possible way to get the sentence commuted. He had interested the best, the highest, and the noblest in the city in the case, but in vain. On going to the gaol on the third day before the execution, my father was refused admission, and was told that an order had been sent not to allow him to see the condemned man again. That evening he received a parcel from the governor of the gaol, containing the Testament and a note, saying, the Priest was going to take it away, but the condemned man had entreated him to return it to his only friend.

This circumstance, and at the same time, the execution of a poor sweep, who, it soon afterwards transpired, was hanged for a crime of which he was not guilty, made a deep impression on my father's mind. He resolved to do what he could towards having those laws changed, which were so cruelly severe. After much serious and prayerful thought on the subject, he wrote (I was his assistant amanuensis) to all the judges, and to most of the influential men in the country, entreating their attention to the unchristian severity of our penal statutes. He acted entirely as an individual, the Society had nothing to do with it. Perhaps, except my mother and myself, no one knew of the efforts he made to have the punishment of death done away with, for all crimes, but murder. He received the kindest replies from all parts; thanks for bringing the subject under notice, and promises of legislative interference. Amongst them was one from the Archbishop of Tuam, which cheered him greatly, and assured him that the work then commenced, would be carried on strenuously, until the desired end was achieved. The Archbishop had been a fellow student at the University with my father. Whilst he was Bishop Trench, he had renewed his acquaintance, and now again these two pious men cemented a friendship which, commenced on earth, they are now doubtless enjoying in the mansions of glory, prepared for Christ's redeemed children.

Our governess having left us, in expectation of being married to a Friend in Yorkshire, to whom she was partly engaged when she came to Ireland, but who finally jilted her, it was resolved to send me to the School for the Daughters of Friends. I greatly dreaded and disliked this plan; for I had heard, alas! too truly, that the Mistress was a very plain, strict Friend, a rigid disciplinarian, and of a somewhat tartaric temper.

The distance from our own happy home was only twenty-five miles; but in those days it was a journey quite long enough for one day. We started, my mother and myself, after an early breakfast; and, having to refresh the horses twice on the road, it was late in the evening when we arrived. But the time passed rapidly; my mother was possessed of an unfailing fund of traditionary stories and anecdotes, and gifted with a happy method of relating them, interspersed with her own wise, and oftentimes droll and quaint observations.

There were forty girls at the school, only a very few older than myself. Two Mistresses, Sisters Betsey and Anne, an English governess, and five young women, half teachers, half pupils. The house was large and convenient; and opening on a lonely road, was surrounded by a large and well stocked garden at the back, and this was separated from the rest of the world by a mill-stream at one side, and the river at the other. We had always the very best plain fare. Sister Anne presided over the housekeeping department. She was a liberal soul, and spared not those ingredients which constitute the essence of good living. She was a simple-minded, gentle, retiring person; affectionately kind to us all, and on several occasions I found her especially so to me.

We all knew that the great aim and object of Sister Anne's life, was to walk humbly before her God, to maintain the principles and peculiarities of her profession, and to promote the comfort and happiness of us girls; and we all loved her.

Betsey was as opposite to her gentle sister as night from day. She was, what is called, a strong-minded woman; and strong in the belief of her own infallibility, she certainly was. She had been selected for the post she held, as being a Model Quakeress—one whom we young ones would do well to copy in all things. She was a personification of peculiarities. Small, neat, and naturally well-looking, but with an unfeminine severity of countenance. The girls told me they had seen her smile. I never did. Her features, as well as her mind, were too sternly disciplined ever to relax. Her dress was neat, and costly too. Her gown, of very dark brown tabinet, was made, as the gowns of our aristocratic Friends always are, so very long, as to require holding up when walking even across a room; and her petticoat, of the same material, was just short enough to show the neat, fine, white cotton stocking, and the highly polished short quartered shoe, with its broad ribbon tie. The muslin of which her caps and neck-kerchiefs were made, was of a fabric fine enough for Majesty to wear. The time bestowed on washing, ironing, clear-starching, and tacking them, was amazing; but they were perfect structures of delicate folds, when completed. The education given at that school was excellent, so far as it went. The governess was a first-rate scholar herself; and though as plain a Friend as either of the sisters, yet she was cast in a very different mould. She was loveable, of a much higher degree of mental culture and refinement than the others. I was very fond of her. She spoke a few kind words to me on my arrival; and there is nothing makes so indelible an impression on the heart as kind words, spoken with a kind look accompanying them, when one is sad, and feels desolate. But besides this, I had another bond of union with my governess. I soon found out that, like myself, she was no great favourite with Sister Betsey.

How strange a thing is that intuitive feeling of liking and disliking a person at first sight. I have experienced it repeatedly; and years after, without intermediate intercourse, I have felt the truthfulness of that mysterious index.

My dress gave me a world of trouble with Sister Betsey. The rule of the school was, to wear whatever clothes the parents sent, provided they were not unfriendly. Mine were always thought to be passably orthodox at home; but Sister Betsey found out much to alter. The hem on my plain muslin collars was too broad; I had to rip, and re-work them the breadth of a straw. My shawl was bound with narrow ribbon, which had to come off, and a broad hem to be put on instead. I had to take the sleeves out of my frocks; she cut them to her own taste, and then I had to put them in again. The gathers were taken out of my Friends' bonnet, and plaits put in. I murmured at the weary, hateful task; spoiling my clothes, for no earthly good. But it was no use; I was not even allowed to study with the other girls, till the clothes were all finished in the prescribed way.

"Pretty schooling, this," said I; "I am sure I was not sent here to learn mantua-making. I will write home, and tell my mother the kind of schooling I am getting."

"Silly child," said a good-humoured girl beside me, "thou must learn Quakerism."

"But," said I, "is it not provoking? I must put a broad hem on one thing, and take it off another."

"Ah! that is only emblematical," said she. "Friends may swallow a camel, sometimes, but they must always strain at gnats. However," said she, "don't grumble about it. Whenever any of the girls want to get into favour with Sister Betsey, they tell her every thing they hear us say. There is Eliza Morland always prowling about now, listening to every one; take care what thou sayest to her, or in her hearing, for it will all go at once to Betsey. And as to the writing home, put that out of thy head at once; for all our letters are read before they leave the house. I never received a letter since I came here, that had not got the seal broken open. But what matter," said the light-hearted girl; "in a year or two it will be all over, and then I'll go home, and I'll get a straw bonnet, and I'll put red ribbons on it."

We had a chapter in the Bible read to us every morning after breakfast, and again at night another. No observation was made, or explanation given; but frequently at night Sister Betsey would preach about her own devotedness, her feelings, her desire to promote our real welfare; and she would give pious slaps at any misdemeanour we had been guilty of during the day. Happy was the girl who, softened by these addresses, could show her susceptibility by tears. No homage was so grateful to Sister Betsey as this; the triumphant proofs of her eloquence—this assurance that her spiritual travail was accomplishing its desired end. I had no tears thus at command, and consequently I never was a favourite.

There were two of the girls given to preaching; these two—both prime pets of Sister Betsey—plagued me sadly. My hair was long. Oh! what concerns Eliza Morland had, that I should not only have it cropped off like her own, but that, influenced by her persuasion, I should ask permission to have it done. She said "it would be an acceptable sacrifice." Then my boots; there was a tassel on my boots, which caused great mental concern to both Eliza and Anne. They entreated me to cut off the Babylonish ornament, and told me "I would have peace in so doing."

Another thing disturbed these righteous girls, as Sister Betsey once called them to me; that was, that before getting into bed, I knelt to repeat the Lord's prayer, as my mother had ever taught me to do. There was not one of all the forty girls, but myself, had been so habituated. Eliza and Anne remonstrated with me on this, which they called a Popish practice; and because I paid no regard to their preachings, they then went and told Sister Betsey, and she forbid me to kneel. She said "it was too solemn an act for any one but an appointed minister of our Society, and wholly unbecoming in one so far from righteousness as I was."

We were regularly marched out to walk every fine day. Two and two—a long string of us paraded through the town; and the same way to Meetings. If the streets were wet, as indeed they generally were, and dirty too, in winter, we were all obliged to wear pattens. What a clatter we made! Unaccustomed to the use of them, I begged to go without, but was told, "my request was the fruit of a corrupt inclination;" so of course I mounted them like the others, and tottered off. The first attempt my ancle turned. As soon as that got well, I was compelled to mount upon them again, and again I fell; and this happened so often, and so often I limped into Meeting, that at last I gained my point, and the abominable pattens were given to another.

The Meeting was not as large as that which I came from. There were but two women ministers, and no man at all. Occasionally a man sitting in the body of the meeting spoke; but they used to pull him down when he stood up, so that he seldom succeeded in unburthening his mind. He was a poor man, a shopkeeper, and his wife and daughter thought he had as good a right to be heard as any one else. One first day he attempted a sermon; and when all the pulling did not keep him quiet, they forced him out of the Meeting. Whilst so doing, his wife rose up, and shouted out—"Quench not the Spirit." She was then subjected to the same summary eviction; and then up rose the daughter, and shrieked out—"Despise not prophesyings." She had to make her exit also in double quick time. These people often broke the silence of our Meetings; the real ministers but rarely. They were very indifferent preachers; or rather, as Friends say, their gifts in the ministry were very small.

Some of our girls could speak on their fingers; we had many a conversation of this kind, which relieved the tedium of the silent Meetings.

The affairs of the Society here, were altogether governed by the women; some of whom possessed great energy of character. Indeed I believe they cared far more for the upholding of the discipline, than did the men; who, engaged as they were in business, were content quietly and honorably to plod on their way; and thus they resigned to the women that supremacy in the Society, which they coveted, and the others disregarded. Out of Meeting I have heard the men say, it was too bad that Sarah Mills should dictate to the Men's Monthly Meeting. But she was a clever woman, and had them all well in hand, and kept them so while she lived. Two women only ever ventured to oppose her will. They were as stout-hearted as herself. Not being so wealthy, their influence was greatly less; but they had many a skirmish, and sometimes a little more than that, in our Women's Monthly Meetings. I often thought I would like to pat Rebecca Wallis on the back, when she stood up to dispute a point with Sarah Mills, who was so fat, and so supreme in her dictatorial capacity, that she would not even pay the Meeting the usual courtesy of rising to address it, but was accustomed to keep her seat, and from it indulge in those tirades she gloried in inflicting on the silent crowd.

One morning we were all aroused from our slumbers earlier that usual, with the astonishing news that robbers had been in the house during the night. We hastened down stairs, and there saw that the work of spoliation had indeed been unsparingly carried on. Our desks and work-boxes had been broken open, and rifled—not one silver thimble was left us. Our purses were emptied. All our treasures were gone. Even our silk umbrellas; the cotton ones were left. Cloaks, shawls, silver spoons, books—all were swept away. The robbers had evidently spent a long time in the house. They had eaten and drunk abundantly; and moreover, after emptying the desks, they had actually sat down and written sentence after sentence on the paper found therein, and even had perpetrated an attempt at congratulatory poetry, to the fair vestals whose sanctuary they were polluting. The leader of the gang—which was afterwards broken up, and most of them transported, but not before they had in a similar manner despoiled more than a dozen Friends' houses—was a young man who had applied for membership in the Society. He had managed to get into service in a Friend's family; then he went to first day Meetings, mounted a broad brim, and made his humble application for membership on the ground of convincement. He was never admitted; but he had access to many Friends' houses, and found out the vulnerable parts of them, and the places where the treasures were kept. When apprehended, he freely told of all his doings, and would laugh heartily at them. His gang consisted of six men, a boy, and one woman. One of them cut out the pane of a window, then the boy went in, and opened it gently for them. The woman carried a candle, which they said, being made of the fat of a dead man, shed a somniferous influence over all in the house. He said it was his attachment to the Society, which led him to give so decided a preference to Friends' houses. But some people thought it was because he imagined they would not prosecute him if he were detected. He was disappointed. No man is so meek and gentle as a Quaker, provided his interest is not molested; touch that, and you touch the apple of his eye. Unregenerate human nature is exactly the same in all men. The outward garb alters not the inward man.

One evening a party of us went by invitation to visit the house and grounds of Friend Draper. I had long wished to go there. The place was kept beautifully neat; it was well situated, commanding fine views of the surrounding country. The flowers, the grotto, made at an enormous cost, the walks, the ponds—all were in keeping, and all beautiful. After seeing them, we were conducted into the house, and there gratified with a sight of an extensive collection of shells, minerals, and curiosities of all kinds; and then shown into a room, where a table was laid out with fruits, cakes, creams, and flowers. Friend Draper bade us "take our seats, and fire away"—his peculiar phraseology, but it meant, pray regale yourselves. He was a very eccentric old bachelor, a very plain Friend, and very wealthy; lived quite solitary, but in great luxury. As he was old, and fanciful, and was not known to have any near relative, there were many people found ready to conform themselves to his will, in the unspoken hope of being made heirs to his possessions. The dear Friend permitted their attentions to him, and when he died he left all his property to his own two illegitimate children.

One of our girls used to make for herself, and wear, most enormous pockets. "Jane," said I, "is it to be thought pious, thou hast such big pockets?" She laughed. "Yes," said she, "Sister Betsey does think them more friendly than thy little scraps of things; but they are very convenient. Look! what I have in them now." I looked and saw a good sized book; it was Ivanhoe. "I can always borrow a book when I go to dine with my cousin on first day," said Jane; and if thou wilt write out my French Exercise for me,

I will let thee read it." I gladly agreed; and whether it was because stolen waters are sweet, or because of the exceeding fascination of the book itself, certainly no one ever enjoyed a book more than I did that, and some more of the same delightful author's works, which I obtained in the same manner. When reading it in the arbour or in the study, I always took care to provide myself with either an Atlas or Sarah Grubb's Journal; and then if either one of the Mistresses or one of the spy girls came in sight, the Novel was popped under, and the Atlas or the Journal looked innocent or edifying.

When the time of probation was ended, and the happy hour came for emancipation from school thraldom, and returm to home, for any of us, it was thought a hardened thing to show any signs of gladness Sister Betsey often told us that our school days were the only happy days we should have in this world. Therefore tears at being removed from her fostering care were becoming; and the pious girls used to weep wonderfully. When my turn came, I felt as if I had been inhaling oxygen gas. I could no more weep, than she could smile at the idea of losing a pupil who had been very well paid for. However, we parted, quite friendly; she kissed me, and said, that though I had always been obdurate, she loved me for my father's sake. That I had made such good progress in my studies, she trusted that she might yet see me devoting my abilities to the good of our Society. That she considered me quite qualified to become clerk to a Monthly Meeting—yes; even to the Yearly Meeting. No commendation could be more flattering than this. The pious girls, who were always doing mean things to worm themselves into her favour, were amazed; and I departed, laughing and triumphant.

CHAPTER IV.

Home—Dress—Piety in pattens—Inanity of Quakerism—Quarterly Meetings—Friend Brown's effrontery—Masquerades—Christ called a principle and not a person—Borrowing money—The sisters—Ben and his breeches pockets—Ignorance of use—Husband and Wife—Intemperance—The Resurrection.

HOME, delightful happy home! what a multitude of blessed joys were garnered there! It seemed as if a halo of peace and happiness encircled my father, and shed its glories on all belonging to him. I have heard a Roman Catholic Priest at one time, and a good old English Quaker at another, say, that when seated beside him, they felt they were in the company of a child of God. I never saw him angry, or heard a hasty word out of his lips. When any one displeased him, he would become very grave, and look sad. The next day he would take a private opportunity of speaking to the offender; and always so kindly, and so reasonably, and so scripturally were those remonstrances and reproofs given, that they were invariably efficacious.

Delighted with my new found liberty, I now indulged myself somewhat too freely in the use of those ribbons and blonds in which young girls take pleasure, but which are so little in accordance with the "simplicity of our Christian professions." At last, my father requested me to lay them aside, and to resume the dress of our people, though not in its extreme plainness and ugliness. To gratify him was far dearer to me than even gay attire, and I arrayed myself accordingly. My looking-glass comforting me with its assurance, that a well-made coquettish Quaker bonnet, was by no means an unbecoming one.

There was a man Friend in our Meeting, who had in his childhood been the object of a simple, well-meaning mother's care. With the view of making him righteous, she had kept him in petticoats until he was over eight years old. She took him regularly by the hand to Meeting thus dressed, with a flat white beaver hat, and pattens like a girl. At the time I speak of, he was a portly man, but still he bore the name of Piety in Pattens.

This man was one much given to the habit of encouraging young people to become "standard bearers." If he saw any one dressed in a new garb, somewhat of a plainer form than that it superseded, he would smile sweetly on the wearer. In shaking hands, he would squeeze your fingers with a significant and pleasing look, at the improved appearance. And if you took it kindly, you might be morally certain, that on the first opportunity, you would be appointed to one of the minor offices in the Society. This system he now began to try on me. Unfortunately for his designs, I had not within me the elements of Quakerism. But, indeed, I sincerely hope, the work I am now writing, may do more good to the Society than I should ever have done, had I remained amongst them, and realized the hope so often expressed to me, of upholding their doctrines by my words and practice. For as

"Sin is a monster of so vile a mien,
As to be hated, needs but to be seen,"

so, I trust the dawdling inanity to which Quakerism is now sunk, needs but to be exposed, to cause the many intelligent, intellectual, and sensible people, who are now bound to it by a species of moral thraldom, to arouse themselves and see, whether those amongst them who are now quietly allowed to take the lead, are such as it is creditable for people possessed of common sense to submit to.

Having expressed a wish to attend the Quarterly Meeting at Youghal, my father asked me had I a concern to go to it? I told him no religious concern, but a good deal of curiosity. He said I should be gratified, and he hoped good would result from it. He would accompany me himself.

I had a week's time to prepare, to get new dresses, and all the needful et ceteras. It would not do at all, to go to a Quarterly or Yearly Meeting without new clothes. The bonnet, shawl, and gown, must have the first gloss unsullied, or you look shabby among the crowd. We had arranged to go as far as Lismore in our own carriage, stop a day or two there, to see the beautiful scenery of the Blackwater, and visit some gentlemen whom my father wished to interest in the business he had for some time on his mind—the abolition of underground dungeons attached to prisons and lock-up houses—and then to post on to Youghal. More than half my anticipated pleasure was in the prospect of that journey with my own dear father.

The day before that fixed for our departure, old Friend Thomas Brown, came to speak to my father. He was showed into the parlour, where we all assembled just after breakfast. After the customary salutations, he sat down, and fell into silence. Of course we all wondered what was coming; but we respectfully waited until he was ready to unburden his mind. At last he began by saying, how greatly he was impressed "with the beauty of the simplicity of the truth; how greatly he longed that his young friends could be made willing to walk in it. That the beauty of the simplicity of the truth, was a doctrine too high for his own comprehension, and therefore he would greatly recommend us to cast away all doubtings, and hold fast by the beauty of the simplicity of the truth." Then he paused a bit longer, and got up, as if to go away; but he stopped short, and addressing my father, said, "I heard thee was going to Youghal Meeting; is any of thy family going with thee?" "Yes," he replied, "my daughter will accompany me, I expect." "Ah!" said he, "I was thinking so; then you will just have room for my cousin, Betty Brown, between you. She has a concern to go, and I did not well know how to manage for her. When will you be starting, and I'll tell her to be ready?" The cool effrontery of the man, took us all by surprise, which was turned into vexation, when my father, after a moment's reflection, agreed to take charge of the old woman. He said afterwards, that certainly she was not the companion he would have chosen, but he did not think it would be kind to refuse.

This Betty Brown was a little mite of a woman, always wrapt up in flannels and cloth shawls; so fearful lest she should catch cold, that the windows of her house were never opened, and she would put on her bonnet when walking from one room to another. Our plans were all disarranged by the unwelcome intrusion; we gave up our visit to Lismore and the Blackwater; and in an old rumbling post-chaise, got over the ground as fast as we could. Betty, scarcely spoke at all, she was not sufficiently at her ease to ask to have both windows shut up, but she drew her multitudinous shawls close around her, and made her wish intelligible. And as we took no notice of this hint, she stuffed her handkerchief into her mouth, to keep out the breath of heaven on a hot, July day. She wanted to accompany us to the lodgings we had ordered to be prepared for us, and said her cousin had told her "she might have half of my bed." There was no use in saying anything to her; so my father ordered the driver to go to Friend Levi's shop, which was near at hand. He jumped out, and saw Friend Levi, and told the circumstance, asking him to procure suitable accommodation for Betty, and engaging to pay for it. "I'll keep her myself," said he, "and if thee will give me three pounds, I'll engage to send her back safely too, without annoying thee any more." It was a cheap riddance, the money was paid on the spot, and Betty handed out of the chaise. Neither she nor her cousin Tom, ever offered to repay this money. She was poor, but he was as rich as he was mean-spirited.

The Meeting was but a small one, only our own preachers, and but very few parties given. An aunt of mine had come up to attend the Meeting, in her own carriage. Whilst my father was attending on the committees, I was driving about the country with her, seeing all that was to be seen. Sir Walter Raleigh's old house, and its beautiful chimney-piece of carved wood—a perfect gem of its kind—and the famous myrtle tree.

Soon after this, I attended a Cork Quarterly Meeting. We lodged at the hotel; there was another Friend's party stopping there also; and, as we had some previous acquaintance with them, we became intimate for the time being. Having one day declined to accompany my father to a tea-party, because I expected it would be a very stupid affair, and these other Friends having heard me say so, as soon as he was gone, they came to my sitting room, and actually proposed to me to accompany them to a public masquerade ball, which was to take place that night. I was horrified at the idea of doing such a thing, and thought they were jesting with me. But they seriously assured me that they had come up from the country, entirely for the sake of it, and attending the Meeting was a capital plan to put the old Friends off from any chance of discovering it, or suspecting them.

Such expedients as this, are often resorted to by young Friends, to enable them to partake in the amusements of the public. I was frequently invited to join with them, and laughed at heartily for my scruples; for as I had not the look of a very plain Friend, they took it for granted I had no principles to regulate my conduct.

The business of the Cork Meeting was as usual, a mere routine of that laid down in the Book of Discipline. In the preaching part, which was far below mediocrity, one Friend told us that "Christ was to be considered as a principle, not as a person," and no one objected to the heresy.

I have, from time to time, attended almost every one of the Irish Meetings. Our own was always the most interesting. We saw a good deal of company; in fact, kept open house for about a week. Our preparations generally commenced about a month beforehand. We were a very large family, and must each, and all, have new dresses in the first place. Then the rooms were revivified, and everything showy put carefully away. Our object was, to have everything and every one, enveloped in a pleasing, delicate, and graceful drab. And as flowers are an allowed indulgence, and we had them in vast profusion, the contrast was elegant and enlivening. There was one minister who regularly came to us at these times. She was elderly, strikingly plain every way, and rich. She was an epicurean, and much time, cost, and thought were given, to have delicate morsels at all times for her This valuable minister, as they called her, had a habit of borrowing money, not for herself, but for the use of different persons in whom she was interested, and she would give her word as security. My poor dear father was often and heavily victimized. After eating a luxurious dinner, she would begin to get very silent; her silence against tea-time came, would mount up to solemnity. When that, with hot muffins and plum cake, had been despatched, she would lay down her knitting, and begin to twirl her thumbs. Then, significant glances at my father; and he, dear credulous creature, would desire us all to lay by our various employments, and drop into silence. After this had continued about eight or ten minutes, she would unburthen herself. Generally beginning with a text of Scripture, such as—"To obey is better than sacrifice." She would give a very good lecture on it for about five minutes. She never could keep on much longer, though she often tried. Then another long silence, and then she would kick the footstool on one side—a method of intimating that we might go about our business. And, addressing my father, she would beg him to oblige her with five minutes' conversation in another room. Well he knew, and we all knew, what was coming now. The amount she would require him to give was the only doubtful point. Rather than we should entertain any disrespectful feeling towards an acknowledged minister of the Society, who professed to be led and guided in all things by the Spirit of Truth, he would yield to her demand. Sometimes it was for one hundred pounds, sometimes fifty; and we, rather than distress him, would pretend we had no suspicion of her trickery. She borrowed from him upwards of five hundred pounds in this manner, and never repaid it, or gave him such guarantees, as would have enabled him to make a legal demand on her executors, when she died, leaving a property of nine hundred a year.

There was a testimony issued by the Meeting, as is generally done for departed ministers, for this Friend. In it she was represented as an ornament to the Society, an experienced and devoted minister of the Gospel of Peace; in short, she was made to appear as if a concentration of all virtue, faith, and godliness, had been perfected in her.

Our Quarterly Meeting parties were often very amusing. I was invited to a large first day dinner, at which I met, amongst others, five sisters. They were aged from about twenty-five to seventeen, all well looking, the youngest quite handsome. They were all dressed exactly alike, in dark greenish tabinets, muslin kerchief, plaited over the dress, and muslin mob caps. The eldest had been a constant attendant of these Meetings; the four others were now brought out for the first time. They had been desired, when leaving home, to behave like Anne, the eldest, to do whatsoever she did, to copy her. The dinner provided for us was at the head of the table—a fine large loin of roast veal, with force-meats, &c. At the foot was a cold joint of roast beef. At one side, a ham; at the other, boiled chickens, and vegetables in variety. The sisters ranged themselves according to their ages, at one side. Friend Tench, the hostess, addressing one of the younger ones, asked—"Jane, may I help thee to some roast veal?" She glanced at Anne, looked timid, and then said, "Oh! I'm obliged to thee, not yet; I'll wait a bit." Friend Tench then addressed another—"Susanna, may I help thee?" "I'll wait a bit, too, if thee please," said Susanna. Friend Tench tried again, "Rebecca, will thee have some veal?" "I'll wait a bit, too, if thee please," said Rebecca. Friend Tench did not know what to make of it, but she tried again, and addressed the eldest. "Anne, what will thee take?" "I'll take some cold roast beef; I like cold meat on first days," said Anne. She was helped. And then again, Jane, and Susanna, and Rebecca, and Martha, were asked, and each one answered in the same words as Anne—"I'll take some cold roast beef, if thee please. I like cold meat on first days." They were all helped, and presently Anne handed up the plate, and said, "Will thee give me a little of that nice gravy, and a bit of force-meat?" She got it, and up came the other plates, one after another, in their regular ages, from the other four, and each saying—

"Will thee give me a little of that nice gravy, and a bit of force-meat?" It was difficult to maintain due gravity. In fact, the effort to do so was painful; and when the second course was placed on the table, and, "I'll take some rice pudding, if thee please, I'm very fond of rice pudding," was again echoed, and re-echoed by the sisters, there was more than one of the company obliged to leave the room, not to annoy Friends by the mal-à-propôs fit of coughing which seized them.

The sisters left the house soon after dinner, and were, as usual, commented on immediately after. "One would think they had no sense," said one Friend, "repeating every word that Anne said, like parrots." "Ah! no," said kind and charitable Friend Tench, "they are young and innocent. They only showed the simplicity of their minds, by copying Anne a little too closely."

Not long after, we heard that Rebecca, the simple-minded innocent, had been detected in the act of eloping with a dragoon soldier, with whom she had made acquaintance in the streets. Anne had her immediately conveyed to a very lonely house in the country, and great pains were taken to keep the affair secret, lest, as the Friends said, it might bring discredit on the cause of truth. "Not so," said my mother, "let it be known; there is no harm done; it is but the act of a silly, ignorant girl, and perhaps it may convince some Friends, that the practice they dwell so much on, of keeping their young people out of temptation, is a very inefficient one. Give them principles to resist temptation; for all you can do is in vain, whilst you neglect to teach them the law of the Lord."

In our drawing-rooms, the elder women Friends were always given the upper and best seats; next to them, sat the younger women and girls, and the men were crowded near the door. A very plain man or two, would be allowed to sit among the elder women—the rest were almost as much apart as on the Meeting's seats. No one seemed ever to think of changing their chair. Once placed, you had to remain fixed the whole evening, so that it was a matter of consequence on coming into the room, to select an agreeable, chatty neighbour for the time being. If you had not that, the only entertainment was listening to others. I was often so placed, and yet had my full share of enjoyment.

There was one Benjamin, a youth of the very straitest. His father had taken him away from school, after the first quarter, because the boy had said *you*, instead of *thee*. The father said, his son had already grown vicious. So poor Benjamin got no more schooling. He told us that the height of his ambition was to be door-keeper to the Meeting, and to be allowed to snuff the candles. Bess Chapman, who knew him well, had heard him one day regretting that no female had ever written to him; and to gratify the simple boy, she wrote him a note, asking him could he tell her was there a copy of the Life of William Penn in the Meeting Library? Ben was delighted; he had at last a woman's letter. He boasted of it. He tantalized his brother Dick by showing him the outside. He looked gloriously happy, and walked more lightly than ever. He met Bess, and thanked her; and she said, "Mind and keep it safe, Ben. It is not every young man I would write to." Soon after, as Bess was seated among her own companions, Dick stumbled across the room. "Well," said he, "I saw thy letter to Ben." Ben was summoned over. "Ah! Ben," said she, "I did not expect thee would show my letter."

"I did not show it to any body," said Ben.

"I saw it," said Dick.

"No, thee did not," replied Ben.

"Indeed I did, Bess," said Dick, again.

"How is this, Ben?" said she; "this is a serious matter, I must know all about it."

Poor Ben was ready to cry. "Don't believe him," said he, "he is telling lies."

"I am not telling lies," said the other, "I read it; it is about William Penn; now did not I read it?"

Bess put on a grave face. "Tell me, Ben," said she severely, "has thee left my note carelessly about for people to read?"

"No," said he, "indeed I did not, I kept it always rammed down into the bottom of my breeches pocket."

"And when thee was asleep at night, I stole it out of thy pocket, and read it," said Dick.

Both of these sensible youths were shortly after promoted in the Meeting.

Ignorance is no disqualification for Friends; on the contrary, when a strong-minded woman is in authority, she likes to have her nominees in the men's Meeting, sufficiently devoid of learning and natural intelligence, to be her willing coadjutors.

As our ministers so constantly reminded us, that we were a more spiritually-minded people than any others—that our profession was the high and holy one, of being "at all times led and guided by the Spirit of Truth"—it was only natural that I should expect to find something superior in the general tone of conversation, and attentively listen when plain Friends were conversing near me.

I was seated between Rebecca Stubbs and Anne Woods, at a large Quarterly Meeting tea party. "Anne," said Rebecca, "it is a long time since I met thee: six or seven years I think. Thee used to attend our Quarterly Meetings much more frequently. How is that? I hope thee has not lost thy interest in the discipline of our Society."

"Oh! no," said Anne, "but I was not married then. I thought when I was marrying Isaac, that there would be nobody to prevent me going to all the Meetings; and indeed, Rebecca, that was a great part of the reason I married him at all, but he wont let me go."

"I am surprised to hear thee saying so," replied Rebecca; "for Isaac is a very consistent Friend; he takes rather a prominent part in the discipline himself, and his judgment is considered to be very sound."

"I know that," said the wife, "but for all that, he is very positive with me. When I told him I wished to go to any of the Quarterly Meetings, and I even told him that it was strongly borne in on my mind, that my concern to go was not altogether of myself: he said, it was fitter for me to stay at home, and mind my children. And more than that, Rebecca, he said, that our Women's Meetings were all humbugs; that it was only for the sake of getting new bonnets, and new gowns, and shawls, and good eating, and talking among ourselves, that we wanted to go at all. He would not have let me come here now, only that I nursed him so well during his long illness, that he said he would not refuse me a little pleasure."

"Thee astonishes me," said Rebecca; "why Anne dear thee is to be pitied. Thee has a great deal to bear with."

"Oh!" replied Anne, "I hope thee does not think I said any thing against my husband. Isaac is very good and kind to me, I have not any fault at all to find with him."

As Friends allow of no pastime whatever at these parties, the only occupation is eating, drinking, and talking. These were often indulged in to excess. I have seen the men reeling into the drawing-room, and heard them boast of having each got through fourteen tumblers of punch. I have heard them taunt a young man, and call him a "paper skull," because he had refused to drink more than one tumbler of punch. I have seen some of these high professors, indulge in unbounded gormandizing; and in eating, though happily not in drinking, some of the women rival the men.

Friends do not approve of talking on religion. They say it is too solemn a subject to be discussed in a familiar manner; and especially conversation on doctrinal points is reprobated. Nevertheless, I sometimes heard opinions expressed, which were charming from their novelty, if nothing else.

"Susanna," said I, "when a person dies, where does the spirit go to?"

"To heaven, my dear, of course."

"What appearance will the spirit have?"

"We do not know, my dear, but it will have wings."

"Will it bear any resemblance to our forms here on earth?"

"Oh! dear, no; for flesh and blood cannot inherit the kingdom of God."

"Can the spirit of a man be seen at all in heaven?"

"Oh! yes, at least the wings will be seen."

Susanna was an elder, and of course competent to explain Friends' views. From her I understood that spirits in heaven were something like butterflies on earth, flying about in great enjoyment, and having nothing to do.

"Martha," said I, to another elder, a nice, dear old woman, of whom I was very fond, "can thee tell me what the Scripture means by the resurrection of the dead?"

"Certainly, dear; it is, that though our bodies must die, and be consigned to the dark tomb, our spirits will live for ever in heaven."

"But, Martha, surely the spirit never dies; it cannot be that; the body dies, but not the spirit. Is it not so?"

"Ah! my dear, we must not take a carnal view of the subject. These bodies of ours are worn out on earth; we shall have prepared bodies given to us; but it is, when we become quickened by the workings of the Spirit of Life within us, that we are raised from the death of sin, and brought into the newness of life."

The doctrine of the resurrection of the dead is not held by Friends generally. They confound it with regeneration. They spiritualize away the words of Scripture, and hold their own mystical interpretation. I do not allude to Friends' writings, or to the authorized expression of their doctrines. I am merely stating what they *are*, as far as my own observation and experience go.

CHAPTER V.

Curious Preachings—Printed Creed—Sermon against shells, corals, and natural curiosities—Unwillingness of Friends to speak in Meetings—Guides—Travelling Friends—Women Preachers' Families—Broad Brims to escape disownment—Poor Committee—Provincial Schools—False Accusation.

ONE of our ministers had been appointed to the office, very much against the judgment of the majority of the meeting. But she had interest and family connections with several of the elders and overseers, and so she attained the acme of her ambition. Her preaching was very extraordinary. She would say, that she knew very well that her preaching was not liked; she expected no less; it was only the spiritually-minded who could understand and value a spiritual ministry. It was not her business to preach such things as would please the carnal heart—carnal ears would want carnal words. She was not bound to please, and she did not want to please, and she would not pin her faith on any man's sleeve. This Friend very rarely attempted to quote Scripture, and when she did, it was often incorrectly. To look at her speaking, you would think she was in a passion, she often stamped her foot, and gesticulated violently. I often tried to make a caricature sketch of her, but in vain; no caricature could equal the original grotesque writhings of her form and features.

There was a man also in our Meetings, who, though he was not an acknowledged minister, was a permitted one. He, too, often gave us very queer sermons; but they were better than the lady's, for if they did no good, they could do but little harm, as nobody could by any possibility understand them. It was not unusual to hear him end thus:—"I don't know whether you understand me. It is very likely you don't. But I know myself what I mean."

In consequence of these odd preachings, a report was spread through the town, that the Quakers were mere ranters, that they were not Christians. My father was deeply grieved about it. He spoke to many of the Friends, but was not satisfied at the indifference they expressed to public opinion. He then consulted with my mother, and the result was that he drew up a creed of what Friends' belief was, taken from that published by William Penn, and caused it to be inserted in each of the newspapers, signed with his own name, and the names of two others, whom he prevailed on to sign it.

The day after it had been published, I was walking with my father, when we met the Dean. He slipped his arm inside my father's, and said—"Well, John, I have been reading your creed this morning. How is it that none of your preachers have signed it?" He replied, that it was not customary for women to sign public documents. "But," said the Dean, "when they perform public acts, and bring discredit on public bodies, ought they not publicly to repair the evil done? Ah! John, I know very well how it is. That creed is your creed, not theirs. Good bye. You are a great deal too good for the people you belong to."

After this, as if to defy public opinion, the same Martha became more violent in her declamations, more absurd in her choice of topics for discourse; may I not say, more blasphemous in her assumptions of Divine inspiration. And yet, there we sat, Sabbath after Sabbath, year after year, silently listening to these atrocious outpourings of a self-righteous and very conceited fanatic. Upwards of three hundred sensible men and women, solemnly respectful hearers of the rankest nonsense.

In our Women's Monthly Meetings, she was even worse, if possible. The minutest trifle in which she knew of any one disagreeing with her opinion, immediately became the subject of invective. Even her own sisters were not spared. One of them had a taste for collecting shells, spars, minerals, and corals; and one day she placed some choice specimens on the chimney-piece of their common sitting-room. Martha saw, but said nothing to her sister at the time. She gathered up, and nursed her wrath until the next Monthly Meeting, and then poured it out. I fancy I can see her now, as she stood on her elevated platform, her bonnet poking at least six inches over her face, her bosom tightly braced in a dark drab skinny shawl. Her long arms, swaying round and round in her excitement, and occasionally a stamp of the angry foot. And when, by her very vehemence, her breathing failed, she would stop a moment, knit her brows, and drawing her thin lips apart, clench her large black teeth. And what was the subject of this invective? "That people professing the high character of spirituality which belonged to the Society of Friends; that the descendants of those worthy predecessors to whom it was given nobly and boldly to testify against the vanities and corruptions of the world; that such highly favoured ones, should blindly fall into the snare of the devil; that the shining of the light within should be so neglected and disregarded; that occasion should be given to the adversary to reproach the true seed, by the specious notion, that it was no harm to indulge a taste for the beauties of nature, by collecting spars, and shells, and corals. Oh! it was a specious device of the arch enemy: first, they are looked at and admired; then they are bought, and the eye gratified with their shining colours. And Satan wont stop there. Oh! no; then they are put on the chimney-piece, and the attention is distracted from its holy meditations; then the enemy triumphs, and the soul is lost—lost forever." She assured us that it was entirely without her own will that she spoke thus; but that the call was so decided, that she dare not be unfaithful, or peril her own peace by keeping silence.

The preachers of the Society—all of them, men and women, the very best of them—are constantly in the habit of saying, that it is against their own will that they stand up to speak in Meetings; that it is very painful to them to have to address their Friends. And that they are compelled to speak, by the fear of the light which is in them being withdrawn, if they sit quiet. They say, "they have been made willing to give up to the requirings of truth." In fact, they give their hearers to understand, that they consider they have conferred a compliment on the Almighty, in consenting to do his work. Instead of being, as good and faithful servants, glad of an opportunity of service, they tell us they perform it unwillingly, and as a distasteful task. How strange! Can it be, that any appointed minister, who has himself drank of the cup of salvation, and who knows the only way which God has revealed to man, whereby atonement for sinners may be made—can such a one, see souls perishing for lack of that knowledge, and feel it irksome to instruct them? Impossible. The true minister of the Gospel delights in his calling; it is his meat and drink to do his Master's work, and to bring sinners to the knowledge of salvation by the blood of the Lord Jesus Christ.

It is customary to draw out a list of the names of all the young men belonging to each Meeting. They are then expected, in rotation, to act as guides to Friends travelling in the ministry; and if these ministers wish it, (as with a few honourable exceptions, they always do,) to pay their travelling expenses for them.

The guide thus acts as courier, and the ministers are raised in general estimation by this deferential attention. Some of the young men do not at all like the office imposed upon them. Others, candidates for office, deem it an honour. An acquaintance of mine had repeatedly tried to evade the disagreeable duty, but in vain; at last he resolved to play them a trick, and did so. The minister and his attendant friend, an elder; they always travel in couples, something on the same plan as the Jesuits, who appoint one of their body to be a guardian angel to their novices, in reality to watch that no cause of scandal shall arise to the Society. These Friends travelled in a very snug close carriage, which only held two. The guide was expected to ride his own horse beside them, a distance of twenty miles, the weather cold and wet. He contrived that both his own horse and theirs, should begin to flag on the road as they approached any town or village; then he kept them shivering in the cold for a time sufficiently long to make them unwilling to refuse the glasses of good strong punch he presented to them. And against the journey was ended, he had them both in a state of uproarious hilarity, which startled the sober quiet family who had been all day expecting them. The guide hurried away; and, as he anticipated, was never again asked to act as courier to travelling Ministers.

When a minister inclines to travel, he, or I should say, she—for there were then only two men ministers in all Ireland, and a host of women—is expected to announce their intention on the First Day Morning Meeting. When the Friends have shaken hands, the way they always break up Meeting, the Clerk calls out, "Members are requested to keep their seats." All who are not Members must walk away. Then the minister rises, and lays her concern before the Meeting; and hopes her Friends will express their feelings on the subject, as though she is made willing to surrender herself to the service required, she is also willing to leave the matter to the decision of her Friends. Then, one after another, the plain Friends will rise, and say, they "feel unity with the dear Friend in her prospect of service;" or, they "hope their dear Friend will be strengthened to perform the arduous undertaking she has laid before them." This is the usual routine. On one occasion in our Meeting, a man Friend rose after these customary speeches had been made, and said, "I think it would be satisfactory, if our Friend would inform us what the duty is to which she considers herself called?" She rose, and somewhat haughtily, replied, "She wished to obtain a certificate from the Monthly Meeting to enable her to visit the families of Friends residing within the compass of the Dublin Monthly Meeting, and also some other parts of the Leinster province." The same Friend, again asked, "Will our Friend inform us, is it her design to visit Friends' families generally through the province of Leinster, or only the Meetings?" She was very much annoyed at these questions, and replied, "She hoped Friends would leave her at liberty to follow the leadings of conscience." Another then stood up, and addressing the questioner, began—"Take off thy shoes from off thy feet, for the place whereon thou standest is holy ground." Another said, "When Ephraim spake trembling, he exalted himself; but when he offended in Baal, he died." Of course nobody else volunteered to question or gainsay the Friend's proposal, for it is not pleasant to get even a pious rebuff in so public a manner.

This was the only occasion on which I heard the slightest demur made at granting the required certificate; but my mother told me, that in another Meeting a woman, one first day, laid before the Meeting, her "concern to perform the arduous undertaking of visiting Meetings in England, and sitting with families as often, and wherever, truth might open the way." Immediately as she resumed her seat in the gallery, her husband far down in the Meeting, an honest, quiet, sensible looking man, rose up and said —"He hoped Friends would not encourage his wife in the plan she had taken into her head of travelling in England. That she was acting in opposition to his known wishes. That it was an unnatural thing of her to leave her baby, three months old, and five small children, to go pleasuring for two years in England, the time she intended to absent herself from her family duties; and that he did not believe the Almighty would approve of her so doing." When he resumed his seat, one after another of the Friends spoke on the subject; one and all expressing deep sympathy with their much tried Friend in her painful situation; hoping she might be strengthened from above, to yield herself to the requirings of duty; and assuring her, that it was given to them to say, she would be favoured with the incomings of peace; and that her devotedness to the service required of her, was a proof that the Society was still a highly favoured one. She got her certificate, a clear one, without any mention of her husband's dissent from it. She travelled about in England for more than two years, and was thought a greal deal of there. She entirely neglected her husband and family; but with our ministers, these minor duties are always subordinate to the public practices of their calling.

It is a very extraordinary fact, that so many of the preachers neglect their families, that the wildest and I believe I might say, the most notoriously irreligious young men in the Society, are the sons of preaching women.

The most scandalous deeds I have ever heard of among Friends, or among any people—immorality in its most hideous forms, licentiousness, and dishonourable conduct—are in ministers' families; and provided public attention is not awakened to them, the sin is covered, and the sinner walks erect among his people. But if the offence become known, then indeed the offender is disowned by the Society, unless there is wealth and interest among the high Friends to assist the guilty in escaping. I have known more than one instance where the delinquent did not wish to be disowned, and to avoid it, put on a plainer garb, and a broader brim than ever; and thus, backed by his mother's influence, not only escaped censure, but actually rose very high in the estimation of our worthies.

The only office my mother could be prevailed on to accept in our Meeting, was that of being on the Committee for the poor. A small subscription was made at each Monthly Meeting, for the support of the few poor Friends who belonged to us. Adjoining our Meeting-house, was the Friends' poor-house, in which five women had each a good room, comfortably furnished; they were allowed a small supply of coals and candles, and three pence half-penny a day, to find themselves in food. Clothing was generally given by one or another of the Friends, independent of the allowance from the Meeting Fund. I often accompanied my mother in her visits to these poor women, and often went of messages from her to them. They complained sadly of the small pittance. And at last, my mother resolved to speak on their behalf in the Meeting. It was the only time I ever heard her speak there; and then she just said, she hoped the allowance would be raised to sixpence, as it was not creditable to the Meeting, or right, she thought, that the very few poor they had to maintain, should have their wants so badly supplied. When she resumed her seat, about half a dozen rose, one after another—fine, fat, well-fed women—to object to any increase. One said, she "had already calculated, and was quite satisfied the allowance made was ample." Another, that "she would not object, but that it would be a precedent, which it might not suit the Meeting to follow at all times." And one saucy creature, who has since joined the White Quakers, said—"I feel called on to say, to the Friend who has thought fit to make this strange proposal—go thou, and sweep before thy own door, but meddle not with those hallowed things which thou understandest not." The poor women were present during this scene; and on our next visit, expressed great regret at having asked her interference, as it had subjected her to insult on their behalf. They were all very grateful to her, she gave them liberty to come walk in our shrubberies whenever they pleased; they often availed themselves of the permission, and returned home, laden with meat, tea, eggs, and such like comforts.

I never knew or heard of a poor man Friend. As poverty generally results from some imprudence, I think the burden is got rid of, by testifying against that imprudence, and disowning the individual. Several cases occurred to my knowledge, which we, who ventured to think and speak too, thought very suspicious. Certainly, the circumstances under which they were disowned, were far more the result of chance, or the conduct of others, than any sinful designs on their own part; and were but trifles light as air, in comparison of the deeds of others who still hold the first places.

The committee for examining into the management of the Provincial Schools, is held at the time of the Quarterly Meeting; and in that Meeting, a dozen or more Friends are appointed to examine the children in their studies, as well as to see to the general arrangement of the establishment.

On one of these occasions, my sister was appointed, and went with the others. A class of about ten girls was given her. The examination of their advancement in secular learning was quite satisfactory to her. Then she asked them questions on religion. They could repeat the words of their catechism, but were ignorant of the meaning. She tried them with the simplest questions, such as she was in the habit of putting to the children at the Infant School, but in vain; they knew nothing. At last she said, "Well, let me hear you repeat the Lord's Prayer." One only out of the ten could do it, and she had only been one month at the school. As she said herself, "she had not had time to forget it." My sister then tried had they been well instructed in the history of Quakerism, and asked them who was the first Friend? They all replied together, "Our Master." It is customary when the examination is ended, for all the visitors to sign a paper for the next Meeting, stating how they found the school affairs, and that they were satisfied, at the instruction given. My sister refused to sign it, because she was not satisfied at all, that the most important part of all education—religion, had been so neglected. The others urged and entreated her to sign it, and said, such a thing was never known as for any one to object to the management in all points of the very consistent Friends who had the care of the school. It was in vain, she would not sign it for them. So that in the report for the Meeting, they were obliged to leave out the word *unanimous*, which was always hitherto inserted.

There is a catechism published for the use of these schools, which has been approved of by the Society. It is the production of Richard Allen, a minister; and in it I find this question and answer, embodied in many words—"Is the sacrifice of our Lord on the cross, sufficient to insure our acceptance with God?" Answer, "No." Such is the teaching given at Provincial Schools. No wonder the pupils so often turn out as they do. No wonder that the Leinster Provincial School, where the vilest sin was practiced, was at last obliged to be given up, and its hypocritical master obliged to fly the country. No wonder that the scores of young Friends educated there should prove irreligious; and, as some of them to my own knowledge, are infidels.

One morning, we were greatly startled and annoyed, by two constables coming to our house with a warrant to arrest my brother, on a charge which had been sworn against him, of shooting at a woman with intent to kill. We were seated at the breakfast table, when the men came in, and very civilly, though firmly, told their business. "George," said my father, "how is this? Explain it." "Father," he replied, "I cannot explain it, for I know nothing about it." They went together to the magistrate, who, knowing our family so well, consented at last to take a very large bail. My brother was in the habit of riding to his farm every morning, and returning late in the evening. He had a large dairy, and had sold the produce of it to Anty Keene, a farmer's daughter, who again retailed it in the town. This Anty Keene had been some twenty pounds in my brother's debt, and he refused to give her further credit, and was about contracting with another woman, who was a rival in the trade with Anty. Oh! how anxiously we waited for the day when the trial should come on. George was the only one of the family who looked calm or happy, his spirits never failed him. Anty Keene swore, that on a certain evening, Mr. George had been riding home from his farm; that he was dressed in a large white over-coat, and mounted on a black mare with a long tail; that a little terrier dog ran beside him; that when he came to the old turnpike gate, he overtook her; that he rode beside her for some distance, demanding his money; that she begged and prayed him to allow her time, and that she would pay him all fairly; that he got into a passion, and said, he would shoot her on the spot if she did not pay him at once; that she became frightened, and ran away, and that then he fired at her with a pistol which he drew from his breast, and that the shots had gone through the hood of the blue cloth cloak she wore. She produced the cloak with six holes, which were very like shot holes. She had one witness, a man, who swore that he was on the road at the time, and hearing the gentleman talking angrily, he had hid himself in the ditch, to listen and watch. He also swore to the horse and the coat, and the dog, and the pistols; and that he saw the shot fired, and the gentleman then put spurs to his horse, and galloped away; and he then ran up to the poor frightened woman, and saw the holes made by the shots quite close to her forehead. This was the charge, and unless he could clear himself of it, the punishment was transportation for life. He confessed that it was true he had been on the road at the time stated; the horse, the coat, the dog—all that was true; he had a brace of pistols in his breast-pocket, but all the rest he denied; he had seen a woman on the road, but he did not speak to her, or know who it was. He had no witness to call; he acknowledged having refused to give Anty further credit; and also, that he had said she would be sorry for her dishonesty, by which he meant, that her rival would get the town business. The general impression on hearing all that could be said on both sides, was, that George was guilty. Many of the gentlemen present, went over to my father, when the first day's investigation was over, and expressed great feeling for him. He thanked them, but said—"I am happy in the belief that my son is innocent of the crime laid to his charge." They did not think so. The lawyers said it was a bad business, and advised George to compromise it with Anty; who they had private reasons to know, would accept of fifty pounds, and drop the prosecution. He indignantly refused. That night few of us could sleep; the sworn evidence against our darling brother was so strong, so incontrovertible. My father did not tell us so, but we all knew that he spent the night in prayer. It was an agonizing thought, that his own dear son, than whom, a more kind, gentle, generous and upright man, never lived, should be transported like a felon. He cast his care upon his God, and found Him strong to save.

On cross-questioning the man witness, at the final hearing, he was observed to tremble violently; and then, most unexpectedly, he declared, that what he and Anty had sworn to, was all false; that she had burnt the holes in her cloak with a knitting needle, while he was standing by her; that she gave him ten shillings to be her false witness; that he and she were on the road together, and saw Mr. George pass by, but had not spoken to him at all; but on that night they planned the accusation to revenge Anty about the dairy. When asked, why he now confessed the truth? he said, "the devil had come to him in the night, and said, 'Ah! I have you now—you have perjured your soul—come off—I have a fine hot hell ready for you.' And that he was so much frightened, he could not help telling, as if others knew it, it would not feel so heavy on himself."

My brother was acquitted and Anty, prosecuted by the crown for perjury, was imprisoned for two years. And when that was over, her relations sent her to America; they were ashamed, they said, to hold up their heads while she was in the country.

CHAPTER VI.

Friend Flannil, the American Minister—Funeral Sermon at the Grave—Sudden Death—Gresham's Hotel—Escape from a Knave—Family Visit—Dress—Visits from the Overseers about Drawing—French—Similarity of Popery and Quakerism.

IN October, 1827, we were sitting one evening around the fire, when two young men of our Meeting walked in. They came to ask could we accommodate the American Friend, James Flannil, and his traveling companion, an English minister, with bed and board for a week or two, as they proposed not only to attend the Quarterly Meeting, but also to visit families. Ours was not the usual house for travelling Friends to come to. We were not plain enough to have that honour in general, at least, not while another house where the fare was equally good, and the dress of the family more consistent, was to be had. On the present occasion, something had occurred to render Friend Flannil's visit inconvenient to others, and a deputation had been sent to try what could be done at our house. My father immediately agreed to receive both the Friends; we were quite delighted, and promised to look sober and plain. The necessary preparations were made; a double bedded room was got ready; an abundant marketing sent home, and a plentiful supply of pastries, jellies, and all such creature comforts laid in. We had several other Friends on a visit with us, and several had come to spend the day with us, when about three o'clock on seventh day, we saw a post chaise drive up the lawn. We all ran to the windows, exclaiming—"Here comes the American." "Oh! no," said one, "it cannot be, the chaise is empty; look, the windows are all blinded." So it was, all shut up—the glass panes down and the blinds up; yet it drove to the door; the steps were let down, and out crawled an enormously large man. He was followed by a nice looking little elderly Friend with a black velvet cap on the top of his head. And after him, stepped out a slight young man, the guide from Youghal Meeting, who merely saw the other two safe into the house, and then stepped back into the chaise, opened the windows, and drove off.

I must describe Friend Flannil. He was six feet four inches high, large boned, and coarse looking in the extreme. A great shapeless white cloth coat, lined with light green, covered him all over. His feet were enveloped in huge moccason boots, and his countenance was indicative, in a remarkable manner, of crossness and discontent. His companion, Isaac Haldwell, was a plain Friend, and a preacher also; a most gentlemanly looking person, and prepossessed us very much by the quiet smile of drollery, with which he watched the impression made on us by the uncouth figure of the American. When the baggage was settled, and Friends seated in the parlour, Friend

Haldwell remarked, how pleasant it was to look about him. He walked to the window, and seemed so uncommonly pleased at gazing on the faded glories of October in the country, that we asked him how it happened, he had arrived with closed blinds. "Why," said he, "that is the very reason I enjoy every thing so much now. It was not very pleasant travelling so far in the dark; and through Lismore, too, that I wished so much to see, and the Blackwater—I was really vexed; but"—and he looked round with a comical smile—"*he* would not let the glasses be up." Somebody in Cork unfortunately asked him, how he liked Ireland? to which he replied, "I did not come from America to see the country." The same question was put to him in Youghal, very naturally, by another Friend. It made him angry, and he said, "he did not look at the country, nor he would not look at it; it was not worth looking at, for the trees were no bigger than American bushes; and he did not like to see so many houses, and no woods." Therefore he had compelled his two unfortunate fellow-travellers to drive all that long way without a glimpse of light. Friend Haldwell whispered—"He does many queer things; but he is a great minister, and we must overlook his little peculiarities."

A smothered laugh induced the speakers to look round. Friend Flannil had drawn his chair close to the fire; he had taken off his moccasons, and the view of his very tattered dirty stockings, accounted for the laugh. We all became silent, watching what he was going to do. The trowsers were drawn up to the knees, (there were several ladies in the room, our usual Quarterly Meeting guests,) a curious garter, made of the bark of a tree and twine, was thrown down on the rug, and the stockings deliberately taken off, exhibiting to our wondering eyes, two of the very dirtiest and biggest feet I had ever beheld. Friend Flannil, perfectly regardless of the presence of any one, held up his feet alternately to the fire, warming and rubbing them, and grumbling that the fire was not good, because it was made of coal, instead of wood, as he said it ought to be. When the feet were warmed and rubbed enough, he began to look about him, and to talk. "Do you call this living in the country? I am sure I don't." Then to my father—"Art thou married? Are these all thy children?" "Oh! no," he replied; (some of the company were as old, and older than himself;) "these young ones here are mine." "Eugh," said Friend Flannil, "they are very puny. I have three sons, and the lowest of them is six feet three; I guess thou can't match that." An irrepressible laugh ran round the room, and poor papa looked miserable, fearing the stranger would be offended; but Friend Haldwell whispered, "Do not be uneasy; he will never imagine it possible any one would laugh at him."

Dinner being announced, a considerable delay took place putting on the old stockings, &c., &c. He was invited to go into another room to wash his hands; but positively refused. "What shall we do with him?"

asked my mother of Friend Haldwell. "Really," said he, "I do not know; but do what thou wilt, he never thinks of taking offence." She then ordered a basin of water, &c. into the room before us all, and said to him—"Dinner is waiting, and thy hands must be washed—pray be quick." "Eugh," said he, "how mighty particular thou art." However, the ablutions were performed in a kind of way, and then he was requested to walk into the dining room. He sat still, and looked about, and seeing the butler standing at the door, he called out—"Here, thee! man, bring in the dinner then, can't thee, if it is ready." With a great deal of difficulty he was induced to go into the dining-room, which at last he did, by running past every one. He was placed at my mother's left hand at table, and the rest of us, twenty-two in number, took our places. Scarce were we seated, when Friend Flannil's tall, awkward form rose; he grasped the salt cellar, stretched it half way down the table, and threw it all about. He said, "I hate them buckets of salt. Mother, never put one near me again! mind, I hate salt." He occasionally used his knife and fork, but much more frequently, his fingers. He called for coffee, which not being ready, he said, "Go, get it; I'll wait for it;" and he went over to the fire until it was prepared. Then he came back to his seat, and ate fish in his fingers, and drank coffee, scolding, and growling incessantly, and ordering "the Mother" to go get him one thing or another.

After dinner, Jane Dalton came in, to pay her respects to the American Friend, and to invite him to dine with her mother on first day. She approached him almost with reverence, as a superior being. She said, "My mother, Mary Dalton—thou hast probably heard her name—sent me to see thee, and to invite thee to dine with us to-morrow, between Meetings. She would wish to become acquainted with thee." "Eugh," said Friend Flannil. "I don't know her, or thee either; nor I don't want to know her; and thee may go back, and tell her that; and I'll not go dine with her; I'll stay with 'the Mother.' Thee may go." Poor Jane!—such a rebuff—from the American Friend too,—so many present—the ill concealed laughter—the gaping, grinning servants—my father's look of agony; for he was pained to the heart, to see "an inspired minister" so rude to a female. It was a most amusing scene; and was ended by my mother most peremptorily desiring Friend Flannil to speak politely; that Friends in Ireland must be treated courteously. He tried to run out of the room; but she insisted that he should sit down, and listen to her. She told him it was very kind of Jane to ask him, and that he must accept her invitation. "Well," said he, "I will, if thou bids me."

The evening wore away; he called for meat at tea, and ate slice after slice of cold roast beef in his fingers, as another person would bread and butter; and when going to bed, said he must have something to eat in the night. He ordered the parlour fire to be kept lighted, and a tray with bread and cheese, and porter, to be left for him. After laughing more than we ever laughed in one day before, we all retired. About three o'clock in the morning, the whole house was alarmed. We started up in our beds, and listened; furniture seemed thrown about, and at last screams were heard from the servants' rooms. My father took a light, and went down stairs, agitated and anxious. The cause of the disturbance was soon discovered. Friend Flannil unclad, had gone from his room in quest of the bread and cheese; he had lost his way in the dark, and wandered into the servant maids' apartment. They were frightened at the great tall white form. It was a moonlight night. They never imagined who it was, but thought it was a ghost, and screamed with terror. He, finding his mistake, threw down a chair in his hurry to be off, and then rushed into another room, rousing the sleepers there too, and then down another stairs, throwing about candlesticks, and every thing he happened to meet with. With difficulty he was got back to his bed, and we finished our sleep.

The following morning Friend Haldwell looked pale, and worn, and wan, and confessed to having had a wretched night. Friend Flannil had disturbed him so often, that he said, "he was quite tired of the duty he had undertaken."

The American disdained to use a spoon eating eggs; and altogether his manners were so revolting, that it was unanimously determined henceforth he should take his meals at a table by himself, my mother persuading him that it was her Irish manner of especially honouring an American guest.

We all went to Meeting, and there Friend Flannil astonished all the assembly with his sermon. After the usual long pause of a Friends' Meeting, his huge gaunt form was seen to rise in the gallery, and to shake itself. Then the queer hat was taken off, and laid on the ground, the coat unbuttoned, and he began in a voice loud and gruff. "There was once an old horse, and he had a sore leg." This strange text drew all eyes on the man. He enlarged for nearly an hour on it, with great volubility; described the appearances as only one could have done who had witnessed the symptoms and treatment of veterinary disease; and drew a kind of moral from it; that we were all as diseased as the old horse, as disgusting as the horrid picture he had drawn, and that Quakerism was the only cure. Of course many comments were made on such a sermon as this, although Friends are often told it is very wrong to make any remark on addresses which are considered to proceed from "immediate inspiration;" but this induced many to disregard the general rule. One said, "it was a wonderfully deep discourse." Another, "that it contained a deal of hidden meaning." Another, "that we must be as far advanced ourselves in Christian experience to be able to understand it." Another, "that it was scandalous to hear such language in a place of worship." And another, "for my part, I think the man is mad." I believe very many agreed in this last opinion, but were timid of saying so.

After Meeting, he went to dine with Mary Dalton; and we had a very large company dining with us, and were amusing ourselves talking of, and laughing at the strange American minister. Whilst we were in the middle of dinner, however, in walked Flannil, with great coat and hat on. We asked him, "was any thing the matter, that he had left Mary Dalton's so soon?" He said, "Yes; I don't like her, she is so fat, and her house has a wall opposite to it, and I like to see something green." We asked had he dined? "Yes; I eat a bit, and then I came away." "Did Mary Dalton know he was going away?" "No; she looked so fat, I only said I was going out for a minute." "But that was rude." "Well, I don't care." Presently after, came a young man up the lawn, looking after him. He told us that Flannil had snatched the leg of a turkey up in his fingers, and gobbled it up, before any one at the table was helped, and then ran out of the house, actually frightening the good Friends.

The next day at dinner we had another scene. He was, as usual, placed at a small side table, by himself, but near my mother. We were all eating, and enjoying ourselves, when suddenly he exclaimed in a loud unearthly voice, that made the knives and forks drop out of our hands—"Something is going to happen." Poor mamma turned pale; the servants stood aghast, and wonder sat on each countenance. We asked—"What, what is the matter?" He slowly replied—"Something dreadful—oh! dreadful!" After what seemed a long time of painful suspense, he said, "I feel all down my leg and foot, like pins and needles pricking me." "Oh!" said one of my brothers, "the man's foot is asleep—that's all." And such a fit of laughter followed, as was, I am very sure, never before heard at a Quarterly Meeting dinner party; even poor papa laughed in spite of himself, and never from that day out, even tried to persuade us to respect this man, who was sent from America with the sanction and approval, by letters and epistles, of three Yearly Meetings there, to preach in this country as an inspired minister of the Christian religion—who was forwarded to Ireland from England, with the full approbation of the English Meetings; and again sent from Dublin down to the South, as something far more holy than common.

In the evenings he would lie on the sofa, full length, and scold any one who came near him; calling old ladies, "child," bidding them "get away";—"young woman, thy breath is not sweet," to one; and when tea was handed round, he addressed one nice English Friend with—"Here thee, go get me some meat." She went, and brought him some slices of cold meat. He turned them over and over again, with his fingers, dashed his tea awkwardly over her nice silk dress, and then scolded her heartily, and greased her with his hands in the most outrageously rude manner. And yet the plain Friends, many of whom were present still looked on him as a holy man, and coveted a word, even a cross word, from him. It would weary to tell all his extravagancies, his dirtiness, his profanation of religion; yet to this man, and the conversations relative to him, I am deeply indebted; for it was these scenes that first opened my eyes to the false pretentions of Quakerism. It was seeing such a man honored—a man who seemed not to possess one redeeming trait of virtue or amiability—who was entirely ignorant of the Scriptures—who was as ignorant as he was selfish, and as selfish as he was knavish and cunning; it was seeing such a disgrace to the name of Christianity honored, and almost reverenced, by the whole body of Friends in America, England, and Ireland; it was seeing this, that first inclined me to think it possible that Friends might be in error, and conviction that they were mistaken in one point, gradually opened the way to look at others, until at length, and not without thought, and prayer, and research, and years of careful study, I am now clearly of opinion, that Quakerism is not what it professes to be—a pure form of Christianity; but a deep and subtle delusion; where some truth is mixed up with great error—where the most soul-deluding doctrines are clothed in the garment of superior sanctity—where imagination is substituted for inspiration—where spiritual pride assumes the form of mock humility, and external forms take the place of dedication of heart—where the ignorant and the hypocritical take the lead, and where the substance, the life of religion

—faith in the blood of Jesus Christ, is never mentioned; at least I can say, after being for forty years a Quakeress, and hearing all the best preachers the Society produces, I never heard in Meetings, either for worship or discipline, "that salvation was to be obtained *only* through that precious blood."

At my father's suggestion, Friend Flannil was sent back to his congenial woods, without finishing his intended visitings; but not before one of our wealthy spinsters had testified against such an unusual quenching of the Spirit, by settling on him an annuity of fifty pounds per annum.

Friend Flannil's text was indeed a very extraordinary one; but quite as strange as his, have been the texts chosen by some of our own countrymen. Dublin Meeting once beheld a venerable patriarchal old man, whose white shining locks fell on his shoulders, rise in the preachers' gallery, and thus commence: "Good morrow morning, my fine, first day morning gallery bucks; what brings you here to-day? A light heart and a thin pair of breeches, will carry you through, my brave boys."

And another time, a tall portly man, in the same place, after slowly rising, and slowly taking off his broad brim, and slowly laying it down on the ground beside him, in the same slow way took off his great coat, folded it up, and laying it down beside the hat, addressed them thus: "Oh! my dear friends, I have a great concern on my mind, that you should take off your sins, and lay them down, as I have done my hat and coat."

One of our preachers having died, we, as usual, attended the funeral. Friends' funerals in Ireland are conducted with great quietness and solemnity—much more so, I think, than in England. On this occasion, the day after we heard of the Friend's death, as she was one for whom we all felt much respect, we went to the house, and sat in silence with the bereaved family for about half an hour. Then we were invited up stairs to see the pallid form. One of her daughters told us of her affection and uprightness, and of her great goodness and kindliness to the poor people in her neighborhood, and that she had always some work for them on her hands. But she did not tell, that which I was greatly wishing to know, whether she died in a happy assurance of pardon, and with the blessed hope of life everlasting. Friends always take it for granted, that a plain Friend when he dies, goes straight to heaven. I have known many cases, in which there was cause for great fear and anxiety; but I never heard of a doubt being expressed, either to the dying or to the survivors. This was certainly a good woman; her short sermons were always scriptural. At her funeral, round the grave, there were many speeches. A large crowd of persons were there. One of those speeches, or sermons, arrested my attention and surprised others not a little. It was Betsey Beater spoke. She eulogized the departed; and said, "that she had honored her Christian name; that she had always been such a consistent Friend; that she had never indulged her daughters in the vain fashions of the world—no; she had never even allowed them to wear silk gowns."

Very soon after this, there was an awfully sudden death in my own family. An aunt had remained up later than usual one night, regulating her house, and then retired apparently in good health; a couple of hours after, she was found dead in her bed. Oh! how I longed to know had she gone to heaven; but it was vain to ask. She was a very consistent Friend; that satisfied every one but myself. Many, many years after, I accidentally heard of her having been a constant reader of the Bible.

My father had some idea of making one of his sons a manufacturer; and before deciding on it, he wrote to some Friends in the north of Ireland to make inquiries. One Friend, who bore a very high character in the Society, amongst others, wrote to him, offering to take the lad as an apprentice, on payment of a fee of £500. Instead of answeriug that letter, my father resolved to go himself to the North: and to my great delight, proposed to make me the companion of his journey. We accordingly set off by the coach, which we had inside all to ourselves, to Dublin. We stopped at Gresham's Hotel for two or three days, attended the Dublin Monthly Meeting, which was nothing but routine business; and by very urgent entreaty, we accompanied a Friend to his house to dinner, that day. He was a very rich man, and had both a town and country house. He had often been feasted at our home, and now he sat us down with a large company, to eat potatoes and cabbage, and fried liver, and nothing else. This was the only bad dinner I ever met with in an Irish Friend's house; therefore I commemorated it. We took an early leave of the party, and hurried to our hotel, where we comforted ourselves with a cup of tea and a mutton chop; and took good care to accept of no more pressing invitations during our stay.

My father always put up at Gresham's Hotel; not only because of its being the best, or one of the best, hotels in Dublin, but because of the exceeding kindness which its master had shown him on the occasion of King George IV.'s visit to Ireland. My father had been one of the Friends appointed to wait on the King, and to present him with a congratulatory address from the Society. A day was fixed for the reception, and afterwards it was postponed for a week. To pass that period, my father and sister, who accompanied him, planned a visit to Lisburn. They set off in one of the northern coaches, drawn by three horses; and when about half the journey was completed, an opposition coach overtook them, and a race commenced, which terminated in the upset of the one in which my father was. It was a dreadful accident; every one on, and in the coach were more or less hurt. My sister's face was sadly cut by the glass; but she was the least hurt of the party. My father's head was cut and bruised, so that he was thought dead for a long time. The outside passengers had some a leg, others an arm broken. A gentleman who lived near, most kindly opened his house for the sufferers. There they had soon the best medical attendance that could be procured, and every domestic care. As soon as he was at all able to move, my father retraced his way in a post-chaise to Dublin. He drove to the Gresham, and was told that the house was full; then to the Bilton—the same answer met him there. From one to another, he went in vain to twenty hotels; and as night was coming on, he returned to the Gresham, and asking to see the proprietor, he told his tale, and begged to be allowed to stay in the coffee-room for the night. When Mr. Gresham had heard him, and seen the poor wounded invalid travellers, he immediately brought them into his own private rooms, gave them all they needed—beds, and care, and comforts; procured medical aid that night for them; and during the week they were compelled to remain, he and his kind family attended them with indefatigable hospitality. Nor would he accept any remuneration whatever; saying, they were guests in his private house, not customers in his hotel.

We proceeded to the North, and called on Friends Ring, the manufacturers. Father and son constituted the Firm; they were exceedingly orthodox Friends, and invited us most politely to their respective houses, both large, good and well furnished. My father spent two long mornings making the inquiries he was so anxious about, with respect to his son. The business appeared satisfactory in every way, and he had no fault to find with the large fee demanded; and yet, there was something on his mind, for which he could not account, that made him hesitate to conclude the arrangement. And at last, after weighing the matter well, he resolved to return home, and consult my mother again, previous to his final decision. Friends Ring urged him to conclude it at once; and asked a question he could not answer even to himself—"Why wilt thou not conclude the arrangement, now that thou art here, and we have mutually agreed to the terms?" On returning home, my mother, whom we feared would be disappointed, said she was well pleased it had so ended. "It was too far off to send the boy; and besides," she added, "they are such *very* plain Friends; and all the plain Friends are not like thee, John dear." This was one of the many instances in which the good hand of our God was upon us. The younger partner in that firm turned out soon after, to be a swindler, and a most unprincipled man. He embezzled a large sum, falsified his books, and fled with his ill-gotten wealth to America, deserting his nice, lady-like wife, and large young family. His conduct brought a scandal on the Society; but as usual, he was read out of the Meeting, and the principles he professed remained intact.

A religious body, certainly, ought not to be judged of, by the bad conduct of individuals; and especially when that body testifies against the evil members, by disowning them. This is the general and very plausible argument; but if it can be proved that the very elements of these unrighteous deeds are component parts of that system—that they are the natural fruits of that specious tree, whose seed germinates in the doctrines and practices of the body—then I conceive it is a work of righteousness to arraign the Society itself. I am not skilled in disquisitions on cause and effect; and leaving that to an abler pen, will simply continue my story of the working of Quakerism as it came before my own eyes. "By their fruits ye shall know them," is a sure criterion of judgment.

Benjamin Sibliman, a minister in great esteem in England, accompanied by the companion appointed to watch over him, paid us a family visit. He had what is called a very weighty concern in our little circle. We were all, with two Friends, our guests at the time, assembled in the large drawing-room. The Friends shook hands with us all round, said what a fine day, what a pleasant situation we lived in, &c. &c., and then sat down in silence for about ten minutes. Friend Benjamin repeatedly drawing out his handkerchief, and applying it to his eyes and nose, and sighing deeply; by which we knew he was labouring under great weight of spiritual burden, and that caused us to feel a kind of creeping solemnity, in expectation of what was coming. At length he spoke, still sitting in his easy chair; (Friends do not ever stand up to speak on family visits.) He told us that he felt great love for us—that he greatly wished us to be blessed of the Lord—that every member of our large and interesting family ought to be a "standard bearer" in our highly favoured Society—that the Lord was only waiting for us to be willing—that if we would yield to the requirings of truth, and come down to that lowly state, which was comparable to Mary in the Gospel, who anointed the Saviour's feet, we should experience a lifting up, and be made the honoured instruments of upholding the principles of our worthy predecessors, some of whom had even suffered martyrdom for the precious cause.

He spoke in this strain for more than half an hour; then paused a few minutes, and knelt down to pray. We all stood up. He first prayed that the dear heads of the family might be strengthened to maintain to the end the Christian warfare, that when the solemn close came, they might have the satisfaction of knowing that they had set a good example, both in words and practices, to their dear children. Then he prayed that the dear eldest daughter of this house, might be so tendered by a feeling of contrition, as to be made willing to give up those outward adornments, which were so calculated to beguile the unstable; that she might feel the great responsibility which rested on her—yes, he felt bold to say, on her—as to the younger members of the family, who were so naturally led by her example. Then he prayed that the Lord would make her willing to give up the vain fashion of wearing curls, and plaiting her hair; and that he would teach her that these were not little things. He also prayed for the strangers amongst us—that they might be gathered into the fold, and never forget that they belonged to that peculiar people, which God had chosen for himself, even the people of a plain language. Then another pause, during which Friend Benjamin wiped his eyes, and nose, again and again, and then he turned round, and shook hands with my father.

A desultory conversation commenced. Abraham, the companion, was an old acquaintance, and told us that Benjamin's concern was much greater in our family than it had been in any other in the town. This was a compliment. It intimated that we were of consequence in the estimation of an English Minister; and Abraham quietly said to the eldest daughter, "Now, my dear, wont thee put on caps? Thy hair is, indeed, very beautiful; but it would look so neat, if closely braided under a small cap. I would like thee better with a cap on, even than I do without. And then these little frills and ornaments: do, my dear young friend, give them up; they are only vain adornings." "Well, now, Aby," she replied, "listen to me. In the first place, I do not want thee to like me better than thee does;" and she smiled archly on the good natured old man—"thee can't help liking me. In the second place, my time is far too valuable to be spent making caps, and wasted day after day, clap-starching them. Besides, it was He who made me who gave me my hair; and I am not so ungrateful as to hide it under a cap, as if I was ashamed of it. The Scripture commands me to adorn myself in modest apparel, not to disfigure myself in an unbecoming sectarian garb. Friend Benjamin has relieved his mind. Thee never was very clever at preaching, my good Friend Aby; so shake hands with me now, and I promise thee the sins of my dress will not be laid at thy door." "Ah!" replied Aby, "thee is a mighty pleasant young woman; and I do think thee is wiser than many of us, for all thee is not so consistent as I wish thee was."

Luncheon was announced, and the worthy Friends set to work with right good will. They were somewhat serious whilst eating the delicate sweetbread; then cold turkey and ham raised their spirits, and against the apple-tarts and cheese-cakes had done their part, Friends Benjamin and Aby were as jocose as plain Friends are permitted to be. One of the lads whispered, just loud enough for Aby to hear. "Does not Friend Benjamin look much happier and more sensible now, than when he was putting his handkerchief to his eyes, and trying to make us think he was oppressed, even to tears, under the weight of his concern? Ask him to take some flummery; I am sure he would like it." Aby contracted his brows, but smiled, and said, "Thee is a very wild boy, I am afraid."

It was wonderful to think of the number of Friends who now began to have concerns on their minds about our dress. The boys they did not interfere about, although my eldest brother was far more unfriendly in his dress than any one of us. He dressed in all points like a gentleman, without any of those righteous spirits rising up to testify against him. But the girls were tormented on the subject; and as my father was an elder, they made him think he was deficient in his duty unless he constrained us to adopt their views. If it had been possible to sow discord in our happy home, they would have done it, by their unceasing efforts to set the father and daughters at variance.

Sarah Mills, of Clonmel, whom I mentioned as having the men's and women's Meetings both under her guidance, thought fit to interfere. She wrote letter after letter to him. I wish I had those letters, that I might copy them here, for they were curious specimens of self-righteous bigotry; but my mother had them burnt, as discreditable to the writer. She wrote to him, that it was his duty to coerce his daughters; and that if his wife would not co-operate with him in doing so, he should exert the authority of a master, and insist upon obedience. That, as an elder in the Society, he was under an especial obligation to see that his family walked consistently. That the Society did expect his daughters to be amongst those who should take an active part in the discipline. And she added, that she had found it often necessary to exercise control over her own family; and she experienced that a firm and decided manner was effective. Even her dear son-in-law, she said, was now obedient to her in everything she could wish. That poor, craven, hen-pecked son-in-law, was a cipher in his own house, as well as everywhere else.

But it is time to mention what our offence was which this worthy woman was so stirred up about. It was, that we wore tortoise-shell side-combs. Incredible as it may seem, that was the burden of her letters. She alluded to the general style of our raiment, but tortoise-shell side-combs was the specified sin. Fortunately, my father had long before told us a story of Sarah Mills, which had brought her meddling and self-satisfied character under our notice; and her wish to dictate to him, on one occasion, in so offensive a manner, though we laughed at the recital of it, was now of great use in nullifying her present attempt to make him coerce us at her instigation.

It was at a Quarterly Meeting party, before my father was married; when he was young, well-looking, and wealthy, and consequently one whom the Friends were anxious to see suitably settled in life. Sarah Mills had unmarried daughters, and wished to bring about a match with one of them. My father was slow at taking the hints so often given him; but he rather avoided the house, feeling that even a casual visit there might be misconstrued; and besides that, he was not only deeply in love, but actually engaged to the bright, intelligent, and highly-educated little woman with whom he afterwards spent his long and happy life. Sarah Mills knew nothing of this engagement, so she invited him very pressingly to her house, and he went. After dinner, when they were all assembled, she said to him, "John, will thee give me two or three shillings? I want them." She held out her hand, and he gave her three tenpenny pieces. She jingled them together, and said, "I like the sound." Then to her daughter Rebecca—"Give me three tenpenny pieces out of thy pocket." Rebecca gave them, and she shook them all together; and, turning to the company, who were looking and wondering what she was about, she said, "I like that music; don't you think they jingle very well together?" "How can thee get over that, John?" said one of her allies, as the laugh ran round the room. "I wish thee joy. She is fine, stout, young woman," said another, "and thy mother-in-law will save thee all the trouble of ordering thy own house." As soon as he could, my father slipped away, without even saying farewell to the fair Rebecca, or her clever, strong-minded mother.

We had a visit from the two women overseers of our meeting, to remonstrate on the impropriety of having a drawing master. They said they would not think of bringing us before the Meeting for it, but it was a relief to their own minds to speak to us on the matter; and they hoped we would weigh it well, and remember, that it was in much love they had spoken.

Another time, the overseers came to say, that they had heard of our having a French master; that they knew it was not generally objected to by Friends, but they felt easier to warn us. There was great danger in it; it was insidious; Friends were tempted to say things in French they would not say in English—such as Monsieur and Madame. They did not wish to be officious, and they hoped we would not think them officious; but their office was a very important one, and they were anxious to fulfil their duty faithfully.

We were always ready to hear them, in silent and respectful attention; and always gave them plenty of cakes and fruit when they had unburdened their minds. We wished to keep them in good humour; for if they had been any way huffed with us, they would have taken a ready revenge, and put us under dealing. This would have so grieved my father, that we made many concessions which we would not otherwise have done. To please them, and keep them quiet, we always wore the "Bonnet" at Meetings, which we attended regularly; and would stay at home of a cold, damp day, rather than put on our out-of-meeting bonnets! and we always used the plain language to Friends, and amongst ourselves.

There is a great similarity between Quakerism and Popery. Both are the religion of the priests, and the people are compelled to an outward conformity. The domineering influence of the Friends who take part in the discipline, over the body, is exactly a counterpart of that which the priests exercise over their flocks. The one requires obedience, because they are inspired, they tell us; the others call themselves the Church, and demand it. The spirit is the same in both!

CHAPTER VII.

Applications for membership—William Abbenger's visit and sermon to persons under twenty-one years of age—Friend Sailors—Shipwrecked Girls—Escape from Quakerism—Dublin Yearly Meeting—Receipt for making a red round of beef.

I remember three applications for membership being made to our Meeting. Two of the applicants were ladies of the highest respectability, the wives of country gentlemen, middle-aged, and wealthy; the other was a poor woman, unmarried, and living in the city. We knew all three personally, and were much interested in the business. They were kept in suspense for several months: visit after visit was appointed to be made to them; and the report of those visits was read to us in the Monthly Meeting. Julia Drevor, one of the ladies, agreed to every thing required; she expressed her entire unity with all our doctrines, practices, and peculiarities; assumed the strictest garb, adopted the language, and came to Meeting whenever she could. She was admitted. A sweet, gentle, amiable lady she was. Tired of the gay frivolities of the fashionable life she had led, she rushed into Quakerism, and flattered herself that the mortifications she underwent from her family and acquaintances was an acceptable sacrifice. She purchased numerous Friends' books, and would pore over them till her sight failed. My mother had many serious conversations with her, and advised her to study the Bible instead, for of that she was very ignorant. She went to live in the country, and we rarely met her. When we did, she was greatly altered; her smile, though still sweet, was very sad. She soon after died, having sent for the Clergyman of the parish on her death-bed, instead of for one of our ministers, as a consistent and converted Friend ought to have done.

Martha Ulveston, the other lady, was also an amiable woman, and was possessed of far more strength of character than Julia. They were relatives, and had worked each other up to the conviction, that it was a required duty of them to become Quakers. Martha was many months longer on our Meeting-books than Julia. She found it more difficult to give the unconditional surrender of all her pre-conceived ideas of religious truth. She was sincere in her wish to be a self-denying, plain Friend; but her husband, an intelligent, sensible man, was greatly averse to her doing so. However, she was at last admitted, and, I believe, continued till her death, a few years after, conformable in all respects to our rules.

The third, poor little Rachel Bates, was visited also. She was reported to unite in all our views of religious truth unconditionally. The visitors said they believed her to be sincere, but that she was very ignorant; and that it was possible her wish to join Friends might be influenced by the knowledge that we supported our own poor. On that supposed possibility she was rejected.

These were the only applications for membership in our Women's Meeting that ever came under my knowledge. I have known three cases of applying to be restored to the membership, which had been lost by marrying in Church. One of them only was re-admitted; for the rule is, you must declare you are sorry for having done so; and two of the ladies refused positively to say this. The third, after holding out for some years, at last said, she was sorry she had married; and then she and her children were all received back again into the fold.

When William Abbenger was travelling the nation, with a certificate from the London Meeting, to visit families, he stayed with us for more than a week. We liked him very much, he was so gentlemanly in his manners and habits, and good-humoured and happy in himself. His conversation was interesting, scientific, and amusing; and he did not trouble us with incessant preachings, like some of the other ministers. One first day morning, at breakfast, he said to us, "I should like very much if some of the young people of your meeting might be invited to meet me this evening in your large room. I think I should like to address them in a less formal manner than in a regularly appointed gathering in the Meeting-house. Am I asking too much? or imposing a burden on thee, my friend?" My father promptly replied, that his wishes should be attended to; and each of us was commissioned to invite the young people up to tea. "Let your invitations," said Friend William, "be limited to persons under twenty-one years of age."

Friends' Meeting-houses are well designated. They are, indeed, places for meeting together; shaking hands, chatting, and communicating all sorts of interesting family and Society news; and it is possible, that during the time they all sit down in silence, many are striving hard to meditate on the things which concern the salvation of their souls; but the Lord has declared, "My house shall be called the house of prayer." In the Friends' Meeting-house, prayer is very seldom heard. Year after year will often pass over, and not one solitary prayer be audibly offered in many of them.

It was to Meeting and to meet our friends we went; and great amusement we had executing Friend William's wishes. "Mary, I can't ask thee to come; thee is over the allowed age, I think; is not thee?" to a young lady of twenty-one and a-half. "Rebecca," to another who looked sixty, "I do not exactly know thy age; but if thou art not over twenty-one, Friend Abbenger has a concern to address thee, this evening, at tea. May I say thee will come?" "Oh! certainly, my dear." "Susanna, how old art thou?" "I am not going to tell thee." "Oh! very well; but I can't ask thee to the English Friend's great tea, unless thee tells me." "Why?" "No one is to be let come, who is over twenty-one." "Oh! well, I'll come;

I'm nineteen." "Ah, Susanna, I do think thee is ten years more than that." "Oh! yes, I'll come; it is this odious bonnet that makes me look old." "James, I am sorry I can't ask thee to our great tea party this evening." "And why, pray, can thee not? My sisters have just told me they are going." "Oh! yes, they are young enough. The English Friend has specified twenty-one as the oldest that he wishes for. Thee is long past that, thee knows." "Nonsense, I am seventeen." "No, James, thee cannot deceive me. I remember those nice black whiskers of thine for many years past." "Oh! yes; but does not thee know that I am a lusus naturæ?"

Altogether we assembled a company of eighty; and, very much against my mother's conscience, she had to send messengers to purchase bread and cakes on the Sabbath day, to feed this unexpected host of juveniles. As soon as the tea things were removed, Friend William, who had been very chatty and pleasant until now, dropped into silence. His face became very grave, and we all ceased to speak, and ranged ourselves in quiet order round the room, and round the table in the centre. The door was open, and many were seated on the landing-place and up the stairs. After a lengthened pause, he asked my brother to read a chapter in the Gospels, but did not say which. Then a short silence, and he addressed us all on the importance of religion; the value of the soul; the uncertainty of life; the necessity for dedication of heart; the high profession which Friends make of inspiration, and the privileges which we enjoyed as members of a chosen and peculiar people. He spoke for nearly an hour, and the Friends left us, greatly pleased with the novelty, and edification, and entertainment they had received.

After they were gone, and the Friend had retired for the night, we began to converse on the events of the day. My mother's remark made a deep impression on my mind. She said, "I was greatly disappointed in Friend Abbenger's address. I do think our ministers will have a great deal to answer for, they all neglect their opportunities of preaching the Gospel so sadly. Here were eighty immortal souls, listening with as much attention as if an angel from heaven was speaking to them. Why did he not tell them they were sinners, and must be washed in the blood of the Lord Jesus, if they would be saved? Why did he not tell them to read their Bibles, and to pray that the Holy Spirit might enable them to understand its truths ? Instead of this, he was puffing them up with the false idea, that they were superior to other denominations of Christians. Our high professions—our highly-privileged Society—our chosen and peculiar people. Our profession is the Christian Religion —nothing more or higher than that of all the Reformed Churches. The highest privilege a mortal can have, is to be allowed access to God in prayer through Christ. This is not certainly peculiar to our Society. The privilege he meant, of being allowed to attend our Monthly Meetings, is unworthy of a preacher's notice. If our ministers knew themselves, that the only way in which a soul can be saved, is by faith in the Lord Jesus; and if they really felt in their own hearts this truth, I am sure they would preach it simply and savingly."

As my father was a Russian merchant, his business often brought him in contact with the captains of vessels. They are a class of men for whom he felt much interest; the comforts of so many homes depending upon their skill and enterprise, and they themselves so completely deprived of all domestic enjoyment. He therefore constantly brought a nautical friend to dine and spend the evening with us; and when the individual happened, as he sometimes was, to be a Quaker, he was allowed to become almost domesticated during his stay in the city. Some of these guests were very interesting, intelligent men—Spaniards, Portuguese, Dutch, and Russian; and as my father could converse with them in their own languages, their happy and gratified looks told of their enjoyment; and many and many a little token of their grateful remembrance of his kindness was sent to him from far-off lands. The parting gift he loved to give them, was a Bible in their own language.

One winter's day, he sent us up a note from town, to say, that a captain and his three daughters were to dine, and stay a few days with us. He added, "their ship was wrecked, they have lost everything, and were picked up by one of the coal ships. Tell the girls to dress them, and make them comfortable." Poor things! they arrived soon after the note—three nice, pretty girls, all under seventeen. One had a man's coat on; another a blanket wrapped round her; and the little thing had on a sailor boy's trowsers, and a piece of canvass sail-cloth like a shawl. We soon attired them in our own dresses, refreshed and cheered them; and against dinner-time came, they were cheerfully smiling, and telling us of their misfortune. They had been run down by a large vessel, and damaged so much, that when the night came on, wild and wet, their ship was unmanageable. The masts were cut down to try and save their lives, but at last they had to get into the boat, as the vessel began to sink, and after tossing for many hours like a cork on the billows, the coal ship had seen and saved them. One man was lost out of the crew; the others, though sadly bruised and frost-bitten, were very thankful to have their lives preserved. They remained our guests about a week, and then left us well clad, and with a considerable sum of money, which my father had collected and raised for them.

Another of our nautical visitors, having inadvertently mentioned the names of some London Friends, was questioned as to his knowledge of them; and at last he was reluctantly brought on to confess, that he was a Friend himself. His mother was an elder or overseer in the Meeting, his father dead, and he, the eldest of several children, could not brook the bondage of Quakerism. To escape it, and the remonstrances and reproofs of his mother and her friends, he had, when quite a lad, run away from home, and gone as cabin-boy on board an East Indiaman. He had worked hard, saved money, and was now part owner of the vessel he commanded. We were the first Friends he had come in contact with since his flight; and his heart warmed to the old familiar language of his childhood, and the names of his unforgotten former acquaintancs. By my father's persuasion and assistance, he renewed his intercourse with his mother, and obtained her forgiveness, which, he repeatedly declared, was a great ease to his mind; but he would not return to Quakerism, of which he had quite a horror.

My mother having occasion to go to Dublin, and it being nearly the time of the Yearly Meeting, there, it was planned to make a pleasant party, and to attend it. My mother, sister, two brothers, and myself, anticipated great pleasure from this trip, and were not disappointed. We travelled in our own carriage and post-horses, and put up at Tuthill's Hotel, in Dawson street, to be near the Meeting-house. It was not what is called an interesting Meeting; that is, there were no American, and only two English ministers, at it; and according to the number and importance of those strangers, is the attendance of our own country Friends; and, consequently, the entertainments and parties were smaller, and less attractive, than Yearly Meeting companies generally are. However, that made no difference to us. The few invitations which we accepted, were given in honor of us, not of the Meeting Friends. We entertained our own company at the Hotel, sometimes at breakfast, sometimes at tea, about half a dozen at a time. Many of our acquaintances were out of the Society; and as my mother's character was well known, she was visited by several of the benevolent and religious leaders of the Societies formed for the benefit of the poor and the ignorant. They endeavoured, and with success, to interest her in the Kildare-street Society, the Hibernian Society, the Bible Society, and several other such like Societies. We attended some of the Rotundo Meetings, and spent altogether a very pleasant six weeks. But I had seen so little of the Friends, and attended so few of the sittings of the Yearly Meeting, that I resolved to persuade my father to bring me with him to the next, as I knew he would attend all regularly, and go among the Friends in their own houses. I found no difficulty in inducing the dear man to gratify my wishes. With one sister for a companion, we came by the coach, and engaged apartments at the Gresham.

This proved an unusually large and interesting Meeting. The names of the celebrated ministers who had applied to their own Meetings for certificates to attend it, had been spoken of all through the country for several weeks previously. John Earl, with his sister, the celebrated Elizabeth Stately, and her sister-in-law, the little Elizabeth Grill; and, besides these, there were seven other strange ministers. The first day Morning Meeting was very large, and several of the preachers, men and women, addressed us. Elizabeth Stately prayed for a blessing on the Yearly Meeting, and that all the sittings might be owned by the Divine Head.

It is not easy to recollect what the Friends say in their sermons; they are so discursive, so rambling, so slovenly in their arrangement, and so mixed up with the expressions of their own feelings, and I may add, so much alike in the one point of exalting Quakerism, and treating it as the only true development of Christianity, that unless you write them down at the time, they soon pass away, unless some peculiar oddity impresses the speaker and the subject on the memory. I had attended Dr. Crook's lectures, and from them learned how to take down the words of the speakers. I have several manuscript volumes of Friends' addresses beside me, which, however, I fear would prove but tiresome reading, if I inserted them. The opinion of Quaker preaching, given by the good William Wilberforce, I entirely agree with—"It leaves behind it no valuable deposit."

After the Morning Meeting, we went by invitation to dine with one of the head Friends of Dublin. There were about eighteen guests. Our entertainment was excellent, choice, substantial, and varied, with most delicious confectionary, and good wines. The company all sedately chatty, and gravely pleasant.

At the Evening Meeting we were favored with five sermons—two men and three women speakers; and then we took tea with another Friend, in a very large company, which had been gathered together, in honor of the great ministers who were of the party. Two rooms were filled with guests. The plain Friends gathered around the English ministers in the best room, listening with devout attention to their remarks, and occasionally venturing to utter a few timid words. I was, of course, among the younger and less important part of the company, in the back room, and yet so near the folding doors, that I could see and hear all that was doing.

"I really am quite pleased I have come to Ireland," said the English Friend, "we had quite a privileged time in both Meetings to-day."

"Yes," replied Joseph, our host, "it was a precious opportunity."

"I am of opinion," she said, "that we English Friends would do well, to be more frequently in the habit of coming amongst you, it feels quite refreshing to me, to be permitted to associate with so many of our dear Friends in the truth, in their own native land."

"Yes," said Joseph; "and it is very gratifying to us, to see you amongst us."

"Canst thou tell me who that female Friend is, that addressed the Meeting this morning; she sat the last in our gallery, and commenced, I think, with the words, 'I do verily believe'?"

"Oh! yes," he answered; "that is Sarah Black—a wonderful woman; she is an acknowledged minister. She is sometimes very large in the exercise of her gift."

"Your ministers, I observe," said she, "are mostly females."

"Yes," he replied, "an American Friend was not long since amongst us; and remarking how the gift of the ministry was so generally bestowed on our women Friends, he was led to speak of it from the gallery, as a symptom of decline in the vigour of our Society. He warned us to stir up the life within us; or, said he, 'the women will take your crowns from you.' Some of our females were not well pleased at the remarks he made."

"Really," she replied, "I am opinion, that it is very desirable, men Friends should share with us in the burden of the ministry. The weight of so serious a calling is too important, to be exclusively laid on the females."

"Yes," said Joseph; "but our men do not seem to apprehend that they are called to speaking in public; and as the women do feel willing to surrender themselves to the service, it appears as if the arrangement was not altogether of our own seeking."

"Ah!" she said, "but I am of opinion, that if our men Friends were faithful to the tender monitions of the divine light, they would be appointed to the service of the ministry. I am really of opinion, that there is danger to be apprehended, when this important office in the Church is wholly delegated to our sex. Some of us may not be well skilled in administering that solid meat, which a healthful body requires, although capable of supplying the milk which is suited for babes."

"Yes," said Joseph; "but thou knowest it is the Spirit that speaks, and the instrument is not to be regarded. The edification which we require, will be administered to us by the Spirit, through that vessel which is dedicated to the service; and perhaps the weaker the vessel, the more glorified may the Spirit be; for there is no distinction of persons."

She paused a few minutes, and then said, "Is that young woman, who was seated on the steps of our gallery, and spoke a few words this evening, an acknowledged minister?"

"Yes," replied Joseph, "she has very lately been acknowledged; she belongs to one of our small country Meetings."

"She appears to be a very simple-minded person; art thou personally acquainted with her?"

"Yes," he replied; "she has been very carefully brought up, by her mother, Anne Butt. Has dedicated herself very early to the work of the ministry: she is only about twenty-four years of age."

"Ah!" she replied, "I am of opinion, there may be a rashness in encouraging what may prove but the zealous desires of a well-meaning young person."

The name Anne Butt, had been heard in the back room; and I turned to listen what the juvenile portion of the company thought of her.

"Mary, I think thee knows all about her; come now, do tell us," said one.

"I do" said Mary; "in the first place, she has been brought up a model of our third query, in plainness of speech, behaviour, and apparel. Her mother was so careful to bring her up consistently, and to keep her from contamination with the world, that poor Anne was never allowed even to sit in the front of the house, lest she should look out at the window and see vanity or wickedness. She was taught her letters out of George Fox's Life, and to read, in Sarah Grubb's Journal. She told me that she had great satisfaction in being able to say, that she had never read any books but Friends' books."

"Consequently," added a plain-looking young man standing by, "she is well calculated to preach to Friends."

"Cousin Edward," said Mary, "thee must not interrupt me with such unbecoming remarks. Anne is an acknowledged minister of our Society, and must be spoken of with respect."

"Go on, Mary, and never mind him. Ah! do; we are all interested."

"I do not think I have much more to tell. She can not only read, but write too, and do sums in a small way. Then she works beautifully; instead of hemming her handkerchiefs, she stitches them all round, two threads to every stitch. She is very fond of needle-work, and spends most of her time at it; but all plain-work of course."

"Consequently she is well calculated to preach," said Edward again.

"I will not condescend to notice thee, Edward," said Mary, smiling. "Anne is far above us all, now.

She used to be very glad to see me; but now she can only speak to the elderly plain Friends. She drops into silence, when any of her old acquaintances are near, and is much given to the practice of admonishing us. She has concerns about so many things, which it is unpleasant to think one may not manage for one's-self, that we rather avoid her company now. My dress—and I am sure I am plain as plain can be —is a constant trouble to her spirit; but she is far beyond me. She is so very plain, she will not even wear fingers in her gloves."

"Indeed," said Edward, "that is plain; I wonder is she too plain to wear toes to her stockings."

This last idea of Edward's upset all our gravity; and a laugh too loud to be quite decorous, was the consequence.

The next morning the Meetings for discipline commenced. The room we met in was very crowded. The business commenced according to the rules of the Book of Discipline, by reading over what had been done last year; and then the clerk was appointed for the present time, with three other Friends to assist her. They sat at one side of an elevated table, which, being covered with a green cloth, and strewn with books, pens, and paper, had quite a business look. The ministers were on the seat exactly behind them, but raised a couple of steps higher; and we so ranged in front, as that every one could see the table and the ministers. Very soon after we had sat down in silence, the English Friend knelt down, and prayed for a blessing on the assembled company, in much the same language as she had used the morning before in the public worship. The names of those who had been sent from distant Meetings as representatives, were called over; each one slowly rising and answering, "Here," when her name was mentioned. Then the clerk read out one query, and each representative in her turn replied to it. Then a second and a third query; that was all the business done at the first sitting; for several Friends had concerns to speak, and took up the time doing so. One said, "She did not feel easy to refrain from mentioning a subject that had very seriously rested on her mind; and which she believed to be of importance; for we were a self-denying people, and it became us to let our light shine. A laxity had crept in among Friends, in the matter of entertaining their country Friends, and the strangers who favored us with their company. She would not wish to put any impediment in the way of due hospitality; but the show, and the extravagance, and the profusion, were calculated to throw a stumbling-block in the way of the unlearned. Sweets after dinner, were a great need-not, and should be abstained from at such a solemn time; and wine was apt to make Friends drowsy, when they came to the Evening Meeting." She then sat down, and in about two minutes rose up again, and said, "I feel easier to add, that cakes at tea are a superfluity, which Friends would do well to avoid."

This meeting lasted for two hours; and after it was over, we all hurried off to dinner. We found ourselves again in a large company, in which some of the English Friends were included. The dinner was a capital good one; fish, flesh, and fowl, and pies and puddings in abundance. The lady of the house apologized for the excellence of the repast she had invited us to; saying, that dinner had been ordered before she went to Meeting; otherwise she would have paid due deference to the advice given in the Yearly Meeting. The guests told her they needed no apology. One of the men guests asked what she alluded to; and when told, said, "Ah! I think I can guess who gave that advice. Was it not Sarah Castle?" "Yes." "She gives very poor entertainments herself, and it vexes her to hear the comparisons which are made. She wants to have you all in the same box with herself."

When dinner was over we all hurried back to Evening Meeting. Two more of the queries were got through, and the certificates of the English Friends were sent by the Men's Meeting, sitting close by, in another room, in to us. These documents were curious in their way. They mentioned that the Friend named in each of them, was a minister in that particular Meeting which issued it; that she was in good esteem amongst them, and that much unity had been felt for her, in the labor of love she was performing, in visiting Ireland. After the clerk had read these papers, in the usual slow, monotonous tone, which the Friends adopt, to give solemnity to their proceedings, one after another, three women rose to express thankfulness that their dear Friends had been led to visit this land—to hope that the Lord would own the dedication of heart which had caused these beloved Friends to leave their native shores, and come to refresh the spirits of the travailing ones—to entreat Friends to prize the precious opportunity now afforded them, and to esteem it as a very plain proof that the Lord was still gracious to us, seeing that he had sent his chosen ones to minister to us, unworthy as we were of so great a privilege. Besides these complimentary preachings, several short remarks, each followed by the usual silence, were made on the queries. That on dress, being, not "clear" from any of the Meetings, caused great affliction; and the outpourings of remonstrances, on the decline of true religion, which was indicated by these deviations from the wholesome rules of our Society. One said, "She was oppressed by witnessing the inroads of the enemy, that she felt very bold to say, the responsibility which rested on mothers was very great. They ought to force obedience from their families; but, alas! alas! she feared that too often they had opened the door for further departure, by putting straw bonnets on their dear children. She was willing to believe they had unintentionally erred by entertaining the fallacious notion, that for young children it was a matter of small moment."

At the end of every one of the sittings, a written message was sent in to the men, to say, the women wished to know had the men any business to communicate to them, and to request information of the time to which the men meant to adjourn. The men would then keep us waiting a long time, and at last send back as formal a note as that they had received, and perhaps two or three printed epistles and testimonies of the dead Friends.

When the Evening Meeting was over, we went to another Friend's house to tea, and were entertained in the same way—plenty of tea, and cakes, and good things; and the conversation, almost invariably, was restricted to comments on the Friends who took part in the Discipline, silly, witty, and pungent as the speaker happened to be. And really, when I call to mind the many, many remarks I have heard made on the slavish subjection of intellect and common sense, which these good Friends demand of their hearers, and the just appreciation of their claims to deferential compliance which was expressed, I am astonished that the mental thraldom is so long endured.

The third morning there was a meeting for worship, when both men and women sat together. We were given several short sermons, and one long one, which was very good of its kind; for John Earl was the very best minister in the Society.

After that was over, we went to another dinner party; but here the fruits of the advice given by Sarah Castle was unpleasantly evident. A leg of mutton and potatoes, and a red round of cold beef, was all the dinner, not even a pudding; and when the cloth was removed, instead of wine, coffee was served up.

There was no danger to be apprehended that evening of our being drowsy in Meeting. A couple more of the queries were gone through, and preached on. One of the English Friends had much to say for the easing of her own mind, on the beauty of our discipline, the value of upholding it in all its primitive loveliness, and the danger of departing from its order. Another English Friend hoped we were careful to study the Holy Scriptures. She had found them a light to her feet, and a lamp to her path. They had comforted her in the hour of bereavement, and counselled her in the path of difficulty. She was jealous of her dear Irish sisters, lest this invaluable treasure of heavenly wisdom had been disregarded, and she was of opinion, that a revival of religion would follow the diligent and prayerful study of that Holy Book. Soon after she had resumed her seat, up rose one of our own country preachers, and said, she could not feel easy to refrain from adding a few words to the instructive counsel our dear Friend had so weightily imparted. She was very fearful there was neglect in the perusal of Friends' books. She was far from wishing to detract from the importance of studying the Holy Scriptures. The one should be done, and the other not undone; for it was the self-same Spirit which dictated the Scriptures, by which our dear predecessors had been enabled to give forth those valuable works. It was the same Spirit which had gathered us as a people, and we ought to make ourselves acquainted with the doctrines by which our highly-favoured Society had been of old distinguished from the ungodly world. It was a truth, which had been in a very remarkable manner borne in upon her mind, that our Society would decline; yea, would become as a thing of naught, if the perusal of Friends' Books was neglected. She said, "It stands us upon, my dear sisters, to look well to our doings in this matter."

We went to another tea party this evening, and heard sad complaints of the poor dinners which, in compliance with Sarah Castle's advice, the Friends had given generally. The men Friends, old and young, gave their opinion, that Sarah Castle "had run before her guiding in the matter."

The fourth morning again found us at Meeting. We had always a very unpleasant ordeal to pass through, to get to our own meeting-room. There is a long vestibule leading to the inner hall, and all along this vestibule the men range themselves, to stare at the women as they pass in. There they make their comments, often audibly, and fix among themselves which is to be called the prettiest girl at the Meeting. In the hall inside is the place where the invitations are given, and, consequently, it is no easy matter to make your way to the interior.

The business was just of the same kind—two more queries, one or two more epistles read, and then a Committee appointed to draw up answers to those epistles, and to bring them to a future sitting to be approved of by the Meeting. All the business which is done might be got over in ten minutes easily; but it is a part of the system to spin out the appearance of doing something for the allotted two hours. At this time two men Friends sent in a note, to say they had a concern to visit the women Friends. A note was returned, saying, that the present appeared a suitable time to receive the proposed visit of men Friends; and as soon as the door-keeper had made her solemn exit with the missive, the Friends in the best seat in the preachers' gallery vacated their places, and settled them comfortably for the men. After a few minutes' waiting, in they came, three tall men, with their hats on. The third had been sent to accompany them, and to see they behaved properly. One of them had a good deal to say; and very good advice he gave on the necessity of being prepared for death, which is sure to come upon each of us, and the miserable state of those who put off till that fearful hour, the most important occupation an immortal being could have, the salvation of the never-dying soul. He said he believed there were some present who would be called on, before the present year had circled its close, to give an account of the deeds done in the body. He warned us, that the time might come when the cup of salvation, if refused now, might not be attainable; and concluded with the words—"A Saviour, or I die! a Redeemer, or I perish for ever!"

The other had a good deal also to say; but it was more for the relief of his own mind than for the edification of ours.

On this evening there was no Meeting held, as so

many of the Friends were appointed on the Committees. For each epistle there were about half a dozen women selected. I was curious to know how they managed to compose them; and after a good deal of coaxing I prevailed on one of the initiated to tell me. Each one wrote out a sentence, in accordance with the epistle they were replying to, and from a sentiment contained in the Book of Discipline; so worded, however, as to appear different. The plainest and most orthodox of the six sisters, was appointed a kind of president, and it fell to her lot to combine the different sentences into one connected whole. There is not much in any of them, and the beginning and ending is always the same—acknowledging the receipt and acceptability of that before them, and concluding with thankfulness for the favoured Meeting now sitting, and the visits of so many ministers, and then the salutation of love.

A friend of mine once tried to bring into the epistle, in her sentence, the idea, that, as sinful creatures, we were hopelessly lost in ourselves, and needed the atoning blood of the Lord Jesus to cleanse us. The others said, that was very beautiful; but it was not usual to depart from the phraseology which had been approved of; and the president put it aside at once, decidedly, by saying, it savoured of new-lightism.

Our dinner party to-day was at the house of a very wealthy Friend. Plain as plain could be, he was; and his wife a model of Quakerism. Every thing in the house was drab, but of the finest and most costly texture. The drawing-room hearth rug, I was told, had cost twenty pounds. We were fifteen at dinner, and had to thank Sarah Castle again for the plain fare. The eldest son of the family, a boy about ten years old, was very communicative with me. "Was not that a horrid dinner," said he; "I wonder thee could eat it? Only for the red round, we would be all starved. Mamma says she can't stand it any longer; so she won't ask any Friends for to-morrow, and then we will have chickens and asparagus."

Wherever we went, we met the "red round;" I remarked on the subject, to my friend, Jane Grey. "Ah!" said she, "it is easy to see thee is not much used to Yearly Meetings. Every house that intends to see company, has a "red round" prepared. It is a very good dish; shall I give thee the receipt for making it?" "Pray do," said I. The next day, soon after I had taken my seat in the Meeting, I felt a gentle hand on my shoulder, and looking round, saw Jane, with a comical smile, handing me a folded paper, containing the promised receipt. "Read it," she whispered; "it contains food for meditation." It was as follows:—

"The Dublin Yearly Meeting's receipt for making a 'Cut and Come again red round.'

"Take a prime round of beef; bone it, and close the hole; tie a tape round it, to keep it firm. Take four ounces of saltpetre pounded, and rub it well with it; let it lie for two or three days; then rub it highly with salt; then let it lie for ten days; drain most of the liquor off. Take half an ounce of cloves powdered, the same of mace, one ounce of pepper, one nutmeg powdered, and rub the beef well with these. Then take half a pound of suet, and flatten it with a rolling pin; put it under and over the beef in a crock; lay a sheet of whitey-brown paper over the meat; then cover it with a plate, and bake it for four or five hours."

We had three more sittings of the Meeting; and in them the business of finishing the queries, and reading the prepared epistles, and signing them with the clerk's name on behalf of the rest of us, was got through. Besides this, we had two lengthy testimonies for dead Friends read aloud, in which the departed were described as having attained to that perfection which the Society holds the doctrine of. There was a great deal more preaching, in the same different styles that I have described; and then the conclusion, in which solemn thanks were recorded to the Divine Head, for the manifestations of continued love, which had been vouchsafed to us in the ministrations of so many of our beloved Friends from another land, and in the love with which the weighty business of the Yearly Meeting had been conducted.

The next day, First day, we had very copious preaching. Even Sarah Black, and Anne Butt, who had been thrown quite in the shade by the brightness of the English luminaries, essayed each a sermon—"a few broken words," as they said themselves.

It was a very pleasant Meeting; we renewed old acquaintances, and made several new ones. We got very good advice on many occasions, and on several subjects; and found the Friends, despite of all their oddities, most friendly, good-humoured, hospitable—(as soon as ever the Meeting was over, the good dinners began again)—and light-hearted. The world goes well with them, and they stand well with the world. But religion, saving religion—alas! alas! that it should be so—is smothered under the load of co-operations which the doctrines of the Society inculcate.

CHAPTER VIII.

Public Meeting at Enniscorthy—Scene at the Inn there—The great Friends visit our city—Establish a Ladies' Society—Government interferes to prevent visiting the Gaols—Quaker scruples—Difficulty of being consistent.

THE Yearly Meeting ended, and our own private business in Dublin transacted, we returned home through the county Wicklow, for the purpose of seeing the far-famed Vale of Avoca, and the exquisitely beautiful scenery of that unrivalled county, with the many objects of interest it contains.

We travelled in a post-chaise, and such a chaise it was as Maria Edgeworth's pen describes. Three times we broke down on the road; and once the horses, or rather the animals they called horses, fell and rolled over. However, as we were all unhurt, and the day very fine, and the road so very lovely, for my part, I rather enjoyed the accidents. It gave me time to climb up the hills, and to obtain a view of the far-off sea and the cloud-capped mountains, which, with the highly cultivated, and well-wooded foreground, formed a landscape replete with life, and teeming with plenty, such as compels a frail mortal to bow his head in marvellous adoration of the goodness and power of the Almighty Creator of so magnificent a scene.

At length we arrived at Enniscorthy late at night, and the following morning, after an early breakfast, and ordering a chaise to be ready the moment it was called for, we went out to take a walk, and see that spot of hateful notoriety, Vinegar Hill. A respectable-looking old man, with a spade on his shoulder, seeing us looking towards the hill, accosted us with the usual "God save you." My father returned his greeting, and entered into conversation with him. He told us of the dreadful scene. He had himself been in the rebel camp. It was an ease to his mind to talk of it, even now, after so many years had passed. He said, the screams and shrieks of the unhappy victims still sounded in his ears, and that, night and day, they were ever before his eyes. "And yet," he added, "I could not help it. I was driven into it. Our own priest was in it, and he made me and a whole lot of us go with him. You are a priest, sir," said he, mistaking my father's dress. "Tell me, for God's sake, wont the blame of it be on him that drove us into it?" Smarting under the lash of an accusing conscience, which for thirty years had embittered every joy of life, and marvelling at the confession of it being made to total strangers, we left him, but not before my father had admonished him to flee from the wrath to come, and to cast himself and his sorrows on the mercy of Christ Jesus the Lord.

On returning to the hotel, we found the English

Friends had arrived there, and were about to hold a public meeting. They had two or three young men in their train, and these were sent through the town, distributing printed papers which they had brought from Dublin, inviting the inhabitants, rich and poor, high and low, to attend the Meeting, which was to be held in about an hour, in a large room hurriedly fitted up for the occasion.

We resolved to delay our departure, and to avail ourselves of the opportunity of again hearing those celebrated Friends' preaching.

There were about two hundred people who came to the Meeting. Not being accustomed to sitting down in silence, it was no wonder they could not understand its being necessary to do so; and John Earl at last rose up on the platform, and explained the necessity for silence being observed. Whilst he was speaking, they were quiet, but as soon as he ceased the chatter began again.

"What did they bring us here for?" said one.

"Faix I don't know," was the answer. "Maybe the decent people are going to treat us genteelly."

"Whist with you," called out a loud voice; "Didn't the gentleman tell you to sit quiet, like the Quakers themselves. Ye'll give a bad impression to the strangers, I'm thinking, in regard of politeness."

"And isn't it yourself is making the noise now?" said another.

"Arrah, now, isn't that too bad? and I only teaching you manners," he answered.

After repeated efforts to obtain silence in vain, one of the women Friends rose up, and in her soft, sweet voice, addressed them on the value of the soul, and the need of a Saviour, the uncertainty of life, and the value of the Bible. When she resumed her seat, I was just wondering whether the Quaker phraseology, in which her ideas were shrouded, would be understood by such an assembly, when I heard a voice close by me audibly whispering—

"She is a fine portly women, God bless her. I wish somebody would insense me into the meaning of what she was trying to say."

"I'll tell you," said another voice. "The decent woman says she has her eye on you, and that you are a big blackguard, and that you are going hot-foot to hell; and she does be crying her eyes out about you and two or three other boys that's going the same way."

"Oh! then," answered the first speaker, "isn't she a knowledgeable creature? She knows more about me than ever I knew about myself. You are clever at the talk, Tom—will you go and tell her I'm obliged for the good opinion she has of me? And tell her she need not be troubling herself about me, for Father Kelly is my own first cousin; and if I am sent there itself, he is the boy will get me out cheap."

The other two Friends also preached. Excellent good advice they gave; but the multitude of words employed were only suited to those who are initiated into the manner of Quakerism. To the assembled auditory there, they might as well have spoken in Greek.

When little Elizabeth had spoken with much energy of manner, I overheard the comment on her.

"Go it, little one; but you are a great game hen, for all you are so weenshe. You got it out very brave; and I'll give you my blessing, for you meant to be kind, I see, only you have a queer way of showing it."

I have been at several public meetings. Those held in barns and large rooms are generally much the same in point of solemnity as this was; those held in Friends' Meeting-houses are more quiet and orderly.

Our chaise was at the door, trunks were packed on it, and we were taking a snack dinner, when we heard a loud altercation under the windows.

The English Friend had ordered the horses to be taken from our carriage and put to his. He travelled with four, and the number he required was not to be had; so, without any ceremony, he was for taking ours. One of the helpers, who happened to know us, objected to obey the order; and blustering very loudly, declared he would not "stand by and see the Englisher lord it over the real gentry that a-way." We ran to the window to see what was the matter, and soon perceived how the case was. "Oh!" said my dear father, "we shall have to remain in this wretched place another night."

"And will thee tamely yield to such unheard-of impertinence?" said my sister.

"Why," he replied, "how can we help it? I did

not think any Friend would do such a thing; but as he has, of course we must yield."

"Of course, no such thing," she said. "Do thee sit quietly here, and do not even show thyself at the window, and I shall go down and manage him."

I was not restricted from looking out, and enjoyed the scene below with interest. Ellen appeared presently, and demanded. "What are you taking the horses off the carriage for?" "'Tis the English gentleman, ma'am," said our acquaintance, the helper. "He says his sister can't travel without four; and when I told him, first come first served, and that the master himself owned this pair, he said, 'they are a better pair of horses than those you are putting to my coach, and I must have them for wheelers;' and more than that he said, Miss, that yee's might stay here till to-morrow, but that it was of consequence for him and his sister to get on their journey."

John Earl then came forward, smiling, though somewhat ruffled by the unusual occurrence of any one daring to dispute his orders.

"Wilt thou please desire this man to put those horses immediately to our coach? He has refused to do so without thy father's orders. Wilt thou give directions, for my sister is already annoyed by this delay? Our carriage is heavy, and we cannot get on without four."

"Oh!" she answered, "you cannot have ours; but cannot you give a few shillings to one of these men, and he will go to the fields and get horses in for you?"

Then turning to the grooms, "Be quick, and fasten all right again. How dare you unharness our horses for any one? Be quick, I say." And quickly indeed that order was obeyed by the grinning men. But Friend John was not content. "I will go speak to thy father," said he, "I am sure he will not refuse to accommodate my sister." She laid her hand gently, but firmly on his arm, and said, "I cannot allow thee to disturb my father now; he is at his dinner. Those horses are mine, thou canst not have them." "But I must;" said he, "I have no alternative, for we cannot get on without them." She turned to the grooms, "Do not let my carriage be disturbed again," she said. "Never fear, Miss, never fear," they answered, "we'll fight for you. The Englishman shan't rough-ride it over you, that a-way, and we to the fore."

My sister then turned again to Friend John, and said, "Is not the scenery of the County Wicklow, through which you passed, very lovely? The journey before us is not so interesting. I hope we shall see you soon in our neighborhood, and that you will arrange to dine with us. Fix the day and hour to suit your own convenience, and we will invite a large company to meet you. Farewell;" and she glided away without giving him time to reply.

We saw no more of our Friend John at Enniscorthy. He was not visible when we started, but his great heavy coach and pair of horses were in attendance.

The groom, as we got into ours, put his head into the window and said, "Say the word now, Miss, and

I'll tackle them garrons of his on for leaders, in a jiffy. Will I Miss, alanna?" "Oh! no; and off we drove, my father, dear man, afraid to ask how the matter had been arranged, glad that it was so, but quite fearful the Friends might be offended.

A few days after, these same Friends arrived in our city, and lodged with my uncle. They arrived on a seventh day afternoon. Their intended visit had been announced, and every preparation made, that the kindest hospitality could devise, to give them a cordial Irish welcome. My uncle was a widower, and although his housekeeper was a clever young woman, and well skilled in the culinary department, still he felt greatly burthened with the honor which had been conferred upon him, in having to entertain these great Friends. At his request my mother had been all over his house, to see that the accommodation provided for them was suitable. Beds of the softest down, and sheets of the finest Irish linen, were prepared for them; and a double-bedded room for the two young men, whom they were in the habit of taking about to swell their train, and run of their messages.

About seven o'clock that evening, we saw my uncle hastening up our lawn; and, knowing from his manner, that something had occurred to ruffle him, my mother went to meet him. "Oh!" said he, "what shall I do; after all, I have not got things right for the Friends, and I am come to thee to help me. They cannot drink anything but London porter, and Elizabeth has called for calf's-foot jelly. I sent to all the confectioners' shops, but there was none to be had; and Debby is kept running about waiting on them, so that she could not make it; and, beside that, the butchers have not got any calves' feet. I sent round to them all to try. Friend John says he is quite distressed on account of his sister, as she requires those things, and that they quite expected to have them at my house, which makes the disappointment greater to them now."

"Could thee get pigs' feet?" said my mother.

"Oh, yes, in plenty."

"Well then, send me two sets of them, and I'll make jelly; she will never know the difference. Thee shall have it by ten o'clock to-morrow, and I would advise thee to tell the young men, and they will manage the porter for thee."

He took my sister home with him to make tea for the Friends, and she told us she had a very pleasant evening. They were chatty, and communicated much that was interesting, about the plans formed in London for ameliorating the condition of the poor, and encouraging women in industry and cleanly habits. Indeed it was to form a Ladies' Association for this purpose, that Elizabeth visited our city. She succeeded in doing so, and in forming another Society for ladies to visit the prisons, and read the Bible to the prisoners.

It was nine o'clock before the pigs' feet came, and then we set to work to manufacture them into jelly. My mother sat up all night, and had her task accomplished by eight o'clock in the morning, when it was sent down in a large cut glass dish; and she had soon after, the pleasure of hearing that the English Friends said it was the nicest calf's-foot jelly they had ever tasted.

This was now first day; the Friends were to dine with us at three o'clock, and to have a Meeting at seven, to which the town's-people were invited.

A dozen of our acquaintances were invited to meet the Friends at dinner; and it fell to my lot to stay from the Morning Meeting, in order to attend to the needful arrangement of this repast, which was as choice and abundant as could be provided on so short a notice. My sister had brought us word the night before, of the honor intended for us.

The Meeting was over at twelve, as usual; and at half-past two, up drove the well-known coach, with its important burden. The ladies were soon seated in the drawing-room, the gentlemen strolled into the garden, and the other guests dropped in one after another. Scarcely had the clock struck three, when Friend John said to my mother, "Three,, I think, is the hour for dinner; shall I ring the bell." "Oh! no," she replied; "some of our friends have not yet arrived." He sat down for about two minutes, and then began again. "My sister will, I fear, be annoyed; she quite expected dinner would be ready at three o'clock. We English Friends are accustomed to be punctual to time." "Dinner is quite ready to be served," said my mother; but we must wait a few minutes for the guests we have invited to meet you." "Probably they will arrive," he said, "whilst dinner is being placed on the table. With thy permission, I will ring for it." And he rose and walked across the room, and rang the bell. The butler entered. "Let dinner be served," he called out. The man looked amazed, but withdrew. I went down stairs to tell my sister how the matter stood. She countermanded the order; and fearing that the Friends were hungry and suffering, called one of the "train-young men," and told him to hand them a glass of wine and a biscuit, to enable them to fast for about ten minutes longer. "Ah! said he, "there is not the slightest occasion; as soon as ever the Meeting was over, they went home, and called for beef-steak and porter; they all three eat heartily of that, and jelly besides." Whilst we were speaking, Friend John himself joined us in the dining-room. "Really," said he, "I am annoyed. This want of punctuality is very trying. My sister's convenience is sadly disregarded."

Ellen at that moment saw the gentleman we were waiting for, entering the gate; and at a quarter after three, Friend John and his sister were satisfying the desires of the inner man with much apparent enjoyment. As soon as the cloth had been removed, and the wines and fruits laid on the table, the Friends dropped into the well-known ominous silence; and one after another preached a domestic sermon. Then they regaled on the dessert, and when satisfied, requested to be shown to bed-rooms, where they might "take a lay," to obviate any tendency to drowsiness in the

Evening Meeting. The ladies were immediately accommodated; but we were somewhat surprised, when the gentleman required the same for himself. His wants too were supplied, even to a night-cap, and a shawl to throw over his shoulders; but ere he composed himself to sleep, he gave orders that tea and coffee should be ready for his sister at half-past five o'clock.

It was made ready as he wished; and then the three resumed their seats on the sofas, gracefully arranging the pillows and stools, and the ample folds of their drab dresses and shawls, so as to form a pleasing tableau vivant. There they were served with tea and coffee; and again we had the satisfaction of thinking their appetites were not impaired. A plate of bread and butter, cut, as we thought, thin, being handed to the little Elizabeth, she helped herself rather superciliously, and then remarked, "Ah! this may pass with me; but certainly it will not with my sister." One of the young people took the loaf to cut some thinner slices for the important lady; and whilst doing so, Friend John leaning forward, said, "Dost thou not feel it a privilege to be permitted to cut bread for my sister?" We were all glad when the weary day was over; for though we fully appreciated the honor of having the company, under our own roof, of these celebrated Friends, still our feelings had been tried, by the manner in which they had received our attentions.

The next morning the public Societies were organized with unparalleled cleverness; and rules and regulations given by Elizabeth herself, in so clear and concise a manner, that there remained no difficulty after she had left, in carrying on the system so admirably set going.

We met again at dinner at my uncle's; he had a very large company assembled in honour of his English guests. At Friends' dinner parties, the fish, soup, and meat are all served together for the first course. We had a boiled turkey at the head of the table, and and a roast loin of veal at the foot; the sides and centre were covered with every variety of food, dressed in the most appetizing forms. After the usual momentary silence, which Friends observe, instead of saying grace, when the covers had been removed, and the viands exposed to view, Friend John turned round to my uncle, and said, "I do wish thou had'st told me what was to be for dinner. My sister always likes turkey to be roast, and veal boiled. This is really very unfortunate." His sister, who always looked greatly pleased when his care for her comforts was openly shown, said, "Yes; and it might so easily have been done right; however, I have no doubt, I shall be able to manage." By this time we had been somewhat accustomed to their oddities; and having often heard that the English Friends were great boors, we rather watched for these developments, and laughed at them.

When the Friends had satisfied their appetites, they retired "to take a lay," ordering tea, as with us the day before ; for there was to be another public Meeting this evening at seven o'clock. The tea passed over without any thing particular; but as soon as the great lady had finished, she dropped into silence. The rest of the company having only just commenced, no notice was taken of her; so she rose silently, and with a stately step walked into the adjoining room, assisted by her brother's arm, and two or three following, to proffer any required service. They soon returned, and said, the dear Friend was under a concern to speak to my sisters and myself, apart from the rest of the company. We had been pouring out tea for them, and had not tasted any ourselves; but though my uncle was distressed, that we should be deprived of what all the others were enjoying, it did not trouble us much, and we hastened in to the great Friend, whom we found on the sofa, as usual, in a graceful attitude. She motioned to each of us where to seat ourselves; one to an arm-chair, on which her arm carelessly reposed; another to a spare morsel of the sofa on which she reclined, and me to a footstool close beside her. After a momentary pause, she addressed us in a kind of familiar preaching, and in a low musical voice. She said, we were a lovely and most interesting trio; she did not blame us for our dress being somewhat smarter than that of most young Friends; for she had herself loved dress with an exceeding love. The time was long past now, but there had been a time, when she had revelled in all the gay seductions of fashionable life. She had frequented balls, and theatres, and concerts; she had drained the cup of earthly pleasure, and could assure us that it was all delusive; and that having been enabled to take up her cross, and to surrender to the requirings of the inward monitor, she had found peace. She had thought it well to tell us these things; for why should we wander on in the enjoyment of the blessings of this life, with which she observed we were surrounded, and not to be told they were fallacious? She told us of her brother's devotion to her—of her brother-in-law's consequence as a member of Parliament—a good deal about the wealth of her family—of the happiness she felt in her own mind because of her Quakerism, and of her devotedness to the service of the Lord. When the address was ended, she presented each of us with a tract, in which her own name was written, as a memento of her visit to Ireland; and said she hoped, before long, that we might feel a drawing to attend the London Yearly Meeting.

These important Friends did not remain many days in our city; and when they were gone, we were told many anecdotes of their manners and queer ways. My uncle told us, that when shown to their rooms the night they arrived, they had felt the beds, as if they were at a doubtful inn; asked were the sheets clean, and desired to be shown what other rooms were in the house, that they might choose which they would prefer. One of the ladies selected my uncle's own room for herself, and ordered her trunks to be removed into it; and as nobody seemed to venture to dispute their wills, he was about to yield to this whim, when it was found that his room was locked, and the key not to be found. One of the lads had overheard the uncourteous order given, and determining that the kind old man should not be robbed of his night's rest, had slipped up stairs, locked the room, put the key in his pocket, and walked out of the house, not returning till they had gone to rest.

In another place they honoured an aunt of mine with their company, and one day kept dinner waiting after it had been placed on the table, for more than an hour, whilst they sent a man on horseback to the town, to purchase Eau de Cologne, in which to bathe their faces, after the fatigue of a few hours drive. We heard many such stories as these. Wherever they went, their odd conduct formed a strange contrast with their preaching and praiseworthy endeavours to rouse the attention of the humane to strenuous efforts for the benefit of their fellow-creatures.

Friends invariably describe their ministers and exalted members as beings who have attained perfection. They carefully suppress every trait of character which they imagine may bring contempt, or disgrace, or disrepute upon the system and the sect. Quaker biography is a record of immaculate devotion, as untrue as it is uninteresting. Sin and frailty are inherent in mortality. You might as well expect a picture to be beautiful, if the light and brilliant foreground was unrelieved by shade and shadow, as expect a sinful mortal to profit by, or appreciate the example of a fellow-sinner, who is represented as freed from those imperfections which we all know and feel to be inseparable from humanity.

It is a great comfort to the soul which is battling with temptations to know, that the best men who ever breathed the breath of this life, have been overtaken by them; and the exquisitely pathetic stories recorded by sacred writers of their fall, and of the compassionate mercy which again raised them up, and kept them until the end, is so corroborative of the Christian's own experience, that he derives hope from the darkest trials, and looking on them as having been, like himself, deeply dyed in sin, like them, too, he hastens to wash, and make himself white in the blood of the Lamb.

My mother entered with much spirit and energy into the management of the Ladies' Societies now formed in our city. One large district was allotted to her and six other ladies. They, however, soon fell off, and the whole care devolved on her, and I was her assistant. Several hundred poor women were employed in manufacturing flax and wool. Their houses were whitewashed, and frequent visits paid them. No religious instruction was allowed to be given; and, therefore, I have no doubt it was, that after several years of most arduous endeavours to improve their condition, no benefit was found to result from them. God was not honoured, and, therefore, His blessing was not on our work.

Once a month, a Committee, composed of all the

ladies from all the districts, was held. They were of all creeds and sects. The Bishop's lady generally presided. Friend Elizabeth's views were carried out to the letter. No pains, no trouble was spared; every thing that could be devised was strenuously done, to promote the temporal benefit of the poor. Alas! it was all in vain. I do not believe that one single individual was raised in the moral scale by all our efforts.

In the Society for visiting the gaols, and reading the Scriptures to the prisoners, we had far more comfort. The result of our labours there may not be revealed until the Judgment Day. What was done was certainly a step in the right direction. Both the women and men to whom we read seemed greatly pleased and interested in what was to them a great novelty—the simple word of Scripture. Anty Whelan, who had perjured herself in her defeated attempt to ruin my dear brother, was one of my daily auditors; and I have seen the tears course each other down her cheek, and beheld the glistening eyes of many others, as they listened to the tale of Jesus' love to man. Several of the prisoners being unable to comprehend the English language, one other lady, a Quakeress, and myself, learned Irish sufficiently well to be able to read the Testament to them. But our work here, too, was but short-lived. The Roman Catholic Priests made a complaint to the Government that we were proselytizing, and an order was forthwith issued, prohibiting us from visiting the gaols.

We incurred censure in another quarter also. The overseers of our Meeting visited, and remonstrated with us on the great danger which, they said, we incurred, in mixing with "people of the world," under the specious idea that we were doing good to our fellow-creatures. They said, that "Friends had best stay quietly away from mixing up." They said, "It was not becoming for my mother, the head of a large family, to sit in a Committee by the side of the Bishop's wife: that to countenance her, in any way at all, was indirectly to countenance the hireling ministry of her husband; and they wondered greatly that a Friend could so far deviate from the principles of our Society as to do so." Besides this they said, "There was a great snare to young people, in looking on the gay dresses of those worldlings who attended the Ladies' Committees, and that my mother had much to answer for, in exposing her daughter to such a temptation." And then they reminded us, "That it was impossible for us to be consistent, and sit quietly by while the Bishop's wife would open the Committee, by saying, 'Ladies met, May 13, 1827.' Surely it was a forsaking of our testimony against the heathen names of the days and months of the year." And another reason why they warned us to give up these associations was, that "Evil communications corrupt good manners;" and sometimes Friends were so led away as to forget themselves, and adopt the language of the world. It was a very deplorable truth, that now-a-days our young people were becoming unguarded.

It was no uncommon thing to hear them say "you," and "ma'am;" and the heads of families would do well to consider were they guiltless in this matter, especially when they themselves countenanced the young, in associating with those by whom they were so liable to be betrayed into a forgetfulness of our Christian peculiarities."

We had to endure very many of these visits. They threatened to bring us under dealing for this matter, but did not. We gave them, as usual, cake and wine, and were most civil and condescending; and then, as the Friend who established those Societies was herself a preacher in good esteem in London, they were fearful of overstraining the discipline, although they took good care to tell us that there were many points in which they did not feel full unity with her.

Some of us knew well, that even the great Elizabeth was not sufficiently orthodox to please our plain Friends. It had been whispered about as a great secret, even during the Dublin Meeting, that the overseers had visited her on the impropriety, of wearing a silk gown, the Irish women preachers having hitherto refrained from silk. Hairbine, stuff, and Irish tabinet, were their approved materials for dress. Now, however, this is altered. The preachers now wear silk; and perhaps few ladies moving in the fashionable circles of life can boast of a greater number of silk dresses, or of more costly fabric either, than they, whose colours, however, are confined to either drab, or very dark shades of purple, brown, and green.

It is really a very difficult thing for a Quaker to be consistent with his own principles; and even the most rigid are often found swallowing them wholesale. For instance, the vain adorning of the person with dress, jewelry, and gold. He considers it a sin to indulge in those things, and yet in his shop he sells them. He makes his money by providing for the sins of his fellow-Christians. He deems it a right thing to wear a broad brim to his hat, but he has no scruple about making and selling hats of a fashionable form for his fellow-Christians to wear. He would not be so wicked as to dress his servant up in livery, with a gold band, &c., but in the way of business he will do it for another. If the "peculiarities" are essential to the salvation of a Quaker, are they not also essential for all Christians? Can it be that "Friends" sell and deal in those forbidden things, because they think "the people of the world" have no chance of salvation at all, and that, therefore, it signifies but little what they indulge in, so that Friends profit by it?

CHAPTER IX.

London Yearly Meeting—Various concerns brought before the Women's Meeting—Bible read in public, and the reader sent to the Mad-house—Great Dinner at Mildred Court—Awful Sermon—King George IV.—Frustrated attempt to penetrate the mysteries of the Women's Meeting.

I HAD often expressed a wish to attend the London Yearly Meeting: for as our Quarterly Meetings were inferior to the Dublin Yearly Meeting, so the Dublin was considered, in comparison to the London. I wished very much to know how the affairs of the Society were managed in the great annual assembly, to which all the smaller Meetings were subordinate; and my father, with his invariable kindness, resolved to gratify my desire. He was appointed one of the Irish representatives, so that my sister and I, accompanying him, had all the opportunities which such good credentials generally bestow.

We had a week only to prepare for the journey, and the Friend who made our bonnets, knowing that she was of unrivalled skill in manufacturing that elaborate costume, and being withal somewhat crazy, was, with great difficulty, prevailed on to have ours ready in time. True, we had plenty of other bonnets, but no respectable Friend ever goes to a Meeting without having, at least, one complete suit, quite new. The rich plain Friends, generally, have a different suit for every day the Meeting lasts. They think it derogatory to wear the same dress two days consecutively. We were not so particular; not being so plain as others, it did not signify for us, but still going to London was an event of no small moment; and preparation was unsparingly made for it. We crossed in the steam-packet to Milford, and had on board one of the great London preachers, and her daughters, with two Englishmen Friends. They were returning, after attending the Dublin Meeting. We had no previous acquaintance with them beyond a mere formal introduction; and as they were not remarkably prepossessing, either in manner or appearance, we kept aloof on the voyage, merely sharing with them the contents of our well-stocked hamper of eatables.

On arriving at Milford, we were met by a Friend, who, grateful for some kindness he had received at our house, where he had been carefully attended during a tedious illness, some time before, now hastened to welcome us, and had his car at the shore ready to convey us to his house, where he said, dinner was prepared, and accommodation for the night, if we would accept it. The dinner was accepted, but we wished to proceed a few stages further on.

When this kind and hospitable man had assisted us to get our luggage landed, he proceeded to conduct us to his car, but Friend Grubly, and her daughters had been before him, and taken possession of it for themselves. He was exceedingly annoyed, and told them they must, at least, make room for us. They refused to do so, and said they wished to have their trunks beside them. Our Friend, Paul, then said to one of the daughters: "Wilt thou look amongst those trunks, and see which is thine?" She got out of the car to do so, and immediately Friend Paul actually lifted me in, shut the door, and ordered the driver to go on. My father and sister had preferred walking. I had suffered from sea sickness, and was not well able to do so; but, indeed, my drive was not over pleasant, for my two companions were somewhat unamiable towards me, and loud in their anger that Paul should have left their dear Hannah to walk. However, she and the rest of the party soon after arrived, and peace was restored by the happy good humour of Paul and his wife. Just before we sat down to dinner, Friend Grubly said to my father, "Dost thou intend to proceed towards London to-night?" He answered "Yes;" and she then hurried out of the room. An hour after dinner was over, the London coach drove up to the door, and she said, in a triumphant way, "My daughters and I have engaged three inside seats; two of you must travel outside, for I will not consent to be crowded." "We are not going by the coach," said he; "we travel post." "Oh! dear," said she, "if I had known that, I need not have sent the young man away from his dinner to secure the places. Thou should'st have told me."

We had a delightful journey, posting with four horses, all the way from Milford to London; stopping a few hours or minutes at the different stages, as inclination led us. In these rail-road days, nobody thinks of travelling by post. A rapid transit is now the only desideratum. A place may have historical interest, or legendary renown, or the scenery may be transcendently lovely, but who, now-a-days, cares for such things? It is only puff, puff, whizz, whizz, and away with speed to the journey's end. The romance of travel is lost and gone; and with it, man has lost one of the purest and most refined enjoyments of this life.

The lamps were lighted when we entered London. The extent amazed, and the noise confused me; the enormous wagons and the ponderous horses astonished me; and the long unbroken line of carriages we met led me to think that the Londoners buried their dead in the evening, and that these were the long funeral trains we were so constantly encountering.

A lodging had been engaged for us in Bishopsgate Street, near the Meeting-house in Devonshire Square.

It was over an apothecary's shop, and redolent with all the abominable smells that could be exhaled from a vast accumulation of unsavory drugs; and morning, noon, and night, the monotonous sound of the pestle and mortar, was heard, thump, thump away. The Friend who had taken this lodging for us, told me, that the smell we so complained of, was the great recommendation to her taste, in selecting them for us.

The great London annoyances, she said, disliked the smell of an apothecary's shop, as much as ourselves; and therefore it was probable we might be able to sleep in peace at nigh. We were in a humour to be content with discomforts; to enjoy every thing that was intended to please us; to relish all that was novel or strange; and, I may add, we anticipated that the Meeting we had come so far to attend, would prove of incalculable benefit to our moral welfare. The Irish preachers did not stand high in our estimation; and we anxiously wished to hear the English, of whose celebrity we had often been told.

The first Meeting we attended was in Gracechurch Street, and we had no less than seven sermons in the two hours it lasted; one short one from a man Friend, the rest all women. One of the women spoke three times. All were much in the same strain; the speakers' feeling of the deep importance of the Yearly Meeting—of the willingness of the Lord to own it, and of the necessity for us all to be silent in the soul, as well as in the body.

After meeting, there was a great shaking of hands, and greetings. We were recognised by one or two, and then introduced to very many, who kindly invited us to their houses, telling us a table was laid at a certain hour every day, and that we were welcome to come and partake as often as we pleased. We thanked them. It is not very flattering to be allowed to go dine with the Friends, instead of the Irish mode of requesting the pleasure of our company; but there was the charm of novelty in it at any rate. As my father had been more cordially invited by one of the men Friends, a preacher, we went with him and his family. They were very rich people. A company of twenty-two assembled—eighteen of us were females.

The table laid would have accommodated more Friends; and the fare provided was good and plentiful; but to our eyes it looked queer. At the top of the table was a fine salmon and lobster sauce; near it, in the middle of the table, was a dish of cut bread; then the long stretch was quite bare to the very end, at which was placed, as close as ever the dishes could be to each other, an enormous surloin of roast beef, a huge round of boiled beef, a large Westphalian ham, and a fine leg of mutton. The women were all at the top of the table, the men in a group at the bottom. Our host Cornelius, informed us, that he had adopted that arrangement of his table, because it was so convenient for the men to carve; and he liked to see his female Friends sitting in the upper seats. We had no pastry, pudding, or wine. When the cloth was removed, coffee was served up, and then we hurried off to Meeting again, at Devonshire House. Oh! what a crowd was assembled in the yard and hall. We used to think the men Friends lining the vestibule in Dublin, to stare at us, as we came in and out of Meeting, an annoyance; but it was nothing to compare to the English men. They stared and pushed, and without any introduction, would catch hold of one's hand, and shake it, and ask our names, with the most outrageous rudeness.

The pushing and driving to get seats was quite an ordeal to get through. We could not manage it, and were consequently left standing at the door. Two of our English acquaintances saw us, and every day after, of the two weeks the Meeting lasted, they contrived to meet us outside, and taking us, one each, under her care, regularly fought the way for us to the foremost and best seats. At the second Meeting, we had sermons from three men, and no women at all—a most unusual circumstance; but so it was. The subject of one of them was—"The true foundation, which was from the beginning of creation to the close of time, and which would lead to a happy eternity." He enlarged much on the subject, but omitted to mention what the true foundation was. It is possible that he did not know; for Friends despise what they contemptuously term, "head knowledge."

Our Women's meetings for Discipline were the same as in the Dublin Meetings, only larger, a greater number of rcpresentatives, from different places, and consequently more answering of queries; frequent preachings on the deficiencies reported in the observance of our rules, and admonitions largely administered for our future conformity to the discipline of the Society, which we were often told, "our worthy predecessors had been enabled, in best wisdom, to give forth."

One Friend was concerned on the subject of Members "deviating from simplicity, by affixing Mr. and Mrs. to names, and thereby opening a door for further departure from our first principles." Another "was impressed," she told us, "in a very remarkable manner, with a view of the wasting and destruction in our borders, by Friends allowing themselves 'latitude in apparel.'" Five others also spoke on the same subject, and pathetically deplored "the inroad which the enemy was making upon us, because of our unfaithfulness, and reluctance to bear this, our cross, in the eyes of the world." Two of these last orators found the burden of this matter so heavy on their minds, that they resigned themselves to the duty of going into the Men's Meeting, sitting hard by, there to impart similar admonition.

One had to inform us that the painful burden of her spirit, was because of the deficiency reported in our peculiar language. "The thee and thou; yes, the thee and thou; it was a stumbling-block to many." And yet she said, "it was the distinctive mark, that we were the Lord's people. It was declared in Holy Writ, that the Lord's called and peculiar people were a little flock, a people of a plain language." She dwelt a good deal on "the duty of mothers to enforce this language on their children, and if need be, to chasten the rebellious."

The propriety of regularly attending Meetings for both worship and discipline, was "spoken to;" and the advantage which would result, if in "the Meetings for Discipline, Friends would try to sit in a waiting state of mind; not absorbed by the business, but in quietness and stillness; then we should find that some amongst us would be raised up, and empowered to offer, it might be, a word in season."

Another hoped "Friends would be careful to regulate their domestic avocations, so that their youth, and that important class amongst them, their apprentices, might not be hindered from duly attending Meetings;" and advised that shops and places of business should be closed during the hours of Meeting on week-days, expressing her "conviction that no ultimate lessening of income would result from the apparent sacrifice of time." She spoke very impressively of the duty which man owed to God, and of the great error of allowing temporal affairs to engross the entire attention. She then went into the Men's Meeting, and laid the same subject, I was told, very weightily before them.

There was a tall, elderly spinster, who very often "spoke to the Discipline." She had a marvellous flow of words. Sometimes, without pausing, she could keep on speaking for an hour at a time. Her "concerns" were numerous, and she united with, and had something to say on the "concerns" of everybody else. Some departures from our rules having been reported by different representatives, on the head of marrying out of Meeting, this spinster Friend had much to say in reprobation of the evil. It was very evident she had no sympathy for the transgressors. She marvelled "how any one could so far forget themselves, or yield to temptation, as to be drawn away from the high privileges which they enjoyed as members, permitting themselves to be joined in marriage with strange men, and thereby sanctioning an hireling ministry." She said, "That wasting and destruction to families had grievously resulted from this evil; and that she had known instances where the transgressor had irretrievably lost her own peace of mind from it." She said, "To her mind it seemed an indelicate thing for a young female Friend, who had been brought up in our habits, and who was accustomed to associate with our worthies in Meetings and elsewhere, to resign herself to the company of those without our pale. People of the world could not be expected to appreciate our customs; and once united to one of them, our dress and our speech must be resigned. A wife was bound to due obedience to her hushand; and these things, which they thought little things, (because too often the light that was in them was darkness,) were obliged to be given up for peace sake; and thus it was, when the hedge was broken down, the wild boar of the wilderness found an easy access, and the adversary triumphed."

There was much said about slavery, and the women and men united in getting up an address to Parliament on the subject. There was also much consultation about receiving an epistle from one of the American Meetings, which it was reported had become New Light or Unitarian in its principles. This was left to a Committee to investigate, and we were only told that it was judged better not to receive that dubious epistle; not to read it in our Meetings, but to return it, which was accordingly done; and both we, and the Men's Meeting also, were cautioned "not to indulge in any conversation on the subject, nor to seek for information about it, as those who were best able to judge had been enabled to do so very wisely."

Drawing up answers to the accepted epistles was, as usual, entrusted to Committees. One day there was what is called an Open Committee, and the young Friends were invited, and indeed urged to attend it. I went with several others; but after long sitting, and nothing done, one of the Friends at the table said, it was not easy to transact the business when so many were present, as it was needful to converse on it; and she therefore proposed that the old plan, of a small number of Friends, of mature understanding, should undertake the business in the usual way—a room by themselves. We had several testimonies for departed Friends, preachers of course. None others are thus honoured; and as they are all "inspired ministers," or they would not have been in our galleries, so also, of course, their ministrations are commemorated in those laudatory records.

We had two Meetings every day for two weeks; and the subjects I have mentioned were scattered over all that time. Each was dwelt on with all the solemnity which was becoming to an assemblage which gravely asserted, and the majority of whom undoubtedly believed, they were listening to admonitions which the speakers were under the immediate inspiration of the

Holy Spirit in giving forth. We had five visits from men Friends, two or three at a time. One of them had travelled to the Ionian Islands, and was grieved at witnessing the degrading worship of saints and images. He advised that large numbers of Friends' tracts should be sent out there, and said, that he had "reason to believe that both in Spain and Portugal a door was opened for usefulness in the same way."

One day, at the close of the Morning Meeting, we were informed that some of our Friends in the ministry were under a concern to have a Meeting that evening, in the large room, for the youth, male and female, and that it was not desirable that any over thirty-five years of age should attend. I went with the other young people, and was led to think that the English atmosphere had some marvellous power to make people look old. Those juveniles of thirty-five actually looked, for the most part, over fifty; but a friend informed me, that unmarried Friends never grow older than thirty-five.

In the Meetings for worship, which were frequent during the session, we had a great deal of preaching from all the best ministers, men and women, in the Society. Our old acquaintance, Joseph John, was, to our mind, infinitely superior to any one else. He rarely descended to the peculiarities of the Society, but preached of faith, and hope, and love. His quotations from Scripture were correct; and, by the way, we may remark, that is a very unusual accomplishment in our ministers. They very often commit slight verbal inaccuracies: sometimes more serious ones.

One day we went to the Borough Meeting-house, and there, to our extreme surprise, an elderly man Friend rose in the gallery to address us; and, drawing from his pocket a small Bible, he commenced reading a chapter in the Gospels; that ended, he spoke on the subject, as he told us, "not by inspiration, but in the simple manner in which a schoolmaster would address his pupils." The elders and overseers became very fidgetty on his saying this, and soon made him sit down; and when he repeated his attempt to speak, they broke up the Meeting. A few days after, I heard he had been sent for care to a Friends' Mad-house. Whether he had ever shown any other symptoms of madness, I never heard. We asked repeatedly, and one very plain Friend, to whom I put the question, for I felt so sorry for the poor man, answered me: "Surely thou must know, every one knows, that a man must be mad who would read the Bible aloud in our Meeting."

The parting Meeting was very large; to get in we had to undergo such pushing, squeezing and jostling, as I never met any where else in all my life. One great, tall awkward Friend, from Wales, with a preposterous broad brim, held his umbrella horizontally out from his chest, and so cleared a path for himself and some women, who held fast by him. An acquaintance of mine was cruelly wounded in the arm by a prod of that umbrella; and I heard the man several times boasting of what an excellent plan he had contrived for getting through the crowd.

As we were of some consequence, it soon became remarked that we had not availed ourselves of the permission given us by so many Friends, to go and take dinner at their houses. We were spoken to about it, and when we said, that we considered as those offers were made to us as a matter of convenience, and as we did not stand in need of any such, having very comfortable dinners at our own apartments, it was of no importance to any one but ourselves. We were told that it was our Irish pride, and that we had given offence. There were some who would not wish it to be said, that a representative from Ireland, and his daughters, had not been entertained at their houses. Hannah Smith, a very nice English girl, an old acquaintance of ours, was especially commissioned to bring us to one of these dinners, given by the great Elizabeth, at her own house. As she had so recently been our guest in Ireland, Hannah urged us very much to go with her; but we told her, whatever was worth having was worth asking for; and if Friend Stately wished for our company, she might take the trouble to invite us, and then we would go. "Ah!" said Hannah, "I told her already, that you, Irish, had ideas of etiquette quite different from us; and that I feared, unless either she, or one of her daughters invited you, you would not come for me. She said, 'she could not understand that anything more was needed, than to let you know that she kept open house during the Meeting; that her table was spread daily for upwards of fifty.' Do come," said Hannah.

"very likely not one of the family will speak to you; but it would never do to say you had not been to Mildred Court." However, we would not go; but coaxed Hannah, instead, to stop with us; and a very pleasant little repast we had, half lunch, half dinner, my father having brought, as usual, two or three of our men Friends to join us. We had quite as much of all the passing news of the Meeting as we wanted. What report of her non-success Hannah gave, I don't know; but two days after, a livery servant was sent with a polite note from Friend Stately herself, requesting the pleasure of our company to dine with her in three days' time. We accepted that invitation, and went.

There were eighty-two guests assembled in two large badly furnished rooms. No lady presided to receive us; we were conducted by our friend Hannah into the room, and with difficulty got chairs. There were more than a dozen standing by the door, who had no seats at all. About five minutes before dinner was announced, the portly mistress of the mansion entered the room, leaning on her brother's arm. She did not take the slightest notice of us, or of any one else; but swept across the room to the uppermost sofa, which was immediately vacated for her, the former occupants retreating to the group at the door. When seated comfortably, her pillows and footstool arranged, and her two daughters, who had followed her into the room, also settled to her mind, she looked round, and nodded to one, and smiled at another.

At length her eye fell on me, and she beckoned me to come over to her. I did so; and had the honour of a cordial shake hands, and a most gracious welcome to her house, and to the London Meeting, and to England in general. She then introduced me to her daughters, one of whom slipped her arm inside mine, and re-conducted me to my seat. My sister underwent the same ceremony, and then my father was summoned in his turn. She was very polite to him, and actually made room for him to sit beside her on the sofa.

Dinner was announced, and the lady and her brother took the lead. The women Friends, with here and there a venturous man, next forced themselves on, each trying to get foremost. My father made his way through the crowd over to us, and held my sister and myself on his arms. We whispered to each other what a strange scene it was, and waited till the crush had passed us by; then we followed into the dining-room. Two long tables were laid, and both were quite filled; and at the first, at which the great Friend herself presided, the work of demolition had commenced. A gentleman at the foot of the second table spied us standing outside the door, jumped up, and quickly and unceremoniously sweeping away three men, he handed us to their seats, and bade them wait until another table was prepared for them. We remonstrated. "Oh!" said he, "never mind them, they know how to take care of themselves." The fare at our table was only middling in quality, and very scanty in quantity. Half a salmon at the head, and a roast leg of lamb at the foot, a small dish of potatoes, and a large silver basket of cut stale bread, was all provided for twenty-five people. The old Friend who carved the lamb was very facetious. He reckoned heads. "Twenty-five," said he, "and the men will surely ask for two helps. I wish I had a compass, to cut it even, share and share for all. A thin slice will do for the females; they sometimes like to be thought delicate in their appetites; so I can only hope, now, they may feel flattered at my supposing them to give a preference to a delicately cut morsel." What was at the best table I do not know, but believe it was more plentiful, as one of the young men who was dining in another room with the residue of the guests, told me, that when the dishes in our room were carried out, they were taken possession of by one of their scouts, and that on one of them there was a bit of beef. It was not from our table that went; we sent nothing away.

Dinner over, one of the daughters came over to me, and said, would I like "to take a lay?"—that there were four bedrooms open for Friends, and if I would go quick, before the crowd, I could be accommodated. Her mother had gone, and she was going, "it was so refreshing before the Evening Meeting." Curiosity induced me to accompany her up stairs, and indeed it was to me a novel sight, to see from three to four dozen women Friends crowded together in the bedrooms, some anxiously searching out their bonnets and shawls, some eagerly securing for themselves a place on the beds "to take a lay," and some, like myself, swelling the throng, for the sake of looking at the ludicrous anxiety of the others. When we left, there were seventeen stretched on the beds, and two humble-minded young women on the floor, seeking their accustomed antidote to drowsiness in the Evening Meeting. Our repast had not been so heavy as to make us dread any danger of transgressing the query. On the contrary, it had been so very sparing, that we complained of actual hunger to my father, who confessed to the same himself; and, therefore, we hurried to our own lodging to get a bit of dinner. As we were going out of the house, we met three young men of our acquaintance, and one lady, and said, "Where are you hurrying to? Come with us." They hesitated a moment, and then said, "The fact is, we scarcely got a bit of dinner, and we are going to a confectioner's to get something to eat." So, finding we were all of the same mind, they came with us, and we had an impromptu dinner, far more plentiful and merrier than the much-talked-of affair at which eighty people were assembled, that it might be said, such vast numbers were daily entertained at Mildred Court. Before leaving London, we received an invitation to dine at the country-house of these great Friends; but the specimen we had had of their style of entertainment sufficed us, and we declined the honour. My aunt was invited at the same time. She went, and told me afterwards, that it was quite a different affair from the Mildred Court dinner. She said, they had a sumptuous entertainment, well served, with abundance of plate, glass, &c. &c., and half a dozen livery servants to attend, and that very few of the guests were Friends. There were Members of Parliament, a Baronet, and two Honourables; and the portly mistress was the graceful, entertaining, courteous, lady-like hostess; not the haughty, supercilious woman she had been to us, who seemed as if she thought herself very condescending to sit for a few minutes in the same room, or breathe the same air with us.

We dined at another Friend's house, with a very large company, and had a most plentiful repast, as, indeed, we had wherever we went, with only the one exception; but these great companies were not pleasant; and having satisfied our curiosity, with four or five of them, we refused to join any more. The English Friends are not nearly so polite or so well-mannered as the Irish; they push and drive to get the best seats for themselves, stretch across you at dinner, help themselves, and think not of others; and except of the Meeting, they had scarcely any other topic to converse on.

"What Meeting wast thou at yesterday?"

"I was at Devonshire house. Elizabeth Dilman was very large in the ministry; and we had quite an awful sermon from Sarah Wormley."

"Indeed! dost thou recollect it? I should so like to hear it."

"Oh! thou knowest we are advised not to speak of those things."

"Well, I know we are in general; but thou says it was an awful sermon. Do tell me; wilt thou not?"

"She said, our Society had fallen very low; and that as we had deserted the cross which was given us to bear, we might look for the time that the cross would be taken from us and given to those who were now as the offscouring of the earth; that we would be sifted, as gold and silver, in the furnace of affliction, and that all the dross and reprobate silver would be cast out; that we had been tried and found wanting. A small burden had been given us to bear—even a peculiar dress, and a peculiar language; and that we had kicked against it; and that unless there was a returning to first principles, and an humble dedication of self, a keeping down of the risings up of the worldly spirit, which was laying waste our borders, she was bold to say we would be cast out as a brand fit for the firing. She said, it was a vain thing to deceive ourselves with false notions—to imagine we had more light than our worthy predecessors. She knew there were reasoners afloat—proud boasters—Bible readers—people who met together to study the Scriptures. They might read the Bible from Genesis to Revelation, and yet be in darkness. It was only Christ in you, the light in you, that can lead you into righteousness; and be assured, that true light will never lead any one into a joining with the vain customs of this wicked world. She said, the Bible should never be read, but in a prepared spirit—in the spirit of prayer; for 'the letter killeth.' That her words might seem harsh; but she did not wish to be a prophet speaking smooth things; for the time was fast coming, when there would be a shaking of the dry bones, an emptying of the whitened sepulchres. The cry was already going forth—Who is on the Lord's side, who? And the day of battle would be a day of clouds, and gloominess, and sorrow."

"Oh! I wish I had been there; that sermon was worth hearing. I was at Gracechurch Street, and we had only four very third-rate sermons—just Friends easing their own minds."

"Dost thou know many of the Friends here today."

"Yes, I know almost all of them; that elderly couple on the sofa are bride and bridegroom; she is seventy-two, he is sixty-eight. Look how lovingly he holds her hand in his. Is it not pleasant to see how the tender feelings of youth outlive the decay of years?"

"Yes, it is pleasant to see that even the stiffest and starchest amongst us can relax their gravity sometimes. That dear aged couple look as happy, as loveing, and as self-absorbed, as if they were actually in love with each other."

"And so they are. No young bride could take more pains to select a becoming and costly dress than our Friend yonder. Look close at her cap, and thou wilt see it is made of Indian muslin, and cost a guinea a yard; her gown is of the richest and softest French silk, and her petticoat matches it. His raiment also, is all super-superior, from his grey silk stockings, and gold knee-buckles, up to his fine cambric cravat. But he has long had a concern not to wear cotton, on account of the slavery question; neither does he eat sugar. He is fond of sweets; but puddings and pies, and tea, and coffee, must all be sweetened with honey for him."

This was the general style of conversation at the London Yearly Meeting convivial parties—what had passed in the Meetings, or talking about the people present.

I was shown in the Women's Meeting-room, the seat on which his Majesty, King George IV. when Prince Regent, had for a moment placed himself, when led by the spirit of adventure, and, as my informant stated, a most unbecoming curiosity, he had, disguised as a woman Friend, made his way into the secret conclave. His dress was all right; a grey silk gown, a brown cloth shawl, a little white silk handkerchief, with hemmed edge, round his neck, and a very well poked Friend's bonnet, with the neatly crimped border of his clear muslin cap tied under the chin, completed the disguise, in which he might have escaped detection very well, were it not for the tell-tale boots, and the unfeminine position in which the arms and legs bestowed themselves. The young women who sat behind him, and saw the heel protruding from its silken robe, slipt quietly out of Meeting and gave the alarm. Two men Friends were speedily summoned, and the Royal intruder felt himself gently tapped on the shoulder, and requested to walk into another room. He made no resistance, but quietly went away; and receiving the usual notice, that the rules of the Society would not allow any but members to be present, he retired, and calling a hackney coach, drove off, perhaps flattering himself that his incognito had not been penetrated; for although his countenance had been instantly recognized, still nothing was said to intimate that it had been so. Resolute that none but the initiated should be present, they were yet careful to treat with courtesy their most unexpected visitant, and even deferentially to respect his assumed character.

CHAPTER X.

Hat Worship—Marriage Ceremony—English Customs—Ignorance of Friends—Method of paying tithes—Tribute of respect to the Established Church—Advice about dealing exclusively with Friends—Evidences—Venerable-looking men chosen to sit in the galleries—Committing the Scriptures to memory, for the sake of repeating in Meeting, forbidden.

We remained in London for six weeks after the Meeting had ended, seeing all the wonderful and interesting sights of that vast city. We had to go by ourselves to Westminster Abbey, and to St. Paul's, on account of the annoyance which results from Friends' testimony against taking off the hat going into a place of worship, or even a private room, which they call "hat worship." We could not prevail on any of our men Friends to accompany us to these places. It is not pleasant when a man feels that he is displaying a moral courage, which it has cost him much to acquire, in upholding the manifestation of his own peculiar views, to have that lofty feeling of self-satisfaction rudely dashed to the ground, by the hand of a Verger quietly and gently removing in silence, and as a matter of course, the hat, the broad-brimmed hat, which he wears as a symbol that he is separated, by peculiar holiness, from the "people of the world." An officer being appointed to take off the hat of a Friend, in courts of law, churches, &c. &c. is, I believe, the very greatest cross which Quakers have, in reality, to bear now-a-days. It is, such a ridiculously simple termination of all their scruples on the subject, and it is so entirely impossible to object to it, that it makes the mortification complete. The young Quakers, for the most part, do violence to their conscience, rather than submit to the humiliation.

We went to the Jews' Synagogue, and there our escort was most courteously treated. In the Synagogue no "hat worship" is allowed. If you take off your hat, some Jew will oblige you either to put it on again, or to go out of the house.

I was one day greatly amused, by watching a very plain man Friend, who was paying us a morning visit. It was a hot summer's day, and he had walked a long distance. He came into our room, as all orthodox Friends do, with his broad brim on, shook hands, and sat down. After bearing his testimony thus for a few minutes, he took off the hat, and laid it on the floor beside him. We were chatting away, when a loud rap at the door announced some more visitors. Friend Hugh in a great hurry popped on his hat, lest any one should see him "shirking his testimony." As soon as he had satisfied himself that his orthodoxy was sufficiently manifested, he yielded again to the natural feeling, and laid the hat beside him. But soon came another visitor, and another, and poor hot-headed Hugh replaced the badge of membership again and again. This happened so often, that at last it became very ludicrous.

We visited all the Meetings in the vicinity of London during our stay; and as we came home slowly, we "sat with" Friends at all the different towns and cities we passed through, when it happened that we were there on Meeting-days. They were one and all silent Meetings. And on remarking how strange that seemed, I was told that ministers had exhausted themselves at the Yearly Meeting; that the exercise of their spirits, during that solemn time, was so great, that they generally needed relaxation and quiet for two or three months after. I have since often observed, that those who spoke most at Yearly Meetings, had the least to say for a long time afterwards.

Soon after my visit to London, I was married. Oh! what an ordeal I had to go through. My intended husband lived in England, and I in Ireland; so that we had to undergo all the formalities which the Society boasts of having instituted, under the "influence of best wisdom," for the performance of the ceremony. First of all I had, in the presence of two men witnesses, to sign a document, stating that the gentleman was authorized by me to stand up in his own Meeting, and to inform his assembled brethren that he had an intention of marrying me, telling them all who I was, and where I lived. His Meeting then made inquiry into his former conduct; and a month after, they gave him a written permission to marry me, as they had satisfied themselves that he was "clear of all other marriage engagements." The second step was then, that he and I, with a large company of our respective relatives, had to walk in together, arm-in-arm, into the women's Monthly Meeting that I belonged to; and there, before the assembled throng, all seated, gazing at us, we had each to make the appointed speech standing, then to sit down, while the Clerk of the Meeting asked the relatives who accompanied us, did they consent to the "presentation of marriage" which had just been made? They answered "Yes;" and then the written permission from the English Meeting was read. We then "paused a bit," and retired from the women's room, in the same solemn procession we had entered it; and, having walked into the men's Meeting-room, there went through the very same formalities.

It is esteemed very desirable that, as soon as the ceremony is over, the presentation party should, one and all of them, return to their respective Meeting-rooms, and "sit out the sitting" with the Friends. We evaded this custom, and returned home. We had a large dinner party that day, and I received many compliments on the elegance of my dress, the beauty of my companion, the satisfactory manner in which we had performed, and admonition on the necessity of speaking louder at the next and final ceremony.

Five weeks after this, another Monthly Meeting was held, and then the two men and the two women Friends who had been appointed to make inquiry, reported, that there did not appear to be any reason for refusing to allow of our marriage; and therefore they gave us formal permission to go on with it. There was then a delay of two weeks more, before the wedding day came. At last it arrived, and then, accompanied by sixteen couple, we were marshaled into the elders' and overseers' gallery, which is two steps lower than the ministers,' and, like it, fronts the whole assembly. As usual on such occasions, a vast number of the town's people flocked to see the show. A Quaker bride is not allowed to wear a veil; and there, for two long weary hours, we had to sit and be stared at. About the middle of the Meeting, an appointed man Friend came over to where we sat, and placed before us the words that we were to stand up and repeat aloud. Then we signed each the long certificate, which was a very elaborate and elegant specimen of penmanship, on vellum, and the man Friend read the whole out very loud. After this was done, three women Friends preached. I was told afterwards that it was to me they preached, and that they had admonished me, and hoped good for me and my consistent walk through life, most beautifully. I did not hear a word of it. I knew somebody was speaking, but the words conveyed to my mind no more meaning than the sound of the waves as they ripple on the shore. One of the speakers was my own new sister-in-law. Even her voice, which was very peculiar, did not rouse me out of that dreamy state which the lengthened restraint I was compelled to keep myself in, while the public exhibition lasted, had sent me into.

Our dinner party was very large. All our respective fathers and mothers, uncles and aunts, brothers and sisters, brother-in-law and sister-in-law, nephews and nieces, and first cousins, had been invited for a month beforehand; and from far and near they came. We assembled over eighty altogether, and the feasting and merry-making continued for nearly a week. Some of my near relatives were not Quakers. They drew me aside from the crowd, and prayed for me, and blessed me; so did my own dear father and mother, but no one else. That such a service is desirable, I believe rarely enters into the head of a true Quaker.

My father had spared no pains or cost to provide an entertainment worthy of the occasion. Even one of his own pet, beautiful peacocks was sacrificed to do us honour. Venison and pine apples, &c. &c., were sent him by his noble acquaintances; and the Lord Bishop of the Diocese actually sent his own French cook to dress the dinner. Quakers boast of being "a self-denying people." It would be curious to analyze in what the self-denial consists. The ministers, elders, and overseers, who rule over each Meeting, are certainly very strict in denying the young people those indulgences, and that liberty of thought and action, which is the inherent birth-right of us all. To maintain their order, to uphold their system, is necessary to them. It is a pleasure, not a cross to them, to wear the garb, and use the language, and live isolated from even Christian communion with their fellows; and it is a pleasure, not a cross, to tyrannize, as they do, over the mass, by enforcing on them those burdens which few, comparatively, have sufficient energy of mind to reject. The great body of the Society tamely submits to the arbitrary dictum of the few; but that cannot be called self-denial. I have asked different individuals, both in England and in Ireland, dozens of times, "Why does thee wear the bonnet or the hat?"—and the general answer was, "I wear it to please my father and mother. I hate it, and can see no earthly good in it; but the overseers would torment us if I left it off." This was not self-denial; and I am sure, that in the matter of appetite, some Friends are the most self-indulgent people in the world.

Soon after I had moved to my new home, near Bristol, I was duly certified to the Meeting there, as a Member.

Some of the customs of the English Friends were strange to me. For instance: it was on a third day morning that I made my first appearance in the Meeting. A seat was appointed for me on the second row of seats, high up. Very many of the Friends shook hands with me; several introduced themselves. Nothing could be more flattering than my reception there. That day, two cousins of mine dined with us. After dinner, my husband and the gentlemen went out for a walk into the city. We sat chatting over the drawing-room fire, which was blazing so brightly that we put out the candles to enjoy it more thoroughly. Seven o'clock came, and immediately carriage after carriage drove up to the door, and, to my utter dismay, in came Friend after Friend, all in best company dress; upwards of thirty of them. I did not know the name of one of the party, but that made no difference; they knew mine, and made themselves quite at home, and ran about the house to find chairs for themselves. I sent one of the servants off in a great hurry to my sister-in-law, who lived near, to tell her of the inundation which had come on me, and how unprepared I was for it. With the greatest kindness and good humour, she promptly set to work, and packed up a large basket of her own china, silver spoons, and all other requisites, which she knew we had not had time, as yet, to provide for ourselves. She sent these things on before her, and then put on her bonnet, and taking another servant, with another large basket with her, she went to the grocer's, confectioner's, fruit-seller's, and purchased for me all things needful for the entertainment; and then she came, and helped me to get tea for them. To do all this took a long time; and when my husband came home at night, he was somewhat surprised to see his house lighted up, and filled with so unexpected a party, just commencing to regale themselves with the refreshment which was at last made ready. Fortunately he knew them all, and introduced them to me by name; and then we found out that it was the custom in that city, when they wished to be very polite, and to form an intimate acquaintance with a newly settled family, to flock in crowds to the house at tea time, on the day of a first appearance in the Meeting. I was also then informed, that my guests were of the richest and highest families belonging to the Society in Bristol; and that they had paid me the greatest possible compliment. Of course, I felt greatly flattered, and could only regret the awkwardness of being so unprepared to receive them as I should have liked. The next evening about a dozen more came, and apologized for having delayed their visit for twenty-four hours longer than they had wished.

I found them, one and all, amiable, kind-hearted, and benevolent; but they did not appear to be religious, or, at least, although they were all plain Friends, they scrupulously avoided religious conversation; and we have it on the authority of Holy writ, that the mouth speaks of those things which the heart cherishes.

Some of the English Friends were very ignorant; they asked me questions which astonished me from persons moving in such a sphere of life. One asked me, "by what conveyance I had travelled from Ireland?" and when I mentioned the steam-packet, she said, "she would have preferred the coach, the sea was so dangerous." Another, who told me she was a botanist, asked me "were there any wild flowers in Ireland?" and another, "was the water in Ireland good and clear?" and numerous such like questions.

The Bristol Friends had another custom which

amused me, it was so unlike our Irish ways. When we went to return our bridal visits, we were received ceremoniously in the state and coldest room—kept waiting until the ladies had time to array themselves in best order; and one good creature actually thought it right to apologize for receiving a bride in her second best gown. Then, after chatting a while, the lady of the house would say, "Wilt thou allow me to call for the tray?" At first, I did not comprehend that this was intended to convey the idea, that I was to consider I had been offered lunch; but having subsequently, for the amusement of the thing, assented to the tray being called for, and seen the neat, tidy servant maid, in answer to the summons, lay on the table a tray, often a silver one, with plates, and knives, and glasses, but nothing else; and watched the mistress of the house pretending not to see her, and to be so engaged in conversation, as to forget the tray until we rose to depart, and then hospitably attract our attention to it, I was able to understand the value of appearances. Except in Bristol, I never met with this custom; there, I have seen it over and over again.

Soon after becoming a housekeeper, I was called on by the tithe collector. Friends annually sum up the amount of all they have lost by this suffering, as they call it; and I was then under the idea, that "our noble testimony against an hireling ministry," was an essential part of all true Christianity, and that our refusal to pay the unholy tax was an acceptable martyrdom, in a small way. I had heard much preaching on the subject, and very much self-laudation on the faithfulness of the Society generally, indeed universally, to this our testimony, which so widely separated us from the hirelings of all other creeds. The two men who called on me, for the purpose of collecting the disputed impost, were exceedingly gentle and polite. They saw at a glance that I was an ignoramus, and kindly volunteered to inform me how other Quakers managed, for I had told them, that my profession would not allow me to pay tithes; and that if they insisted on forcibly taking away my property, though I would not resist, still I would look on it as actual robbery.

"Did you ever pay tithes ma'am?" said one of the men.

"Never," I replied.

"Well, then," said he, "you are a stranger here, I see, and I'll just tell you how the Bristol Quakers manage, for I am going about among them for twenty years past, and I am always glad to accommodate them, and meet their scruples. The sum you must pay is one guinea; so I will call here to-morrow, at eleven o'clock in the morning, and you just leave on the sideboard there some articles of plate—your teapot will do very well, or spoons, or whatever you like—then I come and take it away. You don't give it, and so your conscience is clear. You will then return to your Meeting-people, that your tea-pot, worth ten guineas, was distrained for tithe; and as soon after as you like, you can go to Mr. Jones, the silversmith, and tell him how you lost your tea-pot, and are obliged to buy a new one. He will condole with you; and after showing you a variety of new ones to select from, he will hand you your own identical article, and say, he can sell you that cheap—say one guinea. You pay your guinea, and get your own safe back again, cleaner and brighter than ever; and, if you like, you can purchase some other little trifling article; for Mr. Jones is a very accommodating man."

I was really shocked at the cool proposal of so nefarious and unprincipled a transaction, and indignantly rejected it; declaring, at the same time, my firm belief, that no Quaker would be guilty of so undignified and false an act. The man smiled, and said, "Aye, that is the way they all go on at first; but ma'am, it is a great deal the easiest and best plan in the end;" and then he gave the names of very many, my own acquaintances, who regularly once a year, as he jocularly said, "allowed Mr. Jones to clean their plate." "There is old Mr. R." said he, "has a fine massive silver tea-pot. It is always laid out ready for me; I always give notice before I go; and now, twenty times I have carried it off, and got it brightened for him. He values it at twenty pounds, and his tithe is only one pound ten. And there is young Mr. R. He likes me to get his spoons done for him. He gives so many dinners, he likes to have them bright and new looking." Seeing me still very incredulous, he said, "Well, ma'am I wont call on you for a week, to give you time to think about the matter." During that week I went to old Mr. R.'s, and told his daughter that tithes had been demanded of me, but that I had not paid them, and was expecting another visit from the collector.

"Oh! yes," said she, "this is just the time they go about. They seized a valuable silver tea-pot from us last week. My father values it at twenty guineas, and the demand in money is only about thirty shillings; but it is a noble testimony we are called on to bear; and I trust our faithfulness will yet be the means of opening the eyes of professing Christians to the nature of a pure, free, gospel ministry. I trust, my young Friend, thou wilt be faithful."

She spoke so seriously, that I hesitated to say what I intended about Jones's shop, lest the idea that I for a moment could think her or her father capable of such a deed, might offend.

I then called on young Mrs. R., and mentioned the same thing to her. "They did indeed," said she, "take our spoons; but my William has some way or other to get them back. I can't tell how he manages; but I suppose they are ashamed of taking so much over their demand, and so return them. At any rate, they are sent back beautifully polished; and not only that, but a handsome sugar-spoon, with our crest engraved on it, was also amongst them. I suppose they were sorry, and put in the spoon by way of atonement." I suspected that my Friend William might know more than his wife on the subject, but said nothing.

I then went to Jones's shop, and boldly asked, if they would return me articles of plate which might be distrained for tithe, on paying the exact amount of tithe demanded, and was politely informed, that they would be most happy to do so—to enter into the same arrangement with me as with other Quakers. "But," said I, "what recompense will you require, for afford- me so great an accommodation?"

"None whatever," replied the shopkeeper; "the Friends are very good customers of ours; we are always glad to see them entering our doors."

"And what must I pay the collectors?"

"They make no charge either; you can give them an odd shilling now and then if you like, for they are very honest, civil fellows."

Faithful to their appointment, at the end of the week, the men came to me, walked straight into the parlour, and over to the sideboard, and looked disappointed not to find the plate ready laid out for them. I told them I had to apologize for doubting their veracity. I had inquired, and found that their statement was true; but as I could not see any sense in such a round about way of paying, I thought it simpler, and came to the same thing in the end, to pay the money at once, which I did. They thanked me, and broadly grinning, said, "I was the only Quaker in Bristol who did the thing in a straight forward manner, as most of the Society had a crank in their consciences about it." This first drew my attention to the doctrine of our Friends as relates to tithes. I studied the rules of the Meeting, Barclay's Apology, and various tracts, &c. on the subject; and finding that, in the first place, they assume, that all who receive any pecuniary aid, are hirelings, and preach for the sake of filthy lucre; and in the next place, that the one only Scripture text on which they profess to be called on to bear this testimony, is this—"Freely ye have received, freely give," I imagined, that the first was an uncharitable, as well as a most unwarrantable assumption; and the second seemed to me an actual command to give. Surely it is a curious perversion, to construe, "freely give," into "do not give."

I never was called to account by the Meeting for paying my tithe. The Friends to whom we reported, when called on for the amount of our "sufferings for the cause of truth," merely remarked on the small sum we returned; and at the next Monthly Meeting, I heard the query satisfactorily answered—and by one of those very Friends, whose names had been mentioned to me, as customers of Jones the silver-smith—"that Friends were faithful in bearing their Christian testimony against paying tithes, priests' demands, and church rates."

I really felt that day, that I was an awful hypocrite in the sight of God, to sit quietly by, sanctioning such a mean, cowardly subterfuge. But my conscience soon got hardened again, by listening to the repetition of the thing; and besides, it is only by very slow degrees that the light breaks in upon a mind which has been drilled into a system. When I think now, of the great difficulty I felt in shaking off the mental thraldom of Quakerism, and of the many years that I lived, seeing the fallacies of the system, and alive to the discrepancies between profession and practice, and yet unable to see my way out of the distorted system of Christianity which I knew it to be, I can feel very tenderly for those who are still dwelling in that gloom, from which I was only rescued by the rough hand of adversity, and the persecution which, for ten years past, the Society has condescended to inflict on me; but I am not come to that yet.

There was an elderly female preacher, who sometimes favoured me with a morning call. She always spoke kindly and affectionately to me; although she considered she was in the line of her duty in reproving me for the fashion of my window curtains, and the oil paintings on the walls, still it was not done in an offensive manner, and evidently only for the "easing of her mind." This dear old woman had one conversation with me, which left an indelible impression on my mind. It was in reference to the study of the Scriptures daily, which she was advocating. She said, she greatly admired the Established Church, because in it the Scriptures were so freely and so largely read; and that notwithstanding the many practices therein, with which as a Quaker, she could not unite, still she felt very sure the Lord would honour it, because it honoured his written word. And in conclusion, she said, "If I were not a Friend by birth, and education, and habits, and family ties, I would join myself to the Established Church." Never before, and never but once since, have I heard a plain Friend speak even kindly of the Church of England; and as I had imbibed much of the dissenting spirit myself, these remarks, from one I esteemed highly, surprised and interested me; and it was in consequence of them, I resolved to go to Church, and judge for myself—a resolution I carried into effect, and which has drawn down on me ever since, the wrath of the Society.

Another little elderly female preacher also visited me. She was not of the set I belonged to; for the Bristol Meeting was divided into three sets: the high Friends, or the rich and well born; the rich and low born, and the poor. My visitor, Grace Mann, was in the second set, and consequently her visit was unexpected. But she was a minister, and therefore welcomed with all due gravity. Half preaching, half conversing, she informed me that her concern in visiting me was to urge upon me the propriety of dealing at Friends' shops. She thought, "as a people, we would do well to encourage each other; and besides that, there was a temptation to depart from the plain language, when we resorted to shops kept by the 'people of the world;' it was sometimes hard for young people to be faithful to their testimonies in such exposed situations;" and then she asked, "who was my baker?" I mentioned the name. "Ah!" said she, "now I am coming to the point. My son

Daniel is in the baking business. He makes very good bread; I think Friends ought to deal with him more generally than they do."

Quakers are often said to be a sly set of people; and indeed I often thought our preachers very much so, when they attract one's attention by the words, "a concern," or "an evidence," which conveys the idea of an inspiration from heaven, and which ought to be irresistible in its influences, and then to press, as they so often do, some point which bears, directly or indirectly, on their own individual welfare and interests.

The "evidences" go farther still; they sometimes reach beyond the tomb. There was a young woman, who had a very uneasy conscience as she lay upon her dying bed. She longed for pardon and peace; but knew not where to look for it; and neither her mother or sisters could direct her fainting heart aright. At last they sent for a female minister, a very celebrated one in the Society. She sat with the invalid, and preached to her, and read a chapter in the Bible too; but still no ray of joy beamed on the dying pillow. The poor sufferer told them of her agonized feeling of unforgiven sin. There was a protracted silence; and then the minister spoke, and bade the dying woman not to fear, for that she had "an evidence" that her sin was blotted out, and that the pearl gates of heaven were open to receive her. The invalid did not again speak of her own feelings; whether she felt satisfied with the "evidence," or whether she felt ready to say with Job—"Miserable comforters are ye," no one knows.

An elderly unmarried man Friend, also was dying. His death-bed was attended with unremitting attention by another woman preacher. He, too, was in a pitiable state of mind, dreading to meet the face of an offended God. She nursed, and cared, and read, and preached for him. She told me he had to undergo a great mental conflict; but that she always rejoiced to witness a conflict, as it was a good sign for the departing. After some days witnessing the terrors of death, she told him, that "she had an evidence of his acceptance." He clung to it, as a drowning man would to a straw, and died, relying for pardon and for heaven on her "evidence." He had been always a plain Friend, a regular attender of Meetings; and being well to do in the world, it seemed to Friends unaccountable that he should so tremble at the sight of the grave. Some time after his death, it was discovered, that he had been a clever, but most arrant knave. He had been remarkably obliging, in helping unmarried women and widows in the management of their affairs, and especially kind in relieving them of the unpleasantness of going to the Bank to make their deposits; and sometimes with, but oftener without asking them even, he would good-naturedly receive their dividends, and bring or send the amount to them. Death, that dread revealer of secrets, told, that whilst so kindly paying the dividends, he had put the principal into his own pocket; and the deceived women soon found that their receipts were forged. One poor widow, with a large family, lost her all—two thousand pounds —by this orthodox friend, who was safely sent to heaven on an "evidence."

I was greatly shocked at hearing of another "evidence," and the effect on the survivors from heeding such an unwarrantable assumption of inspiration. An acquaintance of mine died, too proud to talk of his mental agony, which was only known to those about him by an occasional, and apparently uncontrollable outburst of terror. His life had been an irreligious one; and his latest act was a malevolent attempt to sow the seeds of strife and domestic unhappiness in a family over which his wealth had given him influence. The widow and children, whilst they rejoiced in being released from his tyranny, trembled with horror at the idea of the future, on which he had now entered. He left directions that his widow should continue the unhallowed conduct which God had prevented him from finishing. She recoiled from the hateful task, and positively refused to aid in the unrighteous work. She became sadly anxious for the soul of her departed husband, and was daily becoming more and more alive to the necessity of securing her own salvation, and fleeing from the wrath to come. In this state of mind she was visited by a woman preacher, a relative of her own, one who knew well the ungodly character of the deceased. She pitied the poor widow; and having sought in vain to console the wounded spirit by ordinary means, at last resorted to an "evidence."

One morning, whilst dressing, in the act of lacing her stays, she hurried across the lobby into the widow's apartment, and in an excited manner exclaimed, "Oh! I have had an evidence. Whilst lacing my stays, I had a clear evidence, that thy husband is in heaven, and I have hurried here to tell thee, for I knew it would so cheer thee." The widow, from whom I had the story, took the comfort it was designed to give her. She undoubtingly assured me, that such an evidence was incontrovertible. She ceased to sorrow for the soul of her husband; and soon after, imagining, naturally enough, that if his conduct was not so bad as to shut him out of Heaven, it was not so very dangerous for her to continue his ill deeds. She took up the business he had left undone, from which she had at first shrunk with dismay, and soon entered into the spirit of it, with as keen an eagerness, and as reckless a disregard of all righteousness, as he had done.

In the Bristol Meeting, there were two men and half a dozen women preachers. Several other men were accustomed to sit in the gallery; for, both among the English and Irish Friends, it is the custom, when there are not a sufficient number of men preachers, to select a few others, of the most respectable. Grave-looking, white-haired men are preferred to sit in the gallery. The object in doing so is, that if any of "the people of the world" should chance to come into Meeting, they might behold a well-filled preachers' gallery; and as the women everywhere so greatly outnumber the men, it is not deemed desirable that a stranger should, at a glance, be aware of that fact, which is not altogether a satisfactory one.

In consequence of what that good, pious little woman had said to me about the Established Church, I went to see and hear, and judge for myself. By the merest chance I went to St. James', and had the great privilege of hearing that good old saint, the Rev. Mr. Biddulph, preach. In his sermon he introduced the text, "There is no other name given among men, whereby we may be saved, but only the name of Jesus;" and dwelt much on the necessity of the name "Jesus" being reverenced and honored. He said, "It was a test of our being Christians, and that vast numbers of professors were ashamed of it, and avoided the use of it. That it was a stumbling-block over which many fell; and that no one deserved to be called a Minister of the Gospel who did not faithfully and lovingly publish the glad tidings, that faith in the name of Jesus, who shed his precious blood to atone for sin, was the only way whereby salvation might be attained." I was so pleased with the service of the Church, and with the intelligible and reasonable sermons I heard there, that I continued a frequent attender, but only at such times as did not interfere with my own Meeting, to which I still felt bound.

The contrast between the sermons I heard at Church, and those I heard at Meeting, was painfully striking. Our Friends scarcely ever mentioned the name of Jesus. They seemed as if careful to avoid it, or fearful of using it. They would say, our Redeemer, our

Saviour, our Lord, our Heavenly Father, and even Christ, but the name Jesus—the sweetest name that mortal lips have ever breathed—was very rarely mentioned.

There was an old man, Francis Armit, who spoke almost every first day. It was very tiresome to listen to him, he spoke so slow and so sleepily. Whether it was for the sake of appearing solemn, or whether it was that he had to think what word should follow the last he had spoken, I know not; but the effect was exceedingly unpleasant to any one who took the trouble of listening and trying to comprehend the idea, if idea he had. Several Friends told me they never thought of listening to his monotonous drawl; and, indeed, I am very sure, had any one asked him, when it was over, what he had been saying, he could not himself have told. I was often under the impression that he was asleep; and as his eyes generally closed soon after he began, it is not impossible that he may have been so, and just spoke on as he had for so many years been in the habit of doing. I asked one day, after one of his see-saw, sleepy sermons, how it was that such wretched drivelling was tolerated? and was answered, thus, "Oh! we have so few men ministers, sure it is well, for the appearance of the thing, to have him even. Besides, having been acknowledged as an inspired minister, Friends can't go back now. That would intimate that their own inspiration, in electing him, did not come from 'best wisdom.'" As soon as Friend Francis had done, and sat down, up would rise little Grace Mann, and invariably begin with, "And it is given me to add a few words to the valuable instruction we have just been favored with." She would keep on speaking for about five minutes, and her object seemed to be, to make us think the former speaker's address really had some sense in it; and that as she guessed we could not find it out, she would tell us what it was.

The other women were very "small in their gifts." They rarely spoke, and then only "broken words." and I may add, broken sense, too. There was another man speaker too, who gave us, in tolerable good language, an occasional address, a short essay on truth, or on virtue; but from the time I had heard Mr. Biddulph's sermon, I watched closely, and wrote down almost all I heard in that Meeting, and assuredly it was not the Gospel of salvation. Others were aware of this fact as well as myself. One man, the father of a motherless family, having in vain tried to have the Bible read on first days, was actually in the habit of committing to memory a whole chapter in the Gospels, and repeating it. But this gave offence, and he was forbidden to do so any more.

CHAPTER XI.

Speculation—Anecdote illustrative of the value of riches—Theatre better than Church—Quaker idea of what dissipation really is—Manœuvring for a husband—Elopements—Feelings—Education unnecessary for a Preacher—Persecution—Friend Gregory's method of taking revenge—Disownment and its consequences.

SOME of our men Friends were remarkably clever speculators on 'Change, and were particularly noted for making "good hits," after having sat in the usual week day Morning Meeting. They would laughingly tell us, that the two hours quiet mental calculation helped them greatly; and were quite delighted, and took it as a compliment, when a gentleman one day, with a very sober face, remarked, "Indeed I am no match for you, after your Tuesday Meeting."

The printed rules of the Society are good and sound in reference to speculation, but the practice is totally different. So long as a man is fortunate, and that wealth flows into his coffers, he may speculate in every conceivable way; and the richer he becomes, the higher he will rise in the estimation of the Meeting; but should his speculation fail, then, indeed, the overseers will be on the alert, and the rules rigorously enforced. If the unfortunate has lost only a part of his property,

they will "deal with him gently," and not put him out; but if he has lost his all, no mercy is ever shown. The Meeting testifies its displeasure of his infraction of the rules, and he is "disowned," or in other words, excommunicated.

There were two brothers, partners in business, who, at a time when speculation ran high, had entered into the spirit of it, and realized an enormous sum. With them the old adage proved a true one, "Much would have more;" and again they ventured, and lost all, and more than all they had won. Whilst the Fates had been propitious they were loaded with congratulations and compliments on their sagacity and clever management; but when the tide of fortune turned, they were looked coldly on, and the "Rules of our Society," those "inspired Rules," were held up to them in terrorem. The brothers were both married men. The wife of one of them had a moderate annuity settled on herself; the other was now penniless. The overseers visited them in the solemn way in which they always deal with defaulters. How they separated the sin of one brother from that of the other did not transpire; but the result was, that he whose wife had the independence remained a Quaker, and the other unfortunate was disowned.

This is by no means an isolated case, and the practice of the Society is oftentimes really curious.

It is a rule of the Meeting, that you must attend regularly, if in health, all the appointed Meetings. If you neglect to do so, the overseers make inquiry as to the cause of your absence. Should they ascertain that you go to any other place of worship, especially to the Church, or, as they politely call it, "the Steeple House," you are immediately put under the most rigorous "dealing;" but if your absence from Meeting is only the result of perfect indifference; that you stay at home, and do not go to any place of worship, it is all right, and you are in as good estimation as ever. In the same way a Quaker may attend theatres, balls, races, &c. &c., all of which are forbidden by the rules, and he will not be disowned for it; but if he is found to be guilty of going to Church, he must be cut off from the body as a diseased branch, "fit only for the firing."

There was a young Quaker lad, who having formed an acquaintance with a Christian gentleman, was invited to accompany him to a meeting of the Plymouth Brethren. The lad went, and was so pleased with the Christian instruction he there received, that he spoke of it to his mother. She was a minister, and, not satisfied with sharply reprimanding her son, she made it her business to speak to the gentleman who had invited him, to request he would never again lead her son so astray. The gentleman, who was really interested in the welfare of the lad, replied to her thus: "Your son is in danger of being drawn into infidelity. His companions are young men of notoriously incorrect lives; and he is so pleasant a companion, and so easily led, that I should have thought you would rejoice to hear that he took plea-

sure in attending a place of Christian Worship. You know he is constantly at the theatre, and he told me you had reproved him for going there." "Yes," she answered, "I do know he goes to these places; and I know that his companions are wild young men; but I had far rather he should be there with them, than go with thee to a place of 'common worship.' When he grows older he will settle down into a steady Friend; I have no fear of that. But if once he gets into the habit of frequenting thy Church, he will be lost to the Society."

Some of the Friends have very confused ideas of what sin really is. A young friend of mine was about to be married. The intended bridegroom was a total stranger to me, even by name. I asked a mutual friend about him—"Is he a plain Friend? Is he young? and is he rich?" She replied, "He is young enough, and he is rich enough, but I am sorry to say he is not a plain Friend; indeed, I am told he is a very dissipated young man."

"Indeed," said I, "I am sorry to hear thee say so, for our dear Anna's sake. But how is he dissipated?"

"Ah!" she answered, "he wears a collar on his coat, and a diamond ring on his finger; and, worse than that, he often goes to Church."

"Well," I replied, keeping on as grave a face as I could, "If that is the only dissipation he is guilty of, he may make a very good husband. But how

happens it that he has not been disowned for going to Church?"

"For a very good reason," she answered, "because he is rich. They do not like to disown a rich young man, for there is always the hope that such may marry among us; and then so much depends upon the wife, whether they may become steady Friends or not; the chance is, they will. When once they sow their wild oats they settle down quietly, and do not think any more about the religion of other people, which does not concern them at all."

Many amusing stories of love, and marriage, and manœuvring for husbands have come to my knowledge; and in narrating some of them, I am influenced by the desire of showing, that the assumption of being led and guided in all things by the Spirit of truth is an egregious mistake. This, connected with the doctrine of "perfection," invariably leads the Quaker mind into the belief in its own infallibility. True, they do not claim infallibility. They reject the word—it is a Roman Catholic word, and not to be found in "Friends' writings." But what means the constantly repeated phrase, "best wisdom?" What do the preachers mean, when they call upon us for reverential obedience to them, when they tell us "it has been given them" to direct us? What mean the "concerns" which the preachers so very often have, and to which they expect implicit obedience? What mean the "evidences," but that the preacher has some peculiar mode of communicating with the Almighty, which is

of equal, if not greater authority than the Holy Scriptures, the guide of all other Christians? and which they certainly enforce with an authority that infallibility alone can claim.

I was one evening, at a large tea party, introduced to a very beautiful young bride. She had a large figure, well and most gracefully formed; the roseate hue of her cheek, and the soft brilliancy of her downcast eyes, were only equalled in beauty by the exquisitely fair neck, and the rich dark brown hair, banded in the smoothest Madonna style on her lofty brow. Her dress was of the richest dove-coloured satin; and her Quaker cap, and neck-kerchief, folded in neat plaits across her bosom, were of India's most costly muslin. The handkerchief was attached to the dress by a gold pin, with a pearl head; and the belt of her dress was fastened in front by two more gold pins, each with a diamond head. The bridegroom was a very small, thin, awkward, ill-made man; his face—from which every morsel of whisker had been shaved off—was white, flat, and meaningless; and his dress, though quite new, was badly made, and badly put on; it was, however, a strictly Quaker costume.

In the course of the evening I said to the lady who had introduced me, "How ever did that mean-looking little man manage to get such a very lovely bride?" She smiled, and answered, "Strange as it may seem, I assure thee, it was Rachel who courted him, not he her. I will tell thee the story. About four years ago, Rachel's younger sister was married; and she was somewhat annoyed that she, the elder, and so much the handsomer, should have been passed by; so she resolved to provide herself with an husband; and thou knowest when a woman makes up her mind to do a thing, she triumphs over every obstacle. Rachel's first step was to draw out a list of the names of the eligible young men; opposite to each name she placed the amount of his annual income, as correctly as she could ascertain it. The most wealthy was placed at the top of the list, and so on in regular gradation. She had twelve names down. They lived in all parts of England; one in London, one in York, one in Bristol, and so on.

"Sylvanus Otway was at the head of the list. She had never seen him, and he lived near Norwich. He was down for seven thousand a year. Rachel seriously informed her father and mother, that she had "a concern" to attend the Norwich Quarterly Meeting. They had no acquaintances they cared for there, and were disinclined to take so long a journey; but Rachel became so silent and sad, and so often told them she was burdened with the weight of her concern to go, that they at length yielded to her wishes; and father and mother, Rachel and her sister Susanna, and one of the brothers, all went to Norwich. As the father and mother are acknowledged ministers, of course they were taken much notice of, and invited to all the Friends' houses; amongst others, to Friend Otway's, and Rachel soon had the pleasure of being in-

troduced to Sylvanus. She was delighted to find him a fine, handsome, intelligent-looking young man, and to perceive that he was decidedly fascinated with his new acquaintances; and when, at parting, he whispered to her sister, loud enough for Rachel to hear, 'I hope soon to be in your city, and to have the pleasure of calling at your house,' her cheek flushed with triumph, and her heart palpitated with joy, at the success of her scheme. Sylvanus soon followed them, as he had promised, and proposed for Susanna. He was promptly accepted; and they were married as speedily as the rules of our Society would permit. Rachel was exceeding vexed and disappointed; but she is not a person to be discomfited by one failure, so she resolved to try again; but she has never been friendly with Susanna since. The next on her list was Josiah Gumble, of York, and his income was six thousand. Again she informed her father, that she felt it was required of her to attend the York Quarterly Meeting; and she added, 'it had been borne in on her mind, that the ministry of her beloved father, at that solemn assembly, would be blessed to some waiting minds.'

"There is nothing pleases our ministers more than flattery of their preaching gifts. Rachel is an adept at it. I have often found it difficult to keep my features in sober decorum, when I have heard her speaking of the inward peace she had felt from the acceptable service of her much valued Friends. And then she presses the hand of the minister she is flattering,

with so much feeling, as she says; but they like it, and Rachel has her own ends in view. She went to York, and soon obtained the desired introduction to Josiah Gumble; he too, was young, and passably well-looking; Rachel contrived to be very much in his company; but she saw clearly that he could not be caught. She told me she had never met any man who was so coldly insensible to beauty, and so stupidly indifferent to flattery. However, Rachel was not disheartened; for it soon came out, that Josiah was the victim of an unrighteous attachment to the daughter of a clergyman; for love of whom, he deserted our Israel, and is now—alas! that it should be so—with his six thousand a year, gone over to the camp of the alien.

"The third on Rachel's list was John Jones, of London, her bridegroom now; he is worth about two thousand a year; and, as thou must see, no beauty. When Rachel first saw him, she was half inclined to leave him for somebody else; but the next on her list is only six hundred a year. The sacrifice was too great, and besides, James Lewis might be as mean-looking, so she resolved on the conquest of John Jones. It was very easily accomplished, he made no resistance, he at once became the worshipper of her beauty; and now that they are married, I think it will be her own fault if she is not happy. He is not very wise, but he is good-humoured and good-natured."

"How did thou become acquainted with this amusing story?" said I. "Is it not a breach of confidence to tell it?" "No, indeed," she replied, "there were more than a dozen of us in the room when she told it herself, and showed us the list; she said she did not want it now, so she gave it to Martha Elton, and bade her give a copy of it to any of the girls who would like to try the same plan of getting settled in life."

Several years elapsed before I chanced to hear any thing more of the beautiful Rachel Jones. It was a sad termination to her career; but the hypocritical system of her youth had paved the way for her dismal fall. She lived for a couple of years in her husband's splendid domain, surrounded with all the comforts and luxuries which his doating fondness could accumulate about her, and seemed happy, but her temper was not so even, or her spirits so joyous as formerly. Then she took a very pious fancy, spoke in our Meetings for Discipline, and was rising in the Society. She established schools for the poor in her neighbourhood, and being very strict in requiring a regular attendance from her pupils, she would go herself to their cottages to inquire the cause of absence. This often brought her into contact with scenes of poverty, sickness, and sorrow. She gave up attendance at the school, and devoted her time to visiting the poor. There she would go, day after day, attended by her own coachman, carrying food and clothes, for her to distribute, as she saw they were needed. She would read a chapter in the Bible to the sick, and she would kneel down and pray beside the bed of suffering. Then wearied in body, and exhausted in mind, she

would return home, generally leaning on the coachman's arm. This continued for months to be her daily habit, during which time her husband minded the house and children, for she had two fine boys; and though he regretted that the poor, and the coachman should so engross his wife's attention, still he expected that, like the school, the fancy would soon wear itself out.

One day, she did not return as usual; week after week passed, and no tidings came of her. She had taken up, at several times, large sums of money in her husband's name, as he had from the first, resigned to her, as she wished it, the entire management of his property; about ten thousand pounds, it was supposed, she had in her possession when, with the coachman, who was an Irish Roman Catholic, a handsome young man, she sailed for America—there, under the name of Mrs. Patrick Murphy, she terminated her unhappy career before one year had elapsed.

No notice, that I ever heard of, was taken of her conduct by the Monthly Meeting to which she belonged. It was thought more expedient to let her drop away unnoticed, than, by disowning her for immorality, to allow any record to appear on the books, of this sin having ever been heard of amongst us.

Is is, indeed, a rare sin amongst the Women Friends. The few instances of it, that have come under my knowledge, have all been in families in which the mother was a preacher.

A refined purity, in word, thought, and deed, is an

almost universal attribute of the Quaker ladies. Nor must it be thought that the numerous elopements which take place, result from any deficiency of this principle; but the heart will flutter and throb as wildly under the neat folds of a Quaker costume, as beneath gauze and lace, when the shaft of a young love has pierced it deeply.

When a Quaker girl forms an attachment for a person, "not of our Society," no matter how suitable a connection—no matter how good his character, or how unobjectionable he may be, she is required to refuse him. Her father and mother, she knows, would themselves, be turned out of Meeting, were they to consent to the marriage. She feels that although the rules of the Society hedge in her way, yet that no law of God confronts her; and therefore not to subject herself to the possibility of disobeying her parents, she elopes, generally, in the very simplest and least improper of all ways. Her name is called in the Church three times; no Quaker is there to hear of it, or to tell the overseers; and she just walks quietly from her father's house, for an hour or two, and comes home a bride.

The parents, to escape the censure of the Society, and the inquisitorial annoyance of the overseers, invariably assume the appearance of indignation for a short time. The daughter understands their feigned displeasure, but real affection for her and her husband; she keeps at a distance from them, until the overseers have got some other occupation to engage their attention, and then cordiality, both in reality and in appearance, is resumed.

This is very frequently the true state of the case, although, no doubt, many Quaker girls have eloped without so good an excuse. Some, anxious by any means, to escape the disagreeable surveillance they were subjected to by their overstrict relatives, have been too precipitate, and too rashly confiding.

On the occasion of one elopement, the whole Society was thrown into a ferment. It was a young woman who had been educated most guardedly, that is, who had been carefully kept from all communication with "the people of the world;" from books and newspapers, and even from associating with any Friends' families, but those who were of the utmost orthodoxy; whose chief employment was hemming muslin, and attending Meetings, and whose greatest indulgence was to be allowed out to tea with the ministers and overseers.

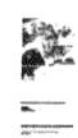

Youth must have some excitement, and she was naturally ambitious of distinction; that inherent trait of her character developed itself, in the only accessible way allowed by the rules; she became a preacher. Her youth, her good looks, and her pleasing voice, combined with her grave and extra-sober demeanor, soon satisfied her Meeting that she was raised up to be what the Society now-a-days sadly wants, "a standard bearer, an inspired minister." Many and many a private meeting was held by ministers and elders, that each might tell the others, what was the feeling of their minds on the important question of allowing her "a seat in our gallery," and after inquiring into the "feeling" of all the plain Friends all over the country, and they unanimously agreeing that Jane ought to be acknowledged as an inspired minister, she was so appointed, and took her seat, to the great delight of her relatives, who were proud of her elevation. To have a preacher in the family, confers a reflected estimation on it.

When the ministers and elders are considering of the suitability of appointing a minister, they make no account of education, that they professedly despise; they make no inquiry, even into the candidate's knowledge of Scripture—no examination whatever is considered necessary. They decide wholly and entirely from their "feelings," and they profess themselves to wait for inspiration, which comes to them always, and only through "feeling." Hence the great difficulty they sometimes suffer under, when an acknowledged minister has proved indisputably, that she is not "inspired;" they must, in testifying against her evil deeds, admit that their own inspiration, when acknowledging her, was not from "unerring and best wisdom." Grave offences are often passed over in a minister, rather than that an open admission should be on record, of the possibility of the Meeting of ministers and elders making a mistake, which strikes at this fundamental doctrine of the Society.

Jane being now a minister, was consequently given a pre-eminence over her parents, and no longer considered herself in subjection to them. She tyrannized over them, as well as the rest of the family, by her numerous "concerns" for their spiritual welfare, to which she required and obtained implicit submission. She had entire liberty to go in and out as she pleased, and might tell or not tell where she had been. Jane enjoyed her new-found liberty, and made full use of it. She soon found out, that "the people of the world" are not all quite so bad as she had been taught to consider them; and having been kept from temptation by the seclusion of her former life, not by sound scriptural principle, which is the only true repellant of temptation, poor Jane could not resist the flattering attentions of a respectable and handsome suitor, who spoke to her of feelings which her woman's heart could well understand, whilst he laughed at her idea of "waiting for a feeling" on which to guide her conduct. She eloped and married him, and was never forgiven by her parents, or by the Society.

Friends, as a body, are extremely vindictive and unforgiving. Parents will often, at the instigation of the Meeting, and to escape blame themselves, persecute their offending children with exceeding severity; and as the Society refuses to take any cognizance of unkindness, or of unchristian severity, or injustice, unless the sufferer be "a member," the persecutor feels encouraged, thinking, that if the Society really consider his conduct improper, the overseers would be only too glad to call upon him.'

So it is in regard of law-suits. The rule is very

stringent, that Friend may not go to law with Friend; but Friends may go to law with "the people of the world," as much and as often as they please. A Friend may be guilty of the meanest, and shabbiest, and most dishonorable conduct, and provided it is only one of "the people of the world" who suffers, his Meeting takes no notice of it, unless there be danger of such publicity as may damage the well-established character of the Society. And if a Friend wishes to go to law with a Friend, he can manage that too. He has only to press his broad brim more tightly on his brow in Meetings; to be more devoted in his attention to the high, plain Friends; squeeze the ministers' hands as they come out of Meeting after speaking, and ingratiate himself with the overseers; and if he is a moneyed man, lay them under pecuniary obligations, and the difficulty which the "rules" opposed to his wishes, vanishes. He can invent, or he can find out, some flaw in his adversary's Quakerism, and have him put under dealing, which being conducted on a most provoking and irritating system of domiciliary visits, generally results in the victim sending in his resignation of membership, for the sake of getting rid of it.

There are other ways of eluding the rules. This I have described is the most common; for when once the resignation is sent in, Friend Broadbrim can go to law, uncensured and unnoticed.

I knew an instance where a man, who was very rich, and of high standing in his Meeting—that is, who was sometimes appointed representative to London, sometimes made clerk of the Quarterly Meeting, who spoke in the meetings of discipline, and kept an excellent table, to which the ministers, elders, and overseers always had a ready access. This man was a violent radical, and quarreled irreconcilably with another Friend, for refusing to join with him in some rather dubious demonstrations in favour of the radical candidate for parliamentary honours. He who refused was a conservative, and well known to be so; but Friend Gregory had found so many only too glad to have it in their power to please him, that he was mortified and indignant that one whom he had the power either to serve or to injure, should refuse, and, more than that, should dare to assign a conscientious reason for not doing his behest. Gregory had evinced on other occasions a somewhat vindictive spirit. He now commenced to work on the plan he had cautiously laid to ruin the offender. He all of a sudden became very friendly with his victim, appeared to enter with kindliness into his affairs, and offered to lend him a considerable sum of money. He thus obtained, easily the knowledge he required of the private history, and the connections of the other, who was unsuspicious, and credulously confiding in what he deemed the wonderful kindliness of Gregory. Trouble after trouble came now upon him. Like the waves of the sea, they followed each other in rapid succession, and in an unaccountable manner; but he was a Christian man, and bore up bravely against the flood. At last a near relative died, and in his will gave strange reasons for alienating some property which he had expected. This led to inquiry, and it was found, by the papers of the deceased, that Gregory had long been in correspondence with him; and, whilst sympathizing hypocritically with his victim's afflictions, had been slandering him most foully. When discovered he threw off the mask, and became an open and formidable enemy. The victim addressed the Monthly Meeting on the subject of the wrongs which Gregory had inflicted on him, and asked the overseers to restrain him, according to the rules, from the persecution he was so wilfully pursuing; but the overseers were Gregory's own people, and the whole Meeting was at his feet. Their letter in reply, which I have seen, was a very curious specimen of Quaker justice. They said, they had been deeply pained to find that any one had accused their esteemed Friend Gregory of persecution; that they had several "solid Meetings" to consider of so grievous a complaint; that the result of their waiting for the inspiration of best wisdom had been, to summon Gregory before them, and to read to him the letter of accusation; that it was done in a very weighty manner, as became so grave a charge; and that they had been exceedingly relieved by that dear Friend informing them that it was all a mistake; that he was incapable of such base conduct as he had been charged with; that so far from his wishing to injure, his heart overflowed with love to his tried Friend; and they added, that as it was impossible to alter the high opinion they entertained of so consistent a Friend as

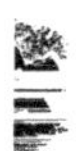

Gregory, it was no use whatever to address them again on the subject.

There was, however, one minister in that Meeting, whom Gregory was fearful had misgivings. The minister was influential, and it would be inconvenient should he look too curiously into the matter. It was necessary to blind his eyes, and none knew better than Gregory how easily that might be done. The minister was poor, comparatively, and had a large family. Gregory was a notoriously benevolent man, a large subscriber to all the charities. It was only what might be expected, that he should call on the minister, express sympathy at the pressure which the wants of so numerous a family entailed on one whose mind ought to be relieved from sublunary cares, that he might the better be enabled to attend to his high calling; and Gregory begged his acceptance of a note for five hundred pounds, which the other accepted, and never since has had misgivings of the rectitude of that ornament of our Society, Friend Gregory.

The illusion caused by the most splendid scenery is dissipated when one gets a peep behind the scenes. Many a house is neat and clean outside, and very dirty within. There is a time coming, when things will be revealed of "that respectable body, the Society of Friends," which the world now little dreams of.

Friends claim for themselves, both publicly and privately, the honour of being free from the sin of persecution. Not long since, I observed a letter

written by some one of them, to one of the periodicals, boldly demanding a public recognition of this claim.

There is nothing in Quakerism to prevent a man persecuting his fellow. On the contrary, there is very much in the system calculated to encourage the growth of that spirit. When the Meeting testifies against any infraction of its rules, and the offender has been "disowned," every relative and connection he has is called upon to persecute him. He is not a Friend now. Friends are advised not to associate with any but Friends. He is cut off from domestic and social companionship. Is not that persecution? What crime has he been guilty of, that he is thus severed from all the associates of youth? Why do all his old friends look so coldly on him? Why do they put an evil construction on his every act and word? Why seem to watch over him for evil? and why prophesy of his ultimate fall? Why do they refuse, with a mysterious reservation, to bear witness to his honourable conduct, to his integrity, or to his moral worth, whilst among them? They profess to cast him off; they do so, in such a way as that, if they can help it, he shall never get on. And what is the crime? Perhaps he has attended the service of the Parish Church; or has allowed his daughters to learn music; or has dressed himself or his family in mourning for a father, a mother, or a wife; or has paid tithes; or has accompanied his sister when she was going to be married in the Church; or, perhaps, he

has brought dishonour on the Society by a failure in his business. True, he has told the overseer how that failure was caused, by some Friends, high in the Meeting, having taken an unfair advantage of him; having advised him to take the unfortunate step he did, with the understanding, that though their names were not to appear, they would back him privately. He has shown that the positive fraud of a "high Friend" has overwhelmed him; he has intreated for mercy, for he dreads the effects of disownment. But all in vain. He is sharply reproved for "highly improper conduct," in mentioning the names of the Friends he has inculpated; and he is tauntingly reminded that he has been lax in the observance of our rules, for a lengthened period. A quick glance at his coat tells him that now a standing collar, and a rounded skirt would have served his cause; and the mention of our overseer, Martha Wrigley's name, brings to his recollection the repeated visits of that "important Friend," to his wife and to himself, to remonstrate with him on the sin of having his daughters taught to play on the piano.

I have seldom known an instance of a member being disowned for sin. But for being unfortunate, and for transgressing the rules of the Society, paying tithes, marrying out of Meeting—often, very often. But for sin, never, unless compelled by publicity. Sin is passed over, rather than have such things recorded on the books.

There is nothing in Quakerism, as I have known

it, to prevent an humble, loving spirit from meekly drinking the waters of salvation. The Holy Scriptures may be freely read in private, and they can accomplish their own mighty work on the hearts of the upright and true followers of the Lamb. But there is nothing in Quakerism, so far as I have known it, to prevent the commission of crime, to preserve from temptation, or to make the road to heaven one whit more accessible, by all the various and specious devices which "the best wisdom of our worthy predecessors" has ordained, than that plain, straightforward way, which Matthew, Mark, Luke, and John, in the good old times, pointed out to us.

I have often met with open infidelity under the name of Quakerism; and a teacher in Friends' families, a pious man, has lately informed me that, with very few exceptions, the young Quakers, his pupils, are growing up infidels.

CHAPTER XII.

Country Meetings in England and Wales—The Ethiopian and the Leopard—Bonnet and Hat essential to Friends' worship—A doubtful Minister—Sleepy old Friend—Dry Meetings—Exhortation to assist in the ministry, and honour promised to reward compliance—Story of poor Mary—St. Paul's want of politeness—Sitting on Dress—Funeral Customs—Schism—Overseers' method of getting Information—Wedding at an Inn.

I HAVE had several opportunities of attending the small country Meetings in England and Wales. In one of them we sat down in number eight persons, one of them was a child of about six years old. The room was large enough to hold a couple of hundred people, and was cold and damp. We took our seats in right order; the plainest dressed man and woman sat fronting the empty room, and the rest of us on the top seats. The silence and the chilly feel soon became painful. The child did not understand or enjoy it. He slipped down quietly off the seat behind his father, and ran over to his mother, saying, audibly, "Oh! Mamma, let us come away." She tried to keep him silent, and succeeded for a few minutes; but there was a very pretty girl near, and he again forgot decorum, and said aloud, "Mamma, that Friend has a very nice face." This unusual breaking of the silence upset the gravity of all. The friends on the raised seat shook hands, and the only public worship which these Friends had on that Sabbath day was concluded. They had sat in the Meeting-room for just one hour. I was sorry to hear afterwards, that the child had been severely punished for his disturbance of the assembly; and not surprised, when told, that the pretty girl had married the Curate of the Parish Church, to which she was in the regular habit of going, as soon as ever the mockery of a Meeting, which her parents constrained her to attend, was over.

At another country Meeting which we were told had the great advantage of a resident minister, we sat down, about forty in number, many of whom, like ourselves, were strangers. After some twenty minutes silence, the minister rose to address us. He did not use any opening text, but in the course of his rambling oration, he made use of these words—" Can the Ethiopian change his skin, or the leopard his spots? No, my friends, they cannot, because they are both brute beasts, and they perish together." When the Meeting was over, many spoke and laughed at the mistake, but none, as if they deemed such ignorance sinful in a professed minister of the Christian Religion.

Travelling through South Wales, we were told one Sabbath morning that there was a Friends' Meeting held in the house of a Friend, and that it was according to law, a registered place of worship. We resolved to attend it, and went there; it a was a gentleman's comfortable house, surrounded by a small, well-kept lawn, and gardens. The owner, his wife, and brother, constituted the usual assembly. We were cordially welcomed at the door, as an acceptable addition to the Meeting. The drawing-room, a very elegant apartment, light, cheerful, and decorated with numerous articles of taste and vertu was the meeting-room. The lady retired for a few moments, and returned with her Friends' bonnet and shawl on, her husband then slipped down stairs, and came back with his hat on. Then we all sat down, and "dropped into silence." It had not continued five minutes, when the owner of the house got fidgetty, and jumping up, said. "I do not think we can manage a silent Meeting well. Shall I read a chapter in the Bible?" We all assented, and he laid on the beautifully inlaid table, a magnificent copy of the Holy Scriptures, from which he read two chapters and a psalm; a two-minutes pause succeeded, and then he turned round on his chair, and gravely shook hands with me. Meeting was over, and we began to chat; he insisted we should remain and dine with him, as he said Friends always did when they attended that Meeting. And his wife proposed a walk, which we all enjoyed very much; the day was fine, and the scenery quite new to me, the mountain air invigorating, and our companions intelligent and exceedingly agreeable.

The lady laughingly told me, that she always put on her bonnet, and her husband his hat, when sitting in their drawing-room—their make-believe Meeting-house, on first days; "but," said she, "it would not feel like a Friends' Meeting, unless we had on those appendages of our Society." She told me that "her husband had subscribed several hundred pounds for the building of a large church which was quite near them; that she often thought it would be more sensible to go there to worship, that the minister was a valued friend of theirs, and that they could not see anything wrong in the service of the Church; but that, as it would expose them to so much annoyance from the Society, they kept on the old way, sitting silent first with hat and bonnet on, for the name of the thing, and then reading the Bible for edification."

I attended for several months a country Meeting, in which there was one woman preacher. She, and one overseer, for company-sake beside her, and an old, plain, white-haired man, who, though he had no appointment, was, on account of his wealth and his orthodox appearance, approved of, sat in the upper or preaching gallery. The Meeting was principally composed of young people, several large families living in the neighbourhood. The preacher's gift was very small. She would sometimes repeat the same sermon over and over again. Some thought she had but one text, so committed to memory as to be able to repeat it aloud. She was a very proud woman, and took offence readily, when not treated with that deference which she conceived her appointment to the ministry entitled her to. Her husband was also a very plain Friend; but there were some rather dubious money transactions, in which both were involved, which made

this Friend's preaching be received more coldly than usual. Plain Friends may do pretty much what they please. The discipline of the Society is never rigidly enforced, when the outward appearance is in all points regulated by the standard of orthodox Quakerism. It is not considered desirable to interfere; for it is so unpleasant to have to put a Friend, whom we have already acknowledged to be an inspired minister of our Society, under dealing, that the sin is covered as much as possible. But if the truth be whispered about, such ministers generally consider it prudent to absent themselves very much from Meeting, under the convenient plea of indisposition; or if they do go, it is to sit up on their elevated seats, but generally in silence.

Sabbath after Sabbath, these young people sat in that Meeting-house, without hearing one word to enlighten their understandings, or to teach them how to attain salvation, or to worship God aright. The old man, after making divers twitchings and contortions, indicative of a determined resistance to the somniferous influence of the silent Meeting, would invariably yield to it. It was almost impossible for any one present to avoid looking at him, as he sat directly raised up in front of us; his head bobbing from side to side, first very gently, then as the sleep grew deeper, down it would sink lower and lower, until at last one great drop down would rouse him up, to open his eyes, and look about him, in a kind of wild way, as if he would say to the bright young eyes he saw gazing up to him —"How dare you think I would go to sleep in Meet-

ing?" He was generally roused to break up Meeting, by the ringing of the Church bell, which was very conveniently timed to do so. But on one occasion, even that did not wake him—he slept soundly; and the Meeting sat on, wearily watching his awaking. Half an hour longer than usual, sitting in a silent Quaker Meeting, is no small trial of patient endurance. At last it became unbearable, and a man Friend, sitting in the middle of the Meeting, shuffled his feet about, and making a noise, rose up to depart. This example was followed by all the rest; and the sleeper awoke to find Meeting broke up, without his usual shake of hands. He was very angry about it; and his sons, tall, stalwart men, threatened to chastise the individual who had infringed on their father's prerogative.

A gentleman told me he had stopped a Friend one day in the street of a large city to speak to him on business. Ah! Robert, said the Quaker, "I am glad to see thee, but I can't talk to thee now; I am just going to our Week Day Meeting. Will thee come and sit a bit with us?" "Well, Sir," replied the gentleman, "I have no objection, since you ask me—I will go with you." They went and sat together; the meeting was a silent one, and lasted an hour. When it was over, the Friend addressed his companion—"Well, Robert, how does thee feel after that? Dry work, is it not? Come with me now, there is a tavern close by, and we'll get something more comfortable for ourselves."

A silent Meeting is technically called, a dry meeting, in contra-distinction to the streams of living waters which are considered as flowing from the lips of acknowledged ministers.

I was now living, as Friends say, within the compass of a highly-favoured meeting, that is, we had an unusually large staff of preachers. We had six acknowledged ministers, and four candidates for that honour; besides this, we often had visits from travelling Friends. Several of these came to our city under "the weight of a concern to sit with Friends in their families," and I, of course, came in for my share of their visitations.

There was a woman Friend, on one of those occasions, whose address pleased me very much. Her concern was to urge on us the frequent and prayerful reading of the Scriptures, and the importance of knowing our own impotence, and our need of the guiding light of the Holy Spirit.

Our old acquaintance, the great John Earl, also paid us a family visit. He honoured us especially by volunteering to dine with us, and was cordially welcomed, as every one was, who came to our house, as a messenger from Christ. To my delight, he came without the usual attendant. His conversation both before, and at dinner, was entertaining and instructive, but at last he dropt into the well-known ominous silence. His concern was different from any of the other Friends; it was, "that my husband might be made willing to yield himself up to the work of the ministry; and that I might be an help-meet for him in so arduous a vocation." He said he had long thought his "dear friend was pre-eminently qualified for a seat in our gallery, that his commanding figure, and his rich deep toned voice, were gifts which ought to be cast into the Lord's treasury." He spoke for several minutes in the most flattering manner of our connections, position in the Society, and of the prominent part which he considered we were both designed to take in the management of it, and he assured me that the trifling sacrifice which would be required of me, in my outward appearance, would be amply compensated for by the delightful feelings I should experience in beholding my husband one of the most honored and most influential men in our Society. He then knelt down, and prayed that the Lord would open our hearts to receive the message which he had been the humble instrument of conveying to us; and especially, that I might be kept from doubting, and from putting any stumbling block in my husband's path. After this, and the usual silence which followed it, had ended, he chatted on different subjects, but before going away, he said he hoped we would not lightly put away the subject he had felt it his duty to speak to us on; and that he would recommend us to study Scott's Bible, with notes and observations, as a peculiarly suitable preparation for that usefulness in the Church to which we are called.

I do not know whether he spoke to others of what he said to us, but about two years afterwards, a woman preacher reproved me very sharply for having, as she said, stood in my husband's path, to impede his service as a minister. And another told me, I had proved a very unfit wife for one, whose early piety and personal beauty, had marked him out for the preacher's gallery. I told them I had never had an opportunity of sinning as they accused me of, for that his own inclination had never been towards preaching, though he certainly was anxious to live as a Christian ought; but it was all in vain, and I had to bear some very hard speeches for it.

The Friend, whom I engaged as governess for my children, was an enthusiastic Quaker. At last she became so carried away by her feelings, as to attempt speaking in Meetings. To her extreme mortification and distress, the overseers visited her, and informed her that her attempt at ministry was not acceptable to the Meeting, and peremptorily told her she would not be allowed to speak there. Poor Mary was overwhelmed with chagrin, and when I soothingly inquired the cause of her distress, she told me all—the feeling of duty which had prompted her to overcome her own natural dislike to speak in a public assembly; the doctrines of the Society which she had studied carefully; she had had visits from travelling Friends, and advices from the overseers, often and often, in which they had warned her of the danger of resisting the guidings of the light within. And now, when she had done so, they blamed her, and spoke harshly to her. Poor Mary! she wept bitterly. I proposed, and she gladly agreed, that we should both search out in the Scriptures, and write down every text we could find on the subject of women's preaching. We did so, and comparing those from which Friends draw an inference, that women's preaching is a part of the Gospel scheme, with St. Paul's positive command—"Let your women keep silence in the churches," (where he immediately afterwards informs us that every one who is spiritual must acknowledge he has written by the commandment of the Lord;) we were both, I believe, satisfied, that for once the overseers had done well. Mary, however, never recovered the painful shock her feelings had received; she was vexed for having exposed herself to the rebuff she had met; she was mortified with the belief, that it was because she was poor in worldly wealth, they had silenced her; and she was intensely grieved to think she had presumed to take upon herself the office of a minister, without being called of God to do so. She had an inherited tendency to consumption; and now, having to work for her living by day, and fretting over these thoughts at night, she soon sunk into the grave. Two days before she died, she told me of the great kindness she had received from a medical Friend, whose purse had been freely opened to her need, and of the peace and joy she felt in heart, at the prospect of so soon seeing her Lord and Saviour.

Some time after her death, I was speaking to an elderly Friend, on the subject of women's preaching, and said, "I cannot understand how our Friends explain away that fourteenth chapter of 1 Cor.; the command is so positive, and so solemnly enforced." She replied, "Ah! my dear, sure thee knows St. Paul was a bachelor; no one could expect that he would be very polite to the females."

There was an overseer in our Meeting, who often paid me a friendly visit, and professed to feel great interest in my welfare, and personal affection for me. She was elderly, unmarried, very rich, and somewhat eccentric. She lived in luxurious comfort and elegance, and indulged freely in her one extravagance, the love of old china. I reckoned eight curious old teapots, one day, ornamenting her plain black marble chimney-piece. One with the handle across, like a kettle, she took down with trembling care, to indulge me with a nearer view of the delicate, semi-transparent china, and told me it was invaluable. She had given ten guineas for it; and would not part with it for ten times that sum.

I used to like my Friend Ennice's visits at first; but when she began to find fault with me, and to dictate what I ought, as a Friend, to do and to wear, I lost her favour, by objecting to comply with her wishes. One morning she came early, and I received her in my common morning attire, a simple blue muslin dress. After the usual salutations, she said, "she wished to sit silently for a bit." I immediately put on my gravest face, and respectfully sat down near her, wondering what was to come. The pause was very long, and then she told me, that for many weeks past, it had been on her mind to sit with me—"On thy dress, my dear, on thy dress." She seemed so overcome with the weight of her burden, and sighed so deeply, and paused so long, that although it is usual to sit perfectly silent, I thought it would relieve and assist her were I to speak; so I said, "What is it that displeases thee in my dress; surely I am now as simply dressed as thyself."

"Ah! my dear"—and she gasped and smiled alternately—"a real Friend ought not to wear blue; but it is not that alone; but look at the vain fashion—look at thy sleeve"—and she drew it out to the full extent;—"and look at thy skirt—what waste of material; it is one half nearly wider than mine."

I could not resist the temptation to say playfully, "Well now, Friend Ennice, let us compare it altogether. Thy dress is just what a real Friend's ought to be, and mine is so unfriendly that it draws down thy censure. Thine is, I see, a dark green, Irish tabinet; blue must have been used to dye the green; blue and yellow, both very unfriendly colours, and mine is only simple blue. My sleeves are too wide; thou hast no sleeves at all, but then thou hast an uncommonly well-shaped arm to show. My skirt is too wide, but look at thine; thou can'st not walk across the room without holding it up, it is so long; so what I have in the width, thou hast in the length, and as to expense, my muslin has not cost me one-tenth the money thy tabinet has cost thee.

She laughed outright, and tapping my cheek said,

"Thou art a strange young woman; who, but thyself, would ever think of commenting on my plain dress; but, my dear, thou should'st not indulge in so unbecoming a levity, on so important a subject; and I am to blame for listening to thee; it was not as an acquaintance, but as an overseer, that I came to speak to thee; and I must do my duty, and inform thee, that Friends are not satisfied with thy general appearance. Really thou must give up thy own will, and take up the cross. Thou wilt only, at first, feel it irksome; and besides, thou wilt be thought much more highly of by Friends."

I was going to speak, but checked myself, lest any reply might annoy her; but she said, in an affectionate voice, "Now, my dear, tell me, wilt thou not yield? Speak to me, and tell me freely, what it is that impedes thy dedication to usefulness amongst us. Would'st thou not like to be one of our representatives to London? I am sure the way might be opened for thee to perform that service."

"Well, my Friend," said I, "in the first place, I am not ambitious of that office; but as thou art so anxious I should take up my cross, and dress myself as thou dost, I will consent to do so, on one condition, that is, that thou wilt set me the example, and take up thy cross, by dressing thyself as I do now. Surely that is only fair. Wilt thou?"

"Me," said she, "dress myself up in a blue muslin! I would be ashamed to be seen in it. A common, vulgar, blue muslin. My dear, how can'st thou speak so lightly of serious matters?"

"Well," said I, "never mind the muslin. Thou shalt have one of my neatest and plainest silk dresses, and my best straw bonnet."

"Nonsense," she sharply answered. "I would not wear thy Babylonish garments for anything in the world. Thou hast distressed me very much by thy levity. I am sorry I came to see thee to-day."

"I should be sorry to offend," said I. "I only wished thee to understand how disagreeable it would be to me to alter my style of dress to please thee; so, perhaps, we had better both stay as we are."

She replied, "Thou hast a most extraordinary way of speaking; but I must make allowance for thee, as thou art Irish. Indeed, I don't feel that I can be offended with thee, although I do not think that any one ever before spoke to an overseer as thou hast to me. Me put on thy dress!" And she laughed at the idea of the appearance she would make. She parted from me with apparent cordiality, and even kissed me, but never honoured me with another visit, and, soon after, ceased to give me even a passing nod of recognition; and I think she must have communicated to the other overseers the result of her interview, for I was never again visited on the subject of dress.

I accepted an invitation to a Friend's funeral, as I wished to know how they managed this matter in England. The printed card of invitation, though not in mourning, was printed in a very sombre style. It informed me that a carriage would be at my door at a certain hour, and that after the funeral, the dinner would be at a specified time. The hearse and eight carriages, which formed the cortege, were painted as dark a colour as possible, without being black. We had three sermons at the grave, expressive of the estimation in which the deceased had been held, and then we went to the dinner. It was just a regular company dinner, plentiful and good, with abundance of sweets and wines. We were all very grave. Who could help being so, whilst the very shadow of the grim monster was over us? But still, conversation was kept up. All the women members of the family were in new dresses, of the very darkest shade of brown; and when I remarked, that it was more than a week since the death had taken place, the eldest young Friend answered, "Yes; but it is a great hurry in a week to get so many dresses made up." And yet the Society considers it a sin to wear mourning! I have known instances of whole families leaving us, in consequence of the displeasure incurred by persisting in wearing that customary tribute of respect to the dead.

How absurd! let a sober man think for an instant, and discover if he can, what connection there is between piety, true spiritual piety, and the colour of our garments—the purity of the soul, and the extent of his head cover!

Can any rational being bring those two things into discernable connection? or show in what way the salvation and sanctity of the soul are confederate with the outward garb of the body? Did any of the apostles indulge in, or appoint such habiliments? Was it made a part and parcel of primitive Christianity?

"What a disgusting contrast to true godliness is there in all this parade of folly. 'Pure religion and undefiled before God and the Father is this, to visit the fatherless and the widow in their affliction, and to keep ourselves unspotted from the world.' These are but Popish mummeries; and when the soul is so besotted as to receive such things as the all in all of godliness, there is no limit to its madness. When it is remembered that an excessive partiality for externals has ever attended an infidel disregard of the letter and spirit of Christianity, we exult in every frank and manly effort that is made to quell and crush the incipient evil of superstitious vanity."

This extract is from an article on Popery, in the Achill Herald. It is equally suited to Quakerism, in which the external appearance is the chief care; and as I have heard some of themselves say, "the foundation stone of the Society."

Whilst I was a member of the Bristol Meeting, there was a great schism in the Society. Some were in the habit of meeting once a week, to read and study the Bible, compare text with text, and converse together on the meaning and teaching of the inspired Word. This led naturally to some great discoveries of the unscriptural doctrines of the Society. With simple uprightness, these Bible-readers imagined that they were doing an acceptable service to the others, by pointing out the discrepancies they had found, and a book, or rather several books, were published: "The Beacon," "Holy Scripture the Test of Truth," &c., &c. The result was very different to what had been expected. The main body held tenaciously to their cherished errors. Meetings for the study of the Scriptures were suppressed, conversations on religion forbidden, and the term "Beaconite" applied in derision to all who dared to think for themselves.

Some of the best preachers, and many of the most enlightened and worthy men and women in all parts of England, on this, seceded from Quakerism. And I may add, the greater number of them, after wavering about amongst the various sects of Dissenters, finally settled down into sober members of the Evangelical Church of England.

Another development of the working of Quakerism was brought under my notice, by a very unexpected and unannounced visit which I received from two of the women overseers—Sally Adams and Anny Draper. They informed me that in consequence of having heard a report that Rebecca Gardiner was supposed to be contemplating a marriage out of the Society, they had called on me to ascertain the truth of it, as they knew that Rebecca was an intimate friend of mine, and that I would be likely to know all about it.

I told them, "I was surprised they should come to me on the subject, and that even if I were, as they imagined, well informed on it, I would certainly refuse to betray the confidence my friend had placed in me."

"Ah! now," said Sally, "it is really trying to hear thee speak so, or use such a word as betray. We have a very arduous office to perform, for thou knowest, as overseers, we are liable to blame unless we impart suitable admonition to the young woman."

"It is thy bounden duty," said Anne, "to give us the information we require. The Monthly Meeting will hold us to have been negligent of our office, unless admonition has been timely given to the young woman."

"Why do you not go to Rebecca herself," said I, "and ask her."

"Oh!" said Sally, "because thee sees, after all, it is only a rumour we have heard; and if it is altogether false, as rumours sometimes are, it would be injudicious to mention it to herself."

"It might put ideas into her head," said Anne, "that maybe never were in it; it would not be prudent to go to herself, until we know more about it. Thee must tell us."

"If I did know all you ask me to tell you," said I, "I would decline doing so. How can you ask me to be guilty of such a breach of friendship?"

"We will not let thy name appear," said Anne.

"No, indeed," echoed Sally, "she shall never know that it was thee told us."

"We never give up the name of an informant," said Anne.

"I can give you no information," said I.

"Sure thee don't mean to say thee will put us off?" said Sally. "Who is there but thyself would be likely to know about it, to tell us? It is astonishing the difficulty we have in getting private information, and we can't put Rebecca under dealing without something more substantial than just bare rumour. It is thy duty to tell us, and really thou must. She shall never hear thy name mentioned in connection with our dealing."

"Suppose," said I, "you dismiss the subject from your minds—why trouble yourselves about a rumour?"

"Come," said Anne, "there is no use in our staying here any longer, she wont tell us. And remember," said she to me, "thou art not to mention to Rebecca that we have called on thee."

"Thou had better not mention it to any one," said Sally.

I was one evening in a company of Friends, when the topic of conversation was the conduct of a lady who had recently fled from her husband's house, The husband himself, and his brother, my old acquaintance, Friend Gregory, were present; and the chief speakers were an elderly lady sitting on the sofa next me, whispered—"Is it not very bad taste in those two men to speak thus publicly of a circumstance which they ought to blush to hear mentioned?" "I do not know the lady they are speaking of," said I, "or what was the cause of her flight." "I knew her very well," she answered, "she was a very nice-looking young woman; but her parents, who are both preachers in our Society, acted very injudiciously towards her. They forced her to marry that man who had nothing on earth to recommend him but his wealth. She was, of course, unhappy. He is an odious man; and perhaps it was to cheer her depression, or perhaps to induce forgetfulness, but certainly she got into the habit of putting a few drops of brandy into her wine, and of taking it a little too often. Then he, and Gregory, and the rest of them, upbraided her, and tormented her so much, that really it was no surprise to me to hear that she had fled from his house. But let us listen to what Gregory is now saying.

"I found out," said he, "that it was to one of the fashionable watering places she had gone; and as I could not trust any one to find out all I wanted for me, I resolved to go myself, and that she might not suspect any thing I disguised myself."

"How didst thou disguise thyself?" asked one of the party.

"I disguised myself," said Gregory, as "a gentleman. I got a black double-breasted coat with a collar on it, a velvet waistcoat, and black trowsers. I bought a gold chain to hang over my waistcoat, and a gentleman's hat; no one would have known me. I soon found out where she was, and by night and by day I watched her, until I found out all I wanted to know." And he chuckled and rubbed his hands with glee, at the idea of having discovered that his sister-in-law was living a life of sin.

"Ah!" said the husband—an ill-shaped, unprepossessing looking plain Friend—"was not Gregory very clever to think of disguising himself?"

"Had he only assumed the habits, as well as the dress of a gentleman, the disguise would indeed have been complete; but perhaps he could not do that," whispered the lady beside me.

I mention this circumstance to show, that there is no meanness which may not be resorted to, when Friends resolve to disown one who has incurred their displeasure. As for thee, poor erring wife, let a veil be drawn over thy sad story. Who can tell the agonizing thoughts which burned thy brain to madness, before the intoxicating draught had touched thy beautiful lips! Who can tell of the floods of tears which drowned the light of thy soft beaming eyes, before the fountain was exhausted which left them dry, cold, and scornful? Who can tell of the bitter words, of the heartless unkindness, which first chilled, and afterwards destroyed, thy woman's feelings and affections? Great as was thy fall, they who witnessed that evening the unmanly triumphing, and indecent garrulity of thy husband and his brother, can well believe thou hadst been more sinned against than sinning.

I was favoured with an invitation to a curious wedding. The dinner was to be at a hotel, not an unusual custom in England. Both bride and bridegroom were very rich; so no expense was spared, and the best fare was ordered. The arranging of the procession into Meeting was not done in the orderly way they conduct these matters in Ireland. The different couples walked in, and sat down just where they pleased. At dinner it was the same—no order, no attention to ceremony, was observed. I never, before or since, dined with so unmannerly a set of people. However, I was highly amused watching the scene, and looking at the awkward attempts at carving, and the visible enjoyment of the eaters. As to the bridegroom, he very nearly devoured the whole of the little roast pig which was before him; and the way some of those Friends spoke was so new to me. "I am glad to see thee. Bee'est thee very well?" "Be'ent thee pleased to see the bride looking so bravely?" "I don't think there be a nicer young woman in our meeting." As soon as dinner was over, we rose from table, and went to the other end of the long ball-room, in a corner of which we had dined; whilst the waiters, who could scarce do their business for laughing at the uncouth company, laid on the tea and bride-cake. Again we sat round the table as at dinner, and the large cake soon vanished before the vigorous onslaught of those wonderful eaters. The whole affair was over, and we had taken leave of the very elegant and graceful bride, by six o'clock in the evening.

CHAPTER XIII.

Retrospect—Radicalism—Devonshire Overseers' Advice—Independents—Wesleyans—Plymouth Brethren—Cathedral—Curious custom—Return to Ireland—Adventure with Smugglers—Jacob rules—A First Day Morning Meeting—Ballyhaganites—Reasons for joining the Society—A Convent—Music mistaken for Hebrew—Ignorance and its results.

WHO can turn over the volume of memory, and not meet many a page blistered with the tears of suffering and sorrow? God has mercifully granted that man shall have a feeling akin to pleasure, in the recollection of bodily pain; and the innocent joys that are past, grow brighter and brighter, as they shine in the light of years gone by. But there are wounds which time can never entirely heal—which still bleed, when the covering is removed, and must continue to do so, until warmed by the dawn of the glorious light of eternity.

My bark had floated lightly over many a stormy wave. The breakers had been around and about me, and I had been many a time drenched with the spray; but I heeded them not;—smooth water was before, and a bright sky above me, and those I loved were by my side.

Death came, and with his unerring arrow pierced my father. I felt then the smart of that keen, sharp cut, which the dread messenger alone can give. I loved him with the most intense affection. I thought him when living—and now, after the lapse of many years, I think him still—to have been the very best and most perfect of all the erring sons of mortality whom I have ever met with. Never was he known to speak an unguarded word; never was he known to do an unkind act. And his death was happy, as his life had been most blessed. The carriage was at the door for him to take his accustomed drive, and he was eating a morsel of bread for his lunch, when the summons came, and found him ready. His lips moved, he faintly uttered the words, "Lord, thou knowest that I love thee," and all was over. My father! my father! thou art not dead. Thou art living in the realms of glory; and often in the dreams of the night, I see thee standing at the gate of the heavenly Jerusalem, waiting to welcome me in, and to lead me to the footstool of the throne of the Redeemer.

My father was most conscientiously a Quaker. For his sake I feel an interest, even now, in the Society he belonged to; and the warmest wish of my heart in writing these sketches is, that "the dry bones may be shaken." That as I have had opportunities, far more than others, of seeing and knowing the way in which the machinery has been worked—as I have been inside the doors which carefully locks up the wheels, and have been well nigh smothered by the dust which is accumulated there, I may, by directing attention to the neglected state of that apartment, be instrumental in causing it to be cleansed.

All nature is progressing, and Friends have been foremost in spending their wealth to promote what they call Radical Reform. And yet—oh! strange inconsistency!—they are the staunchest conservatives of those odd dogmas, which, having been handed down from father to son, endorsed with the words—"best wisdom," are now allowed to pass current amongst them, almost to the exclusion of that pure gold of the realm, on which alone is stamped the king's image.

I was one evening in company with several very orthodox Friends, when Radicalism was the theme of conversation. One said, he had given fifty pounds for the Radical dinner; and another, that he had given one hundred. Said another, "I had not a hundred to give, but I went to it, and it was a glorious scene." "Yes," said another, "I saw thee there; and when Lord John Russell's health was drunk, and the cheering was most uproarious, I saw thee take off thy shoe, and pound upon the table with the iron heel, till the glasses danced again."

These speakers were all men who would have shrunk with horror from the idea of wearing a double-breasted coat, or of going inside the door of a Church. Such is man!

Some of our family being in delicate health, we resolved to go and live in Devonshire, hoping that the soft and balmy air of that beautiful county, might invigorate the invalids.

We were not long settled in our charming home, when I was favoured with a letter from two of the women overseers. They required me to inform them did I attend Friends' Meetings regularly? and asked, did I wish to be still considered a member, for the purpose of having a certificate sent for me. I replied, that of course I was a member, and had not any intention of leaving the Society; but that I did not now attend the Friends' Meeting, as the nearest to my home was forty miles away from me.

Some weeks elapsed, and then came another letter from the same two Friends, telling me that having made anxious and due inquiry, they had ascertained, that although the nearest Meeting-house was forty miles off, still I might be enabled to uphold the precious doctrine of our Society, respecting silent Meetings. They informed me, that in a small country town, eight miles distant from my residence, there lived a man Friend, whose name they kindly gave me. This man, they told me, was in the habit of sitting in his own parlour on first day mornings, and had expressed a more than willingness that I should go, and sit with him at that time. And these wise women—two old maids, by the way—actually required me to comply with their advice—to drive sixteen miles every Sabbath morning, for the ridiculous, not to say indelicate, purpose of sitting in the parlour, back of a cutlery shop, for two hours, with a middle-aged bachelor. To save me from the impiety of attending a place of "common worship," those two steady, highly consistent overseers, wrote this sage advice to me. I did not answer that letter; but I keep it as a curiosity of Quakerism.

They wrote to me a third time on the same subject; but that letter came at a time when my heart was lacerated by a double bereavement, and it escaped my attention. The grave had opened, and in one short week received both my mother and sister to its dark bosom. They descended into it, in the sure and certain hope of a glorious resurrection. Tears for my own loss, and joy for their happiness, banished from my mind the memory of my annoyance from the overseers.

I had still very much of the Quaker feeling of dislike to the Church service; and the Quaker idea, that any form of dissent was to be preferred to the State Church, haunted my mind.

I could not go to Meeting; it was forty miles off. I would not go sit with the man Friend; and for the sake of my young family, if not for conscience sake, I must choose some of the places of "common worship." First, I visited the Independent Meeting-house, and did not like it. The preacher there enforced on his auditors the duty of signing petitions to Parliament for Reform, with more energy than suited my idea of a Christian minister. Then I went to the Methodist preaching-house, and my Quaker feelings were shocked with seeing a fiddler stand up to raise the tunes. Besides this, they had the water for baptism brought into the Church in a common, small, blue, earthenware bowl; and I thought that did not look nice for a place of worship; but the preaching was very good, and I went there regularly, until they changed the preacher. His successor was a politician; so I left. Then I went to the meeting of the Plymouth Brethren; but I could feel no unity with them, in what seemed to me an insult to the Almighty. They would not ask a person of rank to meet them in such a den, as they had thought good enough to consecrate to the service of the King of kings. It was a loft over a stable. You had to pass through a coal-yard to the half-ladder, half-stairs, by which it was gained. A dark, dirty, small, mean room, with an unceiled roof; and, in the evening service, two shabby chamber candlesticks were placed on the top of two men's hats, on a little, ricketty deal table. The brethren were a wealthy body, and built up good houses for themselves.

Not liking any of these places of worship—and I will not say that my dislike to them was a reasonable one—I was compelled either to stay at home, or to go to the Cathedral. I went. The Scriptures of the day were a balm to my soul, and some of the beautiful prayers in the service touched a chord which still vibrates to the sound. The preacher was a sportsman; and when speaking of the sin of maligning our neighbours, he bade us "mind what we were about; and, instead of poaching on other people's manors, to confine ourselves lawfully to our own preserves." I did not like the sermons. We were only favoured with such instructions once a fortnight. Every alternate week the Sacrament was administered, and on that day we had no sermon; but the Scriptures and the service more than compensated me for it. They suited my state of mind; and with them I felt, that let the preacher be what he might, the auditors were independent, and could worship God in spirit and in truth, whilst the instruction of the Scriptures, prevented any one from feeling they had been unedified.

This has always appeared to me to be an inestimable blessing in the Church of England and Ireland. If the preacher is a good man, and an eloquent speaker, it is a privilege to receive instruction from his lips; but if he is deficient in knowledge or in gifts, still the humble, upright Christian is sure to receive some food for his soul, from the appropriate and intelligible prayers of the service, and from the inexhaustible treasury of God's Holy Book. This is the great and blessed peculiarity of that Church. Well may the lover of freedom and independence cherish it! In all the various sects of Dissenters, the people are dependent on their ministers for edification. They may or may not read the Scriptures—I believe all except Friends do; but it is often a very minute portion. Preaching is the important part with them, and the quality of that varies exceedingly.

The Devonshire people have some original customs amongst them. One I will mention, as it is uncommon, and will probably, as the tide of reform sweeps on, become extinct. In the shops, wherever I made purchases amounting to, and over, one pound, I was invariably asked to walk to the upper end of the shop, where was placed a chair on a nice piece of carpet. The shopman would leave me there a moment, and returning with a neat small tray in his hand, he would present me with a glass of wine and a slice of plum cake.

Domestic circumstances having occurred, which rendered it desirable that we should remove to Ireland, we resolved to make the journey a pleasure trip. Sending the rest of our family direct, with our two eldest children, we drove from Devonshire to Liverpool in our own light phaeton, stopping here and there, as fancy or fatigue induced us, and seeing all the beauties and wonders of nature that lay in our path. We were six weeks in accomplishing this most interesting and delightful excursion, and like all other travellers, we met with some adventures.

Our guide-book described the valley of Trentishoe as being delightfully wild scenery; so we turned off the high road to see it. When once you enter on a Devonshire by-road, you must go on, there is no retreating. Every half a mile or so, you will meet with a gateway or a nook, where it is just possible to pass another vehicle; but on you must go through the beautiful high hedges, up and down hills, short, but almost perpendicular, which the country people call "smart pitches," and over ruts and stones, which tried even the temper of our pet black mare. At length we got through the hedges, and emerged on a kind of common; there were car tracks to guide us, but no living being seemed there. The scenery was very lovely all around; hill and dale on one side, purple with the mountain heath, on another, ornamented with plantations. And the sunbeams glittering on the sea, as we caught a glimpse of it occasionally between the hills, reconciled us to the difficulties of our path. The wheel marks that we were following, led us down a hill so steep and winding, as to make us anxious lest our equipage should roll over and over. We had to drag on, and held the back as firmly as we could, to assist our willing steed. We reached the bottom of it in safety; when, to our dismay, we beheld the road-way ascending up another hill, steeper if possible than that we had just come down. Our mare looked up the hill, snorted, and refused to stir. She had never before balked at her task, and we knew she would not now, had it been possible to accomplish it. We had lost our way; evening was coming on, and not a creature near to guide or direct us.

There was a small barn or house in the valley. We went to it. The door was fastened. We called and knocked, no one answered. The window was just under the thatch, and up so high that we could not look in. We unharnessed the horse, and led her to a stream of water hard by, where she could crop the grass banks. Then we seated ourselves on the ground, and, drawing out the basket, which we always took care to have well stored on these nomadic excursions, we eat and drank, and laughed at the dilemma we were in. Whilst so doing, a little child crept near us. Where he came from we did not see, and he was too young to speak. We put into one of his hands the leg of a cold roast chicken, and into the other a piece of bread, and off he ran towards the barn. The door was opened for him, and a tall, bony young woman appeared on the scene. We asked her for meal or oats for the horse; but she was very surly, and said she had not anything, that she was a poor lone creature. We offered her food, she took it, and asked what brought us there? We told her that we must have mistaken the road, and mentioned where we had intended going. She then asked me—"Aint you afraid?" I said, "No, what should I fear? We have done nothing wrong, we have not harmed anybody."

She left us abruptly, and soon returned, bringing a bundle of hay, and a plentiful drink of meal and water for the horse. "Ah!" said I, "you are a kind woman after all, to give us the very things we want most." She smiled, and went back to the barn, bringing this time a tumbler of raw spirits. We tasted it, to show that we appreciated her good intention, and the remainder she tossed off, as one well used to the intoxicating draught. Again she went to the barn, and with her came out, one after another, one, two—aye, six—tall, fierce, daring, resolute-looking men. "Lend a hand here, my good fellows," said my husband; "that decent woman there, I believe, was afraid of me and the children." They touched their caps, and becoming immediately most respectful in manner, lent a ready aid in every way they could. We again tried to mount the hill, but in vain. The horse could not go up it; and yet there was the recent track of wheels on it. The men whispered among themselves, and then told us there was another way out of the valley, and that two of them would accompany us. We thanked them, and they turned the horse's head. One of them led her, and the other pointed out the path we were to walk on, by the side of the stream, which after passing through a grove of tall trees, opened out into a small river. It was into the bed of this river they led the horse and phaeton; and when a large stone impeded the wheels, the second man lifted it out of the way, and returning, kicked it back to its place, as one well practised at such work. For about half a mile we toiled on through the river, and then turned into a field. Our guides pointed out the way we were to go, told us there was either a gateway or a broken hedge to pass through, until we reached the high road, some two miles further off. "It is a poor place, sir," said one of them, "it is not worth coming to again."

"Never fear," he answered, "we will neither come, nor send any one to visit such a lonely place as you have chosen." The man smiled; he saw he was understood; and we parted, mutually well pleased to do so. From one of the hills we passed over, we looked back to the scene of our adventure, and saw the tall spars of a rakish-looking vessel, peeping up in a creek, which could not have been more than a stone's throw from the place where we had dined.

I had been a very short time in Ireland, when I was favoured with a visit from a lady overseer, who told me, she had been desired to call on me, by Friend Oversight, who had received a letter from one of the English overseers respecting me. The lady herself, as well as Reuben Oversight, were strangers to me; at least, I only knew them by name. I begged to be allowed to read the letter; but that was refused me. The lady was very polite. She gave me to understand that the letter from England intimated that I was somewhat deficient in orthodox Quakerism; that I had not made my due appearance at Meetings; and that there would consequently be a difficulty about my certificate. I told her there ought not to be any difficulty, as I had never knowingly transgressed any rules of the Society. "We have been told," said she, "that thou hast frequently gone to Church."

"Yes," I replied, "often and often; but there is no rule to prevent my doing so."

"There is in Ireland," she answered.

To find it acknowledged, that the "inspiration" which had guided Friends to draw up their rules for England and for Ireland was different, surprised me, and led me to inquire the cause, which I ascertained to be this. Some years before, three or four of the Dublin Friends had warmed themselves up to an almost enthusiastic excitement about the minor characteristics of the Society. The principles and the peculiarities had hitherto been considered independent of each other; these ardent Friends wished to see them amalgamated. A peculiar costume was not an original attribute of Quakerism. Nothing of the kind was contemplated in the days of George Fox and William Penn. They recommended a Christian simplicity of dress, in contra-distinction to the extravagant and most foolish fashions of the day, when women would sit up all night lest they should spoil their elaborate head-gear by reposing on a pillow, and men wore chains to fasten the long points of their shoes up to the knee. Dress was now to be made an essential. Two, or perhaps three women, and one man, Joshua Jacob, who is now the leader of the sect of the White Quakers, assumed great power in the Monthly Meetings. They planned out of Meeting, and they professed in it great zeal for the regeneration of the Society. No body took sufficient interest in the matter to oppose these reformers. By a little clever manœuvring, they succeeded in gaining their desired point, of having new rules inserted in the books; and in making them so stringent, as that, whoever refused to submit to them, should be disowned. They decreed, that any one who kept a piano in the house should be cast off. Any one who put on a black dress for a deceased relative, should be disunited. Any one who went to Church, or to any place of worship but Meeting, should be separated from all connection with them.

These, and several other such like rigorous ordinances, are now called, "the Jacob rules;" they are marked in the Irish Book of Discipline, by the date, 1836—that auspicious year, when, as a Friend told me, a new light had dawned on the Society, and fresh vigour been infused into its legislation. It is true, that Joshua Jacob has left the Society himself, and incorporated one in which the primary rule is, that the members attire themselves in undyed garments. They have cast honesty and even morality away, as needless attributes, and are wholly and entirely repudiated by the body they once belonged to. It is also true, that the women who helped him to pass those rules, and who, by their style of preaching, by treating the external forms as the primary duty, were mainly instrumental in having these tyrannical records of ignorance and bigotry placed on the same page as that which inculcates the Christian doctrines, have seen fit to disown all connection with him. Yet the rules remain; and whilst the Society, now, unanimously censure the man, they pertinaciously retain his alterations and additions.

The Pope, claiming infallibility, cannot annul any act. In the same way, I suppose it is, that the Friends, having the "inspiration of best wisdom," cannot recall any of their decisions. I have heard many regret that the rules of 1836 were ever placed on record, but none spoke as if it were possible they could be rescinded. It was on one of those rules that I was to be tried and found guilty.

However, Friends are very slow in coming to their decisions in general; and, as I was a very difficult case, there being no accusation against me except the one, that I sometimes accompanied my husband to Church, he having many years previous'y left the Society, they kept me several years "under dealing," during which time I was earnestly engaged in ascertaining what state the Society was in all over the country. I travelled about a good deal, and attended the Meetings, took notes of the sermons, and made minute inquiries.

I had often heard queer stories told of one of the Northern Meetings, and being in the neighborhood, curiosity led me to attend it. The edification which was one Sabbath morning given to some hundred ignorant people there, was as follows:

A Friend, whom I shall call Tobias, rose up in the gallery to preach; and first pressing his hat firmly on his brows, began thus:—"I have hitherto been in the habit of taking off my hat when addressing you. I yielded to your weakness in doing so, but I cannot any longer do it; for I have heard a voice in mine ears, saying unto me, 'See thou do it not.'" An old man then rose up, and vehemently pounding on the floor with his thick old walking-stick, on the top of which was a ram's head for an ornament, shouted out, "Sit down, Tobias; sit down with thyself, I say. Thou art a ranter; or if thou must speak, go speak to thy own people." But Tobias heeded him not, and went on thus—"The cause is removed, the cause is removed;

therefore the effect must cease. There is an elder," and he pointed with his finger—"she is a liar, and I can prove it to her face." He pointed to another—"There is a Jezebel." And to another—"There is an elder, who climbed up to power on the shoulders of his friend, whom he first cringed to, and then betrayed." During all this, the ram's-horn stick did its duty bravely, and the old man vociferated, "Sit down, Tobias, man, sit down." With such discourses as these, and when the Meeting chanced to be silent, watching the mice as they crept out of their holes, the hours were spent, that were professedly set apart for the worship of the Most High. I have often inquired of those who, being in authority in the Society, ought to have been able to inform me, on what portion of Scripture Friends grounded their practice of holding Meetings for the public worship of God in silence? And I find there is no Scripture warrant for this departure from the order appointed by St. Paul, in his directions to Timothy; but that there is some confusion in Friends' minds between spiritual worship and silent worship, which, however cannot be explained, as they do allow the silence to be broken by both preaching and prayer, and still maintain its spirituality. A dear old Friend, an elder, once told me, the text in the Bible which satisfied his mind was this—"There was silence in Heaven for half an hour." But, he added, "I believe George Fox and William Penn were more likely to know what was right for us to do than either thou or I can be."

There is a class of Friends who are called Ballyhaganites. They are for the most part poor farmers and labourers, ignorant, as might be supposed, of books and men, and manners. Quakers are universally proud of their isolation from the world, and of their fancied superiority in the appreciation of spiritual worship. These Ballyhaganites plume themselves much on their connection. They are very regular attenders of Meetings, and strain a point, whenever they can, to go to the Quarterly Meetings, where they are sure to be invited to the houses of the rich Friends, and where they are as sure to be made great fun of by the young ones. I have heard of a dozen of them being shown into one room where were three beds. "There, boys, sort yourselves," said the conductor, and vanished. Except at Quarterly Meeting dinners, these people never tasted wine. One of them was observed to relish the flavour of it; but he would say, "I'll take some wine, if thee please, for my stomach's sake." The entertainer became impatient, knowing his man, and exclaimed, "Oh! be whipt to thee man; can't thee say at once that thee likes it, and don't be talking to us about thy stomach."

A lady was one day rather annoyed at seeing a troop of the Ballyhaganites come in to join a dinner party, which she had carefully selected of some very aristocratic Friends. She ordered a table to be laid for them in another room, and deputed her son to superintend their repast. This youth, to play a trick on them, and to punish his mother for banishing him from the select company, placed before the "awkward squad," as he called them, a large glass dish-full of calf's-foot jelly. He had previously taken care to have no spoon left in the room; a fork for each man was the only accommodation; and with imperturbable gravity, this youth informed them, there was the dinner, and to help themselves. They had never seen such a dish before, and at first thought it was all glass; but they were hungry, and wished to appear as if not ignorant of the food placed on a rich man's table. Fork, after fork, was struck into the transparent luxury, but all in vain. It would slip back. One said, "Will thee give us a spoon?" "Certainly not," replied the youth, "Thee would not be so ungenteel as to eat that dinner which my mother has taken so much pains to have nice for the Quarterly Meeting, with a spoon. I would be ashamed to tell her thee had asked for one." They tried hard to eat it genteely with the fork; but at last gave up, and hand after hand was plunged into the dish. To see those hands which the day before had held the plough, thus employed, was just what this youth wanted. He laughed aloud. A laugh is infectious, and the Ballyhaganites joined in it most vociferously, whilst they still swallowed the jelly by handfulls. The noise they made brought in a servant from the dinner room, to know was anything the matter; but the youth met him at the door, and bade him say that all was right, and the Friends were only enjoying themselves. It was now time to place the second course on the table, and the lady, in a whisper, directed the servant where to place the dish of jelly. It had vanished from the side table. The truth flashed across her mind, and in an uncontrollable panic, she rushed into the room where the Ballyhaganites were just licking their hands, after demolishing her beautiful and anxiously prepared sweetmeat.

A young man, many of whose connections were Friends, applied to be received into membership. He put on a very broad brim, and took off the collar of his coat. He was admitted. A lady was telling me about him, and saying, that she could not understand what had induced him to join the Society, when he crossed the room and took a seat beside us. She then addressed him, "Well, Richard, I was just saying, that I could not imagine, what had induced thee to join our Society. Do tell me what it was?"

"Well then, Edith, I'll tell thee," he replied: "I have had my fling of pleasure, and am tired of it. The Friends are a very well to do people; they have fine credit; and I thought I could get on better among them."

"But," said Edith, "thee had to be convinced, Richard, how did thee manage the convincement?"

"My coat and my hat," said he, smiling, "were undeniable proofs of convincement. I had not any trouble about that. Cousin Joe was one of the Friends sent to visit me by the Meeting, and he was the very man who first advised me to apply for membership, and told me how well I would be likely to prosper, if I played my cards well."

"Take care," replied she, "thee has some of the old leaven about thee still. To speak of cards in Friends' company! I did not image there was much of religion in thy conversion. Now thee has joined us, I hope thee wont disgrace us. If I had been one of the Committee sent to visit thee, I would not have let thee in so easily."

"Well, Edith, you and I; I beg pardon, thee and I, know two or three things, that we are not going to tell any body, but just wait for two years, and thee will see me a standard bearer. As soon as ever I can, prudently, I'll begin to speak to the Discipline. I'll be very humble, and very tender in my spirit, and I think I'll marry one of the Creidie girls. They have five thousand a-piece I am told, and that will just set me up nicely."

Two years after this, Richard was married to the eldest of the Creidies; and, moreover, was made assistant clerk to the meeting.

One of the queries of the London Yearly Meeting, requires to be informed of the number of persons who have joined the Society by convincement. Many years will often pass over, and no convert have his or her name recorded. When one has been returned, it is a cause of great gratulation; and as the custom is to wait for the leadings of "best wisdom," in admitting a convert, in exactly the same manner as the ministers are appointed to a seat in the gallery; so, if that convert should at any time after his admission, give evidence of being a most unrighteous man, he may be notoriously a hypocrite or a knave; dishonourable in his dealings, or false to his word; yet the Meeting will rather pass over, and cover up his transgressions, than either put him under dealing or disown him; as in so doing, they must admit the possibility of their own "best wisdom" having been an erring guide.

I was lately invited to go to the Dublin Meeting to hear the preaching of a convert who is now all the fashion. I was told that he was a most wonderful speaker; that a short time ago, he had been a common dragoon soldier, who was convinced of Friends' principles in one of the London Meetings; had applied for membership, and had been admitted; and that his preaching now, was so very acceptable, that he had received a certificate expressive of the London Meetings' unity with him, and giving him permission to travel the nation, and to sit with Friends' families as "truth may open the way."

In the year 1836, when the Irish Friends rejoiced in the new light which Joshua Jacob, the leader of the White Quakers, and his female assistants, had conveyed to them, they made a rule to disown any one who should allow music in their houses. Some of the Friends have a natural taste for music; it is one of the gifts of God to them; and they cannot help loving those sweet sounds, which find an echo in their own mysterious being. Some three or four Friends denounced the science; but very many can see no sin in cultivating it, and this leads to many scenes which are altogether Quakerish. A piano is often kept in back and upstairs-rooms, to which no overseer or plain Friend is ever admitted. Musical boxes are very common indulgences; and flutes, French horns, and cornopians—instruments easily put out of sight—are great favourites. But if this departure from Friends' principles is found out, the overseers are on the alert immediately, to visit and remonstrate.

One day an overseer called to visit a young lady. The guitar was easily slipped behind the window curtain; but she entered the room whilst the music still lay open. Her eye glanced round, as an overseer's eye always does; she saw no piano—it fell on the music-book.

"Is that Hebrew," said she; "I often heard it was a very curious character?"

"It is a curious-looking character," answered the young lady.

"Can thee understand it?" said the overseer.

"Oh! yes," she answered, "I can read it very well."

"Thee must be very clever," said the overseer.

Head knowledge is at a discount with the Society. I have been intimately acquainted with many overseers, both in England and Ireland; and I never knew but one, male or female, who was not exceedingly deficient in scholastic acquirements. We read that "the wicked walk on every side, when the vilest men are exalted;" may we not conclude, that the exaltation of ignorance has been a conducing cause of the extreme degeneracy into which Quakerism has now fallen.

CHAPTER XIV.

Dealing—visits to prevail on me to send in my resignation—Yearly Meeting Sermons—The Garret—English Overseer visits in Disguise—Ministers' Sitting—Disowned—Chancery suit a punishment for slighting Women's preaching.

As I was living near the Friends' Meeting-house, and therefore a very frequent attender of it, having still in my mind the fallacious idea, that a disregard to the peculiarities of the Society, whilst I held the doctrines, was compatible with membership, I was surprised to receive notice of an intended visit from no less than four Friends together.

Now that it is all over, and that I have been enabled to shake off the yoke, I can smile at the recollection of this formidable visitation. Then it was not so. I could scarcely sleep or eat for the three intervening days; and being in a nervous, delicate state of health, I was really very ill when I was summoned to appear before these awfully sombre, stern-looking disciplinarians—two men and two women.

With cold formality they shook hands with me all round, and then seated themselves. The silent waiting for "best wisdom" now came on, and lasted unusually long. It was a very cruel suspence to keep me in; for though I had had many visits from overseers before this, still I had never been "under dealing," and I was quite at a loss now to conceive what was the transgression for which I was to be chastised.

The Friends exchanged looks at each other, and then one of the men took off his hat, and laid it slowly on the ground beside him. He fumbled in his pocket, and at last drew out a pair of spectacles, which he duly placed upon his nose, and, looking me in the face, began to speak thus—"We have been appointed by the Monthly Meeting to visit thee. Perhaps it may be well to read to thee the minute of the Meeting."

The other, a very dark-looking man, rose up very slowly, and silently handed a paper to him.

He fumbled again in his pocket, got out another pair of spectacles, and placed them on over the first pair.

People may talk of mesmerism; but the spell which is cast over a poor delinquent when four overseers, one of them with two pair of spectacles on, are sitting in judgment over her, is equally or more enthralling. I could not exactly tell what was my crime, but I felt as if guilty; and it was with a nervous dread that I waited to hear my accusation read by that stern-looking man. I asked for a copy of it when he had done, but he refused it to me, so it was only from memory I could write it down. The purport of it was, that the English Meeting had written a private letter to Reuben Oversight, which gave a bad account of me. I never could get a peep at that letter. Reuben had informed the overseers, and they had, without telling the Monthly Meeting the particulars, got themselves appointed to visit me. In the most respectful and deferential manner, I remonstrated against the injustice of a private letter, which I was not allowed to see, being admitted as any evidence against me.

One of the women then began to speak thus—"Friends are well aware that thou art in the habit of sometimes going to the steeple-house. That of itself is quite enough to cause thee to be put under dealing, and thy general appearance condemns thee. How canst thou reconcile it to thyself, one day to attend to the ministry of an hireling, and another, to sit in our Meeting as a pure spiritual worshipper? Thou canst not serve God and Mammon. Either give up being a Friend entirely, or give up the attendance at the steeple-house. It grieves me greatly to see thee departing from our customs. I had hoped better things of thy father's daughter. Think, my dear Friend, how it would grieve that precious departed relative, if he could see thee living in the neglect of any of our valuable testimonies. He was a light amongst us; thou wilt never find out for thyself a better way. I really cannot imagine how thou canst reconcile to thyself wearing dresses, and going to places, which thou knowest, if he were alive, he would not approve of. Thou shouldst imitate him.

I replied, "I will imitate him. What he was, he was conscientiously. Whatever I am, I will be so too."

The other woman then began—"I do not feel easy to sit here, and not remark on thy very unbecoming interruption. No one wants thee to do anything but what is conscientious. I do not suppose thou art so vain as to imagine thyself wiser than our worthy predecessors were. Thou art placed in a very responsible situation as the head of a family, and it is by submitting thyself to due subordination that thou wilt be enabled to direct thy children aright. I feel well assured that if thy dear father were alive, thou wouldst not act as thou now dost, running after a hireling ministry. Yielding to those imaginings of thine own, may seem very specious; but it will bring thee into trouble; and, when too late, thou wilt repent having refused to take up the cross, which is the only way to secure the crown."

I made no reply. The dark man seemed to fear I might feel hurt, and said, "I hope our Friend will understand, that it is not with a wish to censure her we came here. It is our wish, by a timely remonstrance, to save her from adopting a system which certainly cannot lead to peace. It is for her own sake, and for the sake of her father's memory, that we wish to press upon her the necessity of reconsidering her steps."

There was now another long silence; at its conclusion, the Friend who had the two pair of spectacles on, addressed me. "If our friend has any remark to make, I believe we are prepared to receive it. We feel a great difficulty in the case. It would be very desirable to know from our friend herself, what course she intends to pursue. The meeting would then be in a position to perform its duty."

I then said, that being a member of an English Monthly Meeting, I should think my certificate should, first of all, be sent over, as that was the rule according to the Book of Discipline.

No reply was made to this remark, and after another long pause, they rose up to depart; the visit having lasted altogether more than an hour.

The woman Friend who had first spoken, at parting, drew me to one side, kissed me, and told me the Yearly Meeting would soon be held, and that she hoped I would attend it. I promised her I would do so, and she then kissed me again, and said I had pleased her much by so readily consenting to take her advice. As her manner was so affectionate, I ventured to ask her was I to consider myself as being under dealing. She said, "no, I think not, at least not regularly under dealing, but we have been desired to visit thee, and I wish we had a more satisfactory return to give. I wish thou wouldst promise not to go to church any more." "Oh! no," said I, "I cannot promise to give up my liberty. I have not, that I know of, transgressed any of the English rules, and what more can you require?" "I am sorry for thy own sake," said she, and took her leave.

Not very long after this visit, an elderly lady, with whom I was intimate, was speaking to me about it. She told me the English Meeting had sent my certificate over; but that the Irish Friends had refused to accept it. That the English Meeting did not feel they had ground to disown me on, although my going into a Church was sufficient evidence of my departure from Friends' principles, and the Irish Friends, for many reasons, did not like to have on them the odium of disowning me, as it might look like bigotry, and besides, it could only be done on the "Jacob rules," which many of the Society regretted had ever been inserted on the books. She then said to me—"Thee ought to send in thy resignation; it would relieve Friends from a great difficulty, and be better for thyself. I am sure I would resign, if I were situated as thee is."

The Yearly Meeting came on in due course; and as I had promised, I went to the first sitting on second day morning. The routine was just the same as I have already described. Two of the sermons or preachings were curious, I thought. One lady said, "her mind had been awfully impressed, since she had taken her seat, with the conviction, that there was one amongst us who, neglecting the shinings of the light of truth in her own heart, had fallen into temptation. There was one, and she felt as if she could walk over and lay her hand on the individual, who had tampered with duty, and who was, even at this moment, entertaining the idea of uniting herself in marriage with a person not of our Society. She said it was painful to her, to feel called on to speak on this weighty matter, and she hoped the dear individual would be kept from the snare which now entangled her. For her own part, she had resisted as long as she dared, the pointings of her own mind; and now she felt she was clear, having, as a faithful watchman, given notice of the approach of the enemy."

The other lady, whose sermon particularly attracted my attention, was an English minister of very high reputation, who had come over to attend the Yearly Meeting. She said, "it was deplorable to witness the wasting in our highly favoured Society, which had crept in, she felt bold to say, from our culpable neglect of what some deemed the minor doctrines, which had been given us to uphold. As it was minutes that composed the day, and days that composed the year; so it was the minor doctrines being faithfully upheld, that led the exercised mind on, step by step, to the high appreciation of our doctrine of pure spiritual worship. And it was when the door was opened, by departing from the minor doctrines—she might say the peculiarities—that the enemy came in like a flood, and swept away even our most precious testimonies." She said much about the value of our sectarian dress; it being a shield to defend us from the allurements of the world. And then she expressed great surprise that any who fancied themselves to be religious, could bring themselves to think it was compatible with Christian duty, to frequent places of public worship. She paused a moment, to rivet attention, and add solemnity to the words, and then added—"They who do so, I have no hesitation in saying, sully their souls with a dangerous iniquity." This English minister had been informed of the difficulty Friends felt about poor me; and some of them told me afterwards, that it was very remarkable how she had been led to speak words so exactly suited to my state; and how they hoped better things of me, than that I should pertinaciously resist the spiritual travail of so exalted a minister.

As I was leaving the Meeting-room, the same two women who had visited me with the men some time before, pushed their way through the crowd, and tapping me on the shoulder, said, they requested me to accompany them to a private room, as they had somewhat to say unto me.

They led me up stairs into a small garret. As I passed along with them, marvelling what was to come, I received several sly glances from my acquaintances, and one whispered audibly, "There goes a naughty child."

Up in the little garret, these two Friends, speaking alternately, slowly and in a half-stifled voice, informed me that I was not to attempt to go to Meeting ever again. They had been desired to inform me, that I had forfeited my privilege of sitting with Friends; that Friends were not comfortable at having me among them. I was amazed, and said, "Why, it is only a month since you yourselves came to visit me, with the two men Friends, to remonstrate with me, for not going to Meeting often enough; and now, when I come, you tell me I must not come."

"It seems contradictory," said one of them, "and I greatly regret it; but my very dear friend"—and she squeezed my hand—"if thou would'st give up going to Church these trying things would not happen. Thou must not blame us; we are only informing thee as we have been desired to do."

"If thou art resolved to attend a place of common worship," said the other, "thou should'st send in thy resignation at once; it would save thyself and us much trouble, and be more creditable for thee."

"I was born a Friend," I replied; "I do not intend to send in my resignation. If I have transgressed any of the rules of the Society, you can disown me; if not, what is my offence?"

"That is our great difficulty," said the first speaker; "if thou wast a gay, fashionable woman, and frequented balls and theatres, the way would be easy for us; but we all know thee to be a religious character. However, thee must not attend Meeting again." And again she kissed me.

As I came down from the garret most of the Friends were gone. Those who remained, were curiously watching how I would take the "wholesome discipline" I had been receiving. There was one whose eyes shot out a gleam of malicious triumph as I passed; and I felt assured she had been the prompter of the disgrace I had endured. Every body knows that it is only very bad people indeed, who are taken up to the garret, and I had been so in the most public manner.

I was agitated and annoyed, and somewhat indignant too, at the wanton insult I had received, but said nothing. Fortunately, as soon as I went into the street, I met a gentleman who knew me. Seeing me ready to faint, he gave me his arm and conducted me safely home. I told him and several others of my acquaintances the circumstances; and, acting on their advice, I wrote to some of the most influential Friends, requesting the protection, which, by the rules, I knew I was entitled to. I received no written reply; but was told that the two women had acted injudiciously; that it was only one individual in the Meeting who had objected to my presence there, and that she had taken too much upon her in directing the overseers to lead me up to the garret, or in any way to prevent my going to Meeting. Two or three told me they had been desired to convey me an intimation that nothing of the kind should happen if I went again, and that Friends would be glad to see me there.

The originator of this intended insult, was soon found out; her eye, as she caught mine, when descending from the garret, had truly told her enmity. She was reprimanded in the gentlest way possible, for having increased the difficulty Friends were under about me; and then she said, I had surprised and disappointed her very much. She thought I had "some spirit, and would, whilst smarting under the insult, have sent in an angry resignation."

This lady had often professed a more than common friendship for me, nor had any act or word of discourtesy or unkindness ever passed between us. But she was an acknowledged minister; and my attending on the ministry of an "hireling," as she called all preachers, except Friends, in preference to her "inspiration of best wisdom," was an unpardonable offence.

I was now subjected to almost daily annoyance; cold greetings and averted looks met me on all sides. My nearest relatives became unkind; the trustees of my marriage settlement refused to perform the duty they had undertaken in my father's life-time. My correspondents wrote me angry invectives, at the conclusion of which, I was in the most polite and friendly language unmistakably given over to the enemy of all righteousness.

These things tried me very much, and I became so ill that my life was despaired of. The Friends did not wish that I should actually die. They wished to punish me, to make me feel I had done an evil thing, but they did not desire that it should be known so publicly. Some awkward whispers had been heard, that the Quakers were persecuting to death one of their body, for having gone to Church. They relaxed a little; they would send messengers to the house of the Doctor who attended me, to inquire of my chance of recovery; and, when I was convalescent, they allowed nearly a year to pass over without annoying me.

One evening, in the dusk, an English man Friend called on me. He had, when we lived at Clifton, been a frequent guest at our table, and now, under the guise of friendship, he obtained admission.

He chatted of all the passing news, told me of his marriage and such-like affairs, and then abruptly asked me why I had not sent in my resignation to the Meeting, as he had heard that I was inclined to leave the Society? I smiled, and asked him, was he an overseer, and had he been desired by the English people to visit me? He was altogether a man of business, when I had known him before; and now, being enveloped in a fashionable roquelaire, with large fancy tassels hanging down, I had not suspected what he afterwards acknowledged, that he was now an overseer himself, and come to find out some accessible point of attack. He became very angry when I put those questions to him; he lost both his temper and his manners—he never had a large stock of either; and assuring me I should deeply repent my folly if I persisted, and that if I would resign, and save Friends the annoyance of disowning me, I should find it much better to my interest. He withdrew.

This was the only visit, of the very many I received, in which the Friends were not studiously polite. They were often cold, and stiff, and stern, harsh and unbending, but, with this one exception, they were polite.

I was soon after this informed, by note, that two ministers wished to "sit with me," and that at twelve o'clock the following morning they would be at my house.

Disagreeable as these kind of visits had ever been to me, still I was really desirous of hearing any thing they had to say. My prejudices were all in favour of the Quaker doctrines, as I had learned them from books; and whilst quite resolved not to surrender my liberty to love and associate, even in what is slightingly called "common worship," with other denominations of Christians, I was determined to submit to all the legitimate authority of the sect to which I belonged. It was very evident that the overseers were seeking occasion against me, and it was notorious that they were prompted to do so by some parties influential in the Meeting, who had never forgiven my husband for leaving the Society, and, moreover, "spoken slightingly of the ministry" of one of the preaching women.

The two ladies duly came. One was affectionate in her manner, the other chilly. They invited me to sit between them, and the silence commenced. It lasted for about a quarter of an hour, and then the English Friend spoke. She said—"That a painful feeling had been the covering of her mind, and that she felt an unusual difficulty in breaking the silence. It was a strange thing for her to sit in solemn, silent, spiritual waiting with one who had been nurtured in our highly-privileged Society, and who was related to a gifted minister in it; who had been the object of great travail to many exercised minds, and was yet unwilling to take up the cross. She was free to say, that it was incomprehensible to her mind, how one who had been so laboured with, could walk, and feel peace in so doing, in the way that was not good—walking like a lame man leaning on crutches, unable to go alone; depending on the arm of flesh; drinking out of the muddy water of a man-made ministry, and deserting the pure fountain of living water. People might flatter themselves that they had found a safe path for their feet; they might reason, and delude themselves with their specious reasonings. There were some who, even in reading the Holy Scriptures, thought a light had come on them, which would give them a greater liberty in what they called Christian communion. These things were very specious and soul-deluding. The arch-enemy was ever busy putting a gloss on them, to attract the unstable, who wrest the Scriptures to their own destruction. It would be well, if those who think themselves enlightened, would carefully peruse the writings of our valuable predecessors, and submit their judgment to the experience of those devoted founders of our Society. Depending upon our own unfinished imaginations, was not wisdom—it was rashness. The wisdom of this world was foolishness. They who had most peacefully trod the path of life, who finished the work that was given them to do, and who had passed from works to rewards, were humble-minded; they were willing to be taught; whilst many, who had indulged in the fashions and customs of the world, had, in the hour of sickness and death, to endure great conflicts, because of their inconsistency. And she hoped the dear Friend for whose welfare her soul now travailed, would be made willing to come down, and to sit as a little child at the feet of the Lord. To do this, there must be a yielding; there must be an entrance into silence; there must be a forsaking of the outward form of man-made worship; there must be consistency in all things with the precious testimonies, which we, as a people, are called upon to bear in the sight of the world." She paused for a couple of minutes, and then knelt down to pray, that her "dear, dear Friend might have her eyes anointed with eye-salve, to see how piercing was the reed on which she had been leaning—to see the beauty of holiness—and to understand, that peace and happiness were only to be found in the path of duty. That the proud heart and the stiff neck might be taken away—and that, with the beautiful humility of a little child, she might be made willing to follow Christ, as she herself had done, and in so doing to find peace."

She then rose up from her knees, and resumed her seat in silence. It had not lasted long, when her companion commenced, and spoke thus—:

"The feeling of my mind in this interview, is that of love and sympathy, and Gospel fellowship. That my dear Friend should have thought it right to follow on some paths in which I do not walk, may be a source of regret to me; but I do believe, that as she has, I am convinced, endeavoured to walk uprightly according to the light she has received, her intention will be accepted. The peculiar spirituality of our worship cannot be duly appreciated, except by the spiritually-minded; and some, even of that number, there are, who do not see as we do, on this all-important subject. The blind man, when partially enlightened, could see men, but they appeared to him as trees walking; yet it was the healing touch of Christ's hand that had been on him; and so, my dear friend, it seems to be with thee. Thou must submit to a further operation, before thou canst perceive the glory and the beauty of true spiritual worship. The desire of my heart for thee is, that thy spirit may be introduced into that silence, in which alone thou canst scripturally expect that the Sun of righteousness shall ascend with healing on his wings for thy salvation. Oh! think, I entreat thee, how vain it is to seek for peace in the rites and ceremonies which poor, frail, ignorant men have devised. How vain to hope for light or instruction from the ministry of those, who are themselves ignorant of the Spirit's work."

About a fortnight after this visit had elapsed, when I was sent a formal notice, that two of the men overseers were appointed by the Monthly Meeting to visit me. They were, neither of them, men of whose piety or wisdom I had had reason to think highly, but the reverse. Nevertheless they were respectfully received, as messengers from the meeting.

After faithfully bearing their testimony against taking off their hats, as other men do when they come into a house, and have no need of out of door covering for the head; these two attempted the usual silence, and tried their very best to look solemn. The attempt was a failure, and soon given up.

One of them said, "They had been desired to inform me, that Friends had been told, that I had deviated from the doctrines of the Society, so far as to suffer myself to be baptized, and to take what was called the Lord's Supper, and that they had been desired to ask me, was that the case? as I must be aware that I could not hold my membership, and that Friends would much prefer that I should send in my resignation, than compel them to disown me."

I said, "Will you be so kind as to tell me who it was that informed you I was baptized, or had taken the Lord's Supper?"

"Oh!" replied one of them; "I believe it is unnecessary to mention the name of our informant. As it has come to the knowledge of Friends, I trust thou wilt now see the propriety of sending in thy resignation."

"I do not see the propriety of doing so," I replied; "and I request, and I have a right to know, who has told you this of me."

They looked at each other, and seemed much annoyed. "I think it would not be right to mention any name," said one. "Thou knowest it cannot alter the fact; and as thou hast departed from our Scriptural views on these important doctrines, and that it is therefore impossible for thee to remain in membership, thou wilt relieve Friends from what is really a very great difficulty to them. Friends feel it very unpleasant to disown thee; and really for thy own sake, we hope thou wilt, now that this matter has been revealed to us, feel the propriety of writing to the Monthly Meeting."

"If," said I, "you have really been told these things, it seems to me strange, that you should object to mention the name of your informant. I beg you will tell me who it is? If you still refuse, I must only draw the very natural inference, that you suspect me of having done these things, and by intimating that you have already had information, you expect to obtain from me the confession that your suspicions are correct."

"Thou must not think this," said he; "we do not mention any name, no good could result from so doing. It is contrary to our invariable practice. And thou canst not deny that it is the truth; therefore, really I cannot understand why thou shouldst care to know more than we have told thee."

"If," I replied, "any person told you that I have been baptized, or taken the Lord's Supper, they told you so, falsely. It is not true."

The two overseers looked very blank, and exceedingly annoyed. One of them opened his mouth so wide in his surprise, that I could scarce help laughing, for all I was so annoyed, at what seemed to me the meanness of the trap they had, as they thought, so artfully laid for me.

Before long, another visit was announced to me. The Meeting now sent two different men, to try if they could find out some salient point, at which I might advantageously be attacked.

If I had refused to receive these visits, I knew that I should be disowned immediately. That was a principal reason why so many of them were inflicted on me. The Friends knew that I was in very delicate health, and that those interviews were painfully disagreeable to me. Nothing would have gratified them more than that I should have refused to receive them.

On the present occasion, as well as at all the other interviews, I had insisted on having a friend in the room with me, as it did not suit my ideas of propriety to meet them, as they requested I would, according to the custom of Friends, all alone. And besides, I was anxious to have a witness of what passed.

My present visitors did not attempt the usual silence, they chatted of the weather, &c., &c., at first; and then, just as a matter of business, said, they "had been desired by the Monthly Meeting, in consequence of a communication from England, to visit me. That my attendance on an hireling ministry was incompatible with the rules of the Society, and they merely wished to ask had I determined to continue such attendance."

I replied, that I certainly often did attend at different places of worship; but I added, no Friend could more object than I did to an hireling ministry; that I denied ever having knowingly attended.

"Oh!" said one of them, "If thou acknowledges going to Church, that is all we want; it is the same thing. Those who preach in Churches, must be hirelings, for they take money for preaching. It is absurd to deny thy approval of an hireling ministry, and to acknowledge going to listen to the preaching of men, who give up their whole time to doing it, and then take money for it." "Do you consider," said I, "that every one who derives his support from the congregation to which he preaches, is an hireling?"

"Certainly," he answered.

"Then," said I, "is not your own Friend, Sarah Dwyer, an hireling? She has been, for nearly two years, I think, receiving her entire support from the Meeting. I have been told that both herself and her daughter are liberally maintained, and their travelling expenses paid. Is she an hireling?"

He laughed. "How did thee hear that?" said he. "We did not think it was generally known. But she is not a hireling, oh! no. Only her expenses are paid. Indeed it is time for her to go home; for she is very heavy upon Friends."

He then said, that "the rules of the Society were framed by men who were especially enlightened with divine wisdom, and that they must be obeyed. That the rules were very clear, and that any one who countenanced an hireling ministry, must be separated from the body."

"Are all the rules," I asked, of equal importance?"

"Undoubtedly," he replied, "the rules of our Society, as they appear in the Book of Minutes, have all proceeded from the Spirit of truth, and are, one and all, equally essential."

"Some of the rules," I said, "are not attended to by any of the Friends; how is that, if they are all of equal authority?"

"Thou art mistaken," he said, "there is no rule neglected."

I rose up from my seat, and handing over the Book of Minutes which I happened to have near at hand, I pointed out the rule that all Friends should have their children taught to speak and to write both High and Low Dutch.

He laughed, and said, "He did not before know there was such a rule on the books, but that really he did not know much about the book; it was not very interesting, and he must say, he had never read it all through." He and his companion then chatted about politics, the prospects of the country, &c., &c.; and on shaking hands to go away, they said, "they had a very interesting and agreeable visit, and they would report it to the Monthly Meeting as most satisfactory."

I had not the least idea of what they meant by the expression of "an agreeable visit," and "most satisfactory;" but before long it was made clear enough. They returned an account to the Meeting, by which it was sent on to England, that I had confessed to my encouragement of an hireling ministry, and that I had joined the Church. Now I was to be condemned by my own words, and as quickly as they could hurry it through the Meeting, my disownment was to be issued. And it was with words of regret, but with looks of intense satisfaction, that on the next visit they handed me "the testimony of disunion." There was very much that seemed to me unaccountable, in the desire these people evidently had to turn me out of the Society, for up to the time they disowned me, and for long after it, I had not transgressed any of the rules, nor had I been justly or fairly treated. As a member of an English Meeting, the Irish Friends had no right to put me under dealing at all, even had I transgressed.

The truth was, the woman Friend, of whose ministry we had spoken slightingly, a very long time ago, had resolved to punish us for doing so. She and some others, concocted a plan; they contrived to ingratiate themselves into the favour of a very old lady, who as well as themselves, had a kind of claim on some of our landed property. She poor lady did not believe that "an inspired minister" could do wrong; and consented to do as they wished, which was in her name, to put us into the Court of Chancery—which is described in the Times Newspaper as being "a devouring gulf, a den from whence no footsteps return; a name of terror, a bloodless arena for mutual destruction. A Chancery suit which is endless, bottomless, and insatiable; an organized iniquity; an incurable evil; an inveterate wrong. A Chancery suit which starves the education and spirit of youth, consumes the energies of manhood, and makes a clean wreck of old age. As for a thousand pounds, it is but as the morning dew before the burning sun of a Chancery Suit, amongst the evils of which are the multiplicity of forms, and the opportunities it affords for vexatious and malicious delay."

Nobody can leave the Society of Friends, without enduring some species of persecution; and we were to be made examples of, that none might ever again dare "to despise women's preaching." To put us into Chancery, which was a notoriously suitable way of ruining our temporal affairs, and, at the same time, to preserve the testimony of Friends against going to law with each other, it was necessary to disown me.

They claimed a small portion of our property, by virtue of a will made in 1839, under their own dictatorial influence, and when the reasoning powers of the dying man were plastic in their hands—a will, of which they told the old lady, with sanctimonious audacity, that it bore the evidence of divine aid in its composition. We claimed it, and had possession of it, by virtue of a marriage settlement made in 1829. Nothing could have been better devised for a Chancery cause.

As we were not then aware of the animus of the suit, we complained to the overseers of the injustice of it; and to avert the ruinous waste of property, offered to pay their demands out of other properties, without any dispute as to the legality of their claims.

This they all acknowledged to have been a fair offer; but it would not have ruined or wasted us sufficiently; we must be punished. And whilst they persecuted us, they wished to keep a fair face on the matter, and constantly made excuses for the litigation. "It was a minister who conducted it, therefore it could not be wrong." "It was too complicated a case for Friends to interfere in." "The Court of Chancery would surely do us justice." "The Friends who had instituted the suit were most consistent Friends; it was incredible to say they were actuated by any unworthy motives." We "belonged not to the Society, and had no claim on their interference." "They did not believe it was for the purpose of persecution, and they regretted we should be so unkind as to say it was." "They had full confidence that the parties we had thought fit to censure, would do no act without waiting for the manifestation of divine light to guide them." "It would be a curtailment of the liberty of the subject to prevent Friends going to law with persons not Friends." And, "They could not see what claim we had on the Society, or why we should expect them to interfere for our protection."

So for ten years the suit went on, and still seems as far off being settled in the Court of Chancery as it was the day it began. But many and many a long bill of costs had told us, that to speak slightingly of a woman Friend's preaching, is an unpardonable offence to the whole Society. The case had been officially brought before them; and though they certainly abstained from openly sanctioning it, they positively refused to interfere, although, privately and indirectly, they put the whole weight of the Society in the scale against us.

CHAPTER XV.

Stories of the Sand-man, the Meal-man, and the Elder—Adoration of the Quaker Dress - Cleverly Scroggins—Slipping into Heaven —Disbelief of eternal punishment—Appeal—Petty persecution— Tithe Stories—Chancery Suit—Munificent Donations—Vindictive Punishments.

EVERY body has heard of the story told of a Quaker, who called aloud to his apprentice to come listen to the Bible reading, as soon as he had finished sanding the sugar. The story may not be so generally known, of the Quaker who contracted to supply meal for the poor, during the time of famine, struck a good bargain for himself in so doing, and then adulterated it with some atrocious mixture, expecting that none would care to look after the interests of the poor.

What rank in the Society was held by the sand-man, I do not know, but the meal-man was, and perhaps is still, an elder, in good esteem. That—and for which he was in open court indignantly reprimanded—was not thought of sufficient consequence to draw down any notice from the Society.

Roman Catholics openly profess to keep no faith with heretics, and with them, all are heretics who are not Roman Catholics. Quakers do not, as a body, disregard fair dealing, and the laity of the Society in general, act as other Christians in their communication with their neighbors; but the overseers are very slow to take up an accusation of fraud against either an overseer, elder, or minister. I have heard of no less than seven charges against one elder, for dishonorable conduct in his business. His Meeting professed to give due attention to the complaints, dismissed the several complainants as quietly as they could; but the guilty elder was not subjected to any "dealing," nor did he in any wise sink in the general estimation of the Society.

I have known of a gentleman who was grossly wronged by a plain Friend; and who, having in vain sought redress at the hands of the overseers privately, at length went one first day morning into the Meeting for public worship, and told his grievance there. Then indeed, he was attended to. The sin was now public, and the aggrieved gentleman, all heretic as he was, got compensation.

The adoration with which the Friends regard their peculiar dress, often exposes them to imposition. I do not mean that they actually worship their garb; but the morbid sensitiveness with which they regard it, is similar to that feeling with which the Romanist regards, or professes to regard, the pictures and relics of saints. When the notorious John Tawell was about to suffer the just punishment of his ill deeds, Friends petitioned the magistrate to grant them as a favour, that he might not be hanged in his Quaker dress. Was it not a feeling of adoration for their peculiar attire that prompted this request? Otherwise, could it signify in which of the rags of earth his form was clad? The people thought his conduct a disgrace to manhood; the Friends looked on it as a disgrace to their costume.

Hundreds of times I have heard Friends speaking of the dress, call it "a hedge," which separated us from the "people of the world," which preserved us from the snares and temptations to which they were exposed, and which kept us in safety, so long as we remained within its enclosure. Perhaps if they had been able to build the hedge up high enough, it might be so; if its top had reached to heaven, the enemy of man might not have been able to get into its enclosure. But low and earth-born as it is, it offers no obstruction to his advances.

Let a story, in illustration of the system, exemplify this fact.

Cleverly Scroggins, from being a bad boy, grew up into a dissolute man. Gifted with good natural abilities, shrewd, calculating, and clever, he had the art of adapting himself to his company, and made himself so agreeable, as to ensure a welcome wherever he went. Cleverly and his brother James, his inseparable companion, were neither of them rich. Their tastes were expensive; and honest industry was too plodding a method to suit their soaring genius. The two wise heads devised a plan which they hastened to carry into effect. To the extreme surprise of those who knew them, they all at once assumed the Quaker dress in its extreme, and with it the Quaker manner. No hats had broader brims than theirs, and none were more pressed down upon their brows in Meetings. No faces were better tutored to look grave, and none were more obsequious in their attention to the overseers. No Friends were more ready to "drop into silence;" and none more capable of "centering into nothingness." The spell soon began to work. The preachers were delighted to see these two dear young men so "tendered under their ministry." The elders were pleased with their gravity, and the overseers rejoiced in their "consistent deportment."

Friends generally, felt bound to notice, and invite to their houses, the brothers. The women Friends especially liked to have such convenient additions to their convivial parties. Nothing could exceed the good-nature with which they made themselves useful. They carved well, and thought nothing of going a mile or two out of their way at night, to escort a lady home. It was very natural that wealthy Friends should lend a helping hand to such interesting and "consistent" young men; and equally natural that to those wealthy benefactors they should assiduously devote themselves.

Cleverly's father often said, that the Friends would one day or other find out the true character of his sons, whom he was wont to call a pair of unprincipled scape-graces. And when he was told of their exemplary conduct, and of their "consistent" dress, he would shake his head, and say, that a bad son, could not be a good man.

James was taken into the counting-house of a rich Friend, and gave entire satisfaction to his employer, until some unaccountable deficiencies led to an examination of the books under his care, and it became evident that he had been embezzling from the day he had entered on the employment. Excited at his loss, vexed at being duped, and annoyed at the disgrace which his unprincipled conduct had brought on the dress of a Quaker, James was dismissed unceremoniously—told he was as vile a hypocrite, and as great a villain as could be found in the land; and that unless he left the country of his own accord, he should be brought before the magistrate. He fled, no one knew where.

Cleverly was loud in reprobation of his brother, whilst he timidly and humbly expressed a hope, that "they who attended to the shinings of the light of truth in their hearts, might be preserved from falling." He rose in general estimation. His brother's fall made his uprightness stand out in bold relief.

Cleverly managed to ingratiate himself into favour with a rich old man, whose grand-daughter was expected to inherit a vast portion. With minute and unwearied attentions, with well-timed gifts, and conversations interesting, amusing, and yet skillfully interwoven with the pious slang of the Society, he won his way, and soon obtained a young and wealthy bride. He was now a rich man. His house became the resort of the plain Friends; his appearance was so orthodox, and his frequent "weighty observations" in the Monthly Meetings, gave so much satisfaction, that many said, they felt it a privilege to be seated near him, and to meet him in company. Still his father would say, "Wait a while; he is a hypocrite, and will yet be found out." Whether this oft-repeated opinion of his father's was the cause, or whether the Friends had any other reason, did not transpire, but certain it is, that when Cleverly commenced to speak on first day Morning Meetings, with a view to obtaining a seat in the gallery, he was visited by the overseers, and admonished to refrain from public preaching. With most deferential humility, he yielded to their desire. It was, he said, in his "anxious zeal to promote the good cause, that he had overstepped the line of duty, and he was most grateful to his kind Friends for the judicious counsel they had imparted to him." Cleverly rose higher than ever in general estimation. If his zeal had led him astray, his humility had more than atoned for the error. Years rolled on, and Cleverly was still referred to as a triumphant evidence of the superiority of Quaker principles in converting a sinner from the evil of his ways.

Cleverly was very wealthy; he kept both town and country house, and drove his carriage. But Friends were soon called on to sympathize with him, for now he became a bankrupt. The occurrence was a surprise to all; but his deportment under the "trying dispensation" as he called it, was so exemplary, that a subscription was made for him, and feelingly presented by an elder who esteemed him marvellously well. It seemed curious that he should have managed to pay off every one of his Quaker creditors to the full, and that the only sufferers by his bankruptcy should be young children. One who had an opportunity of knowing something about it, did indeed accuse him of dishonesty, and offered to show the overseers convincing proof of it. They refused to listen to any accusation; they said he stood too high in general estimation, and was so exemplary in his appearance, that it was uncharitable to say such a thing of him. According to the rule, he was put "under dealing," as bankrupts always are, and whilst the visitings continued he was deprived of course, of the liberty of sitting in Meetings for discipline.

The Yearly Meeting was soon to be held, and Cleverly entreated the overseers that he might be allowed to attend it. Bankrupts are generally disowned summarily. And now to release him altogether from censure, was unheard of leniency; but the overseers did not feel it right to refuse his request; his "concern" to attend the Yearly Meeting was so strong, his humble demeanour was so edifying, and he had so faithfully maintained "our Christian testimony against oaths," when called on to swear as to the return of his assets, that really Friends felt unwilling to put any impediment in the way of one whom they considered so great an ornament to the Society. So Cleverly's bankruptcy passed over uncensured, and what is still more extraordinary, he was thought better of than ever. His bankruptcy had not lessened his wealth. It had, on the contrary, very much increased it. A month or two before it happened, he had transferred his right to some property to a dear plain Friend of his. And a month or two after it was all over, the dear plain Friend had transferred it back again to Cleverly.

Some vulgar people had hinted at roguery in the transaction. Friends regretted it had transpired; but did not feel themselves called on to take any notice of what they said was most probably only an error in judgment.

Cleverly's skill in surmounting such kind of difficulties became notorious, and he was employed, at ample remuneration, to assist others who wished to accomplish similar ends, but lacked the ability to do so, and retain their unblemished Quakerism at the same time.

Money was indispensable to Cleverly; his nice, lady-like Quaker wife was supplied lavishly with all needful comforts, and his devoted attention to her was often remarked on, and applauded. With an extra shawl for her use hung on his arm, lest an extra breath of wind should arise to render its warmth desirable, Cleverly would escort her to Meetings, and to pay visits to Friends, looking so meek, so serious, and so respectable, that the very sight of him was edifying. Besides his wife's establishment, Cleverly had another, and another to keep up. He loved variety; but whilst he managed to avoid open shame being brought on the Society by his licentiousness, the overseers did not feel it required of them to notice the frailty of his nature.

He was so candid, so bland, so simple-minded, and so willing to explain his conduct, which he represented to the women Friends as being a kind of extra-righteousness on his part, being willing, as he said, to have a misconstruction put by base-minded people on the platonic liasons which he had formed for the interesting young females, on whose behalf he tried to influence them; that the viler he became, the better he succeeded in blinding the eyes of those who were so credulous as to listen to him.

It suited the views of the overseers to affect disbelief of his immorality. They deemed it more for the welfare of the Society to suffer his wickedness to go on under the flimsy covering he and they had spread over it, than by disowning him, to allow the women and young people to hear mention of the truth. "Oh! do not let our women and young people hear of it, anything but that," said one. "It is far more desirable, bad as he is, to leave him alone, than to allow such discreditable things to transpire," said another. "He is a wicked old man," said a third; "but still the young women are not Friends; and there was lately a very much worse case, thou knows; so perhaps it would be more desirable not to take notice of him now, than to have the young people talking about it."

The very much worse case was, that of two elderly delinquents, who were both, not only members of the Society, but also both ministers, who, whilst sitting side by side in the gallery, clothed in all the paraphernalia of the Society's most consistent costume, and for many years preaching to the entire satisfaction of the Meeting, were yet, during all that time, living together a life of sin.

Many there were who had an interest in Cleverly's escape from censure; he would, and could do anything they wanted, in "a pious way." Was it needed that a widowed mother should be set at variance with her legitimate heirs, Cleverly was the man to do it. How tenderly and feelingly would he break to her the sad intelligence of her own beloved son's crimes; it was true, nobody but himself had heard of those crimes; that only showed his kindness in not allowing her to be surprised by the public report. It was entirely owing to his care that her ears were never pained by hearing of it through any other channel, and it was by his advice that she banished her son from her presence, that he might be spared the temptation of sinning in an effort to regain her lost favour. It was Cleverly's wisdom that suggested to her the idea, that to alienate from her son the property which he had a right to, was a good and charitable deed; for how could she reconcile it to her conscience to give so bad a man the means of living in open defiance of the testimonies of Friends! And the reaction was so natural; her feelings embittered against her child, whose crime being enveloped in an impenetrable cloud only made it seem the darker, how could she better bestow her wealth than on her kind, sympathizing friend, Cleverly? He had need of it all; his ladies were often importunate, and had to be paid well to keep quiet.

Friends belonging to different and far apart Meetings, all knew their man; it was marvellous the number who employed him, to do what the lawyers call "dirty work;" and it was equally marvellous how he did actually accomplish their ends for them. Their way was to give him plenty of money, and he was to keep their names as much as possible out of sight. Cleverly made very much money by these little jobs; he liked them too; he felt his skill in accomplishing what others could not; and it placed them so much in his power, that they were, for their own sakes, obliged to conceal his hypocrisy. The magistrates, the police, an innumerable number of persons knew of his immorality; the overseers were made aware of it; but they said, his dress and his standing in the Society was such as inclined them to think "the cause of truth would not suffer in his hands." Cleverly has been known to go from the house of one of his mistresses, to that of a respectable man, to remonstrate with him on having neglected to attend the preceding week-day Meeting—to another, to express a hope that his dear friend would leave off the vain fashion of wearing the gold chain of his watch outside his waistcoat; and another he would, with ready tears, entreat to take up the cross, and leave off the practice of saying "you and mister." What, but the adoration of his dress, preserved this man from reprobation? How else can we account for the fact, that for six-and-twenty years he was, though known to be both immoral and dishonest, held in the greatest esteem by the rulers of the Society appointed to offices in the Meeting; invited to their houses, and actually supported by a subscription in his infamous career?

Many of the men Friends do not consider it any harm to be immoral; they are never censured by the overseers for this sin, unless it becomes public. Horrified by the depths of Quaker licentiousness, I shrink from polluting my pages with any other tale in exemplification of it. Whilst I was in the Society, like other Quaker ladies, I was comparatively ignorant of its existence; a succession of those fortuitous circumstances which men call chance, has revealed it to me to an extent which it is awful to think of.

The mass of the Society cheat themselves with the idea, that because so many whom they esteem, and who assume the appearance of religion, follow on a way which pretends, or which they may in truth believe, to be good, that therefore it cannot be dangerous for them. Men do not risk their temporal prosperity thus rashly; and surely if they were convinced that religion was a matter which did really concern them, they would not rest satisfied with merely going to Meeting, and dressing up their poor bodies in all the outward forms and fashions of the sect, without examining and ascertaining their own individual standing in the sight of God.

I have heard a Friend say he expected, all sinner as he was, that his aunt, who was a preacher, and very fond of him, would manage to slip him "into heaven under her petticoats." Alas! do not most of the Friends hope to slip into heaven under the shadow of their hats and bonnets? Heaven and hell, the day of judgment, and the kingdom of Christ, are subjects which move them not. Is it not a just inference, that they do not believe in them? Why do they studiously avoid conversation on these subjects?

There is a deep-rooted infidelity in the minds of the Friends on the subject of hell. I have seen it oozing out in the apathy of many, who live as if there was no eternity. It is manifest in the utter indifference displayed for the souls of their fellow-creatures; and I have heard it openly declared in a large company, without any one gainsaying it, that there was no eternity of punishment. It was a woman Friend, high in the Meeting, who said, "that it was an insult to the Almighty, to believe he could be so devoid of mercy and love to the creatures he had made, as to condemn them to hell, to eternal fire." She said, "the idea was right to be taught to the profligate and to the open sinner, as we would frighten a child with the threat of a punishment we had no idea of inflicting; but that it was incompatible with the good and gracious character of the Lord, of whom we are told, that 'he is love,' and that he is the Saviour of all men." She added, "Let us believe in the Scriptures, and lead an innocent and useful life, and we need not torment ourselves with the fear of eternal burnings; for if Friends live consistently, there is not the slightest danger but that an entrance will be ministered for them within the pearl gates; and perhaps it would be wise not to disturb our minds with diving into affairs which do not concern us as a people. As we know that God will act right to all men, let us act our part well; for nothing will be required at our hands, but an account of our own walk through life."

After carefully considering the testimony of disunion which the English Friends had issued against me, I resolved to appeal against it. I can scarcely explain why I did so; nor is it necessary that I should. The "testimony" gave four reasons for disowning me —a very unusual thing, for one is generally considered enough. The first was, that I had joined the National Church; the second, that I had refused the dealing of the Monthly Meeting to which I belonged; the third, that I approved of, and encouraged an hireling ministry; and the fourth, that I never went to Friends' Meetings.

Every one of these four sins laid to my charge happened to be false. I had not joined any Church; indeed I did not well know, as I was living in Ireland, whether they meant the Protestant Church or the Roman Catholic. I had never been under dealing of the Monthly Meeting to which I belonged. It was the Irish Friends who had put me under dealing, on their own "Jacob rules," without any precedent, and for the sole purpose of pleasing those individuals whom I had unfortunately offended. I had never approved of, or encouraged an hireling ministry; although I had refused to apply the insulting epithet to all the honoured clergymen of the Church of England and Ireland. And it was equally untrue, that I had ceased to attend Friends' Meetings; for I went there almost regularly once a week. So I gave the regular notice of appeal, and demanded a copy of all the minutes of the Monthly Meeting which had reference to my case. This I had a right to. The English Friends threw every possible impediment in my way; and gave me the different "minutes" one by one, with an interval of a month between each. By chance I found out that the individuals who wanted to have me disunited, had much difficulty in making out a case sufficiently strong for the Monthly Meeting to act on; for although the Irish Quakers were most willing to assist them, they had not been able to overcome the "difficulty" they found in my case, as I had not transgressed any legitimate rule. The plan they finally adopted was—they desired their assistant clerk to write a private letter to a person living near me, who they knew was trying to rise in the Meeting, and would therefore be likely to accept the office. He was to watch me narrowly, to find out some flaw in my conduct and character; and if he could not do so, he was to invent something which would satisfy the Meeting, and induce them to disown me. The plan succeeded; and on those letters I was found guilty, and cast off from all Christian communion with the Society in which I was born, and in which still remained many of my nearest and dearest relatives. One of the letters I obtained, and was able to refute; the other was positively refused. They said, "it was burnt"—"it was lost"—"it did not bear on the case"—"it was of no consequence." I appealed, according to all due forms, to the Quarterly Meeting, and was immediately reinstated in membership.

The Friends were very angry with me. It was as if I had disturbed an hornet's nest—I was stung on all sides. They do not like appeals. It was, in their "best wisdom" they had disowned me. The Quartely Meeting, in reinstating me, had declared, as plainly as in words, that "the best wisdom" was not good at all, and I became an object of inveterate hatred to the overseers and elders, who considered themselves disgraced by the mere mention of my name. One of them said, "The name was like a thorn in his side, and prevented him from sleeping."

I will just relate one of the many instances in which Friends tried to punish me, for my hardihood in daring publicly to dispute their infallibility. It was on the occasion of my brother's marriage. According to the usual etiquette, I should have gone with him and his bride into the Monthly Meetings, to hear their declaration. These points of etiquette are deemed of great importance in the Society; and to disgrace me by it, they resolved I should not be permitted to enter the Monthly Meeting with the bridal train. One after another near relative was invited to take my place, and refused, because they would not be a party to the slight intended on me. The bride's family were unwilling I should imagine they were individually capable of insulting me; and they informed me, that it was two high Friends who objected to my company, and who felt reluctance to allow me to sit ten minutes in the house appointed for worship with them.

In innumerable such-like little trifling, and almost indescribable ways I was persecuted, to say nothing of the great persecution of the Chancery suit, which was, term after term wasting our property, and by which we have lost already several thousand pounds, both directly and indirectly.

When any Friend incurs the hatred of the Society, it is an easy matter to punish him. His connections being still amongst them, of course his property is more or less liable to be influenced; and they are stirred up—in some cases by slander, as in mine—in others, by a scruple of conscience to maintain any dealings with those who have incurred the censure of Friends—and in others, by a feeling of personal gratification, in chastening the delinquent.

There was another appeal to the Society, just at the same time as mine, which interested me much, and which afforded another curious development of

Quakerism. A gentleman of the most upright and irreproachable character was disowned by the Society, because he had not, as they considered, faithfully maintained their "testimony against paying tithes." He was agent to a nobleman, a large landed proprietor, and, in the discharge of his duty, he had paid the tithe rent-charge legally due. It was on his employer's account, not his own; but for not suffering a distraint on the property, as Friends do, he was ignominiously turned out of the Society. He appealed against the sentence, and the Yearly Meeting, after long and serious investigation, decided against him. They decided, that he should have refused to pay tithes under any circumstances whatever. But it transpired that they were a little bit ashamed of their own decision; for they caused it to be intimated to him, and to all of us, that if he wished to be reinstated in membership, and would apply for it by letter, no impediment would be placed in his way.

Friends find it very difficult "to maintain their testimony against paying tithes," in Ireland, where landed property is so much more in their possession than in England. Many have been disowned, because they had not a sufficient elasticity of conscience to enable them, for the sake of upholding this most untenable doctrine of the Society—to resist their own sense of right and wrong—their personal advantage—the law of the land, and the command of Scripture, "Submit yourselves to every ordinance of man for the Lord's sake."

I have heard many stories, told by the actors themselves, of how they managed "to cheat the devil in the dark," as one of them laughingly expressed it. In my English Quaker experience, I have told how "the testimony" is sometimes managed there. The Irish Friends are quite as clever in a different way.

Thus, a sack of wheat was once placed in a very conspicuous position in a barn, when it was known the tithe collectors were coming to distrain. The owner stood by, and said to them, "Look at that sack of wheat; I would not for five pounds seven and sixpence lose that." Five pounds seven and sixpence was the exact sum demanded. The men immediately lifted it up on the car they had brought with them, and drove off a little beyond the end of the avenue; they then turned back again. The Quaker had not moved from the spot he stood in. They said, "Sir, will you buy a fine sack of wheat from us? "What is the price?" asked Broadbrim; "let me look at it." He opened the sack, rubbed the grain in his hand, and said, it was very prime.

"Come, Sir, be quick, will you buy it for five pounds seven and sixpence."

"Yes," he replied, "I will," and drew the amount out of his pocket. The sack was restored to its proper place. The collectors received an extra shilling, with which to drink the Friend's health, and very likely to laugh heartily at the curious anomaly, a Quaker's conscience.

A gentleman who has now left the Friends, and

joined the Church of England and Ireland, told me, that when he was a Quaker, his plan of evading the payment, and supporting the testimony, was, to leave —as if by chance, cartridges of half-pence rolled up in papers to a larger amount than the sum demanded, in a conspicuous place. The collectors would only take the right sum, and the testimony was upheld most satisfactorily.

Conscience works in another way in some. A very plain Friend, who once refused to accept an invitation to dine at the house of an elder in the Society, because I was one of the invited guests also; and he said, he could not reconcile it to his conscience, to sit at the same hospitable board with one who had incurred the censure of the Society; he was a landed proprietor. He scrupled either to pay or to evade the tithe rent-charge. He was of course distrained—his horse one year, his jaunting-car another. This was unpleasant —it was unendurable. Martyrdom any way is very trying—martyrdom of the pocket especially so. This plain Friend resolved to sell his property, and did so. He sold it to his own younger brother. That younger brother was disowned by the Society for paying tithes. Now if it was a crime for the elder brother to pay them, was he not doubly culpable in putting the temptation to sin in his younger brother's way. But this is not the end of the story. The younger brother, disowned by the Society, and now proprietor of the land, was in want of a tenant for a nice little farm on it. The elder came forward and offered himself. He was accepted; and no scruple of his tender conscience impeded his enjoyment of the land.

Oh! Friends! Friends! God cannot be mocked. You will assuredly have much to answer for, in the day of judgment, for your hypocritical evasions in paying tithes, if it is a sin against God's law to do so; and for your refusal to pay them, if that springs from your imagined "inconsistency of tithes with the nature of the Gospel dispensation," or even from your "firm conviction, that to abide faithful in your testimony against paying tithes, steeple-house rates, and priests' maintenance, has greatly tended to the opening of the eyes of many, not only in this, but also in other countries," unless you can show, that by refusing to submit to this ordinance of man, you have obeyed the law of God.

There is only one text of Scripture given by Friends as the ground on which they have built up their testimony, in which they say, in their Book of Minutes, "We believe that this testimony to the purity and freedom of genuine Gospel ministry, strongly evinces that the formation of our Society was not an effort of human wisdom; neither is there anything more calculated to sap our foundation, and render us a degenerate church, than a departure from this principle"—the text, "Freely ye have received, freely give." My vision is too opaque to discover the connection between "Freely give," and "This Meeting declares it is its sense and judgment that no Friend in truth can pay tithes, it being inconsistent with our Christian testimony."

To return to my own story. I had often heard it said, that it was never worth any one's while to appeal to the Society, for that even if the appeal was successful, you would have to leave the sect sooner or later. That you would be tormented into a voluntary resignation. It was literally so with me. I still had an unaccountable hankering after the silent Meeting, an indestructible affection for very many of the Friends, and an intense anxiety to be a true spiritual worshipper of the Mighty God, who I knew was present everywhere that his Spirit was invoked. But I was soon obliged to give up going to Meeting; cold looks from some, chilly salutations from others, and rude pushes from more, were unpleasant; and in addition to this, the one solitary minister in the Meeting, would not preach when I was present. I did not therefore like, or think it right, to go where I was evidently so unwelcome, and where my presence presented an impediment to "the immediate teaching and influence of the Holy Spirit, whereby acceptable worship is performed, and all true Gospel ministry supplied." I therefore sent in my resignation, although even when doing so, I held many of the Quaker doctrines, and would gladly have remained, had they allowed me quietly and unmolested, to live in peace amongst them. I felt very indignant at the injustice done us; and in my letter of resignation, I recapitulated our wrongs, and openly and by name charged our persecutors with dishonest, disreputable, and unchristian conduct. My letter was received most meekly; and I was told it was quite satisfactory.

Acting under advice, I then sent a concise statement of the persecution which a few Friends, backed by three Monthly Meetings, had so annoyed and injured us by, to every single one of the leading Friends in England and Ireland, and also to the Meeting for Sufferings; and entreated them to restrain their members from entirely ruining us by the vexatious Chancery suit they had so long carried on, requesting them to look into the characters of our persecutors, one at least of whom, though of so very high standing in the Society, was a notoriously disreputable and false man, and offering to leave the decision of our cause to any two Christian men, either in or out of the Society. The answers we received were all intimating that the punishment inflicted on us was not at all greater than we deserved, and that our persecutors had the entire sympathy of the Society in their treatment of us.

The plea of the suit is of course to recover money claimed; whilst the real reason is, to punish us for going to Church and for speaking slightingly of women's preaching. The plaintiffs are are all wealthy Friends; the newspapers now and then record their munificent donations to hospitals, infirmaries, &c. &c., sometimes amounting to a thousand pounds at a time. Indeed these public donations have followed, like cause and effect, after some peculiar injustice inflicted on us.

No one could believe that for the sum of fourteen pounds five shillings per annum, these benevolent individuals, whose liberality is so notorious, would institute a Chancery suit, especially where their claim was never denied, although it might have been.

Friends often claim for themselves credit for being free from the sin of persecution; and therefore it is that I relate this, my experience, of their tender mercy.

Sad stories have been told me of the misery and destitution which Friends have unpityingly caused to others who have offended them.

One young man, for "neglecting to bear his testimony against an hireling ministry, by suffering himself to be joined in marriage by a priest," was deprived of property amounting to fifteen thousand pounds.

Another, for the same unpardonable offence, died for want of proper food and clothing, whilst his parents rolled to Meeting in their carriage.

I think it was O'Connell who said, "that one fact was worth a cart-load of arguments." I do not feel at all competent to argue; but I can supply an abundant store more of facts, if those I have already narrated are not considered sufficiently demonstrative of my assertion, that Quakers, as a sect, are unrivalled in their vindictive persecution of those, who once belonging to their body, have dared to separate, either from conscience sake, or from any other motive.

CHAPTER XVI.

White Quakers—Favourite Texts—Sidcot School—Providential Thunder Storm—Indifference to Sin—Youth's Meetings—Sunday Schools—Baptism and the Lord's Supper—Conclusion.

Having repeatedly had occasion to speak of the "Jacob Rules," it is necessary to explain something about the origin of them. It was, I think, in the years 1835 and 1836, that a Friend, named Joshua Jacob, took a very prominent part in the Dublin Monthly Meeting. His wife also became particularly efficient in the women's Meeting. In some respects, like the modern Puseyites, they were for reviving the obsolete customs of the early Quakers. To adhere strictly to the phraseology of George Fox, to imitate his eccentricities—to throw back the innovations which had crept in, and to revivify the Society in all its original quaintness—appeared to be their object. As George Fox had been "inspired by the shining of the light within" to originate, and had been enabled, in "best wisdom," to establish the Society, and, aided by Robert Barclay, William Penn, and some others, who were equally gifted, had published rules, and laws, and by-laws; and as their teaching was principally directed to exalt the work of the Holy Spirit in the heart of man, in contra-distinction to the great error of the day—an exaltation of the outward forms and ceremonies of religious worship; so these Friends, Jacob and a few others, claimed for themselves the same "inspiration," and the same "best wisdom," with which now to dictate, and to govern.

The Dublin Friends were greatly pleased with what they deemed and called a "New Light, which had been vouchsafed to the Society, to preserve it from the degeneracy which, for some previous years, had been assimilating them to Christians of other Churches." With deferential submission, they accepted "the leadings and guidings" of those "gifted individuals;" and at their suggestion, the Yearly Meeting added to the Book of Discipline several stringent rules, which, according to the custom of Friends, being once inserted there, must remain until the end.

The Jacobs, mistaking their imaginings for the inspiration of the Holy Spirit, and greatly puffed up in their own estimation by the deference conceded to them, yielded very naturally to that inherent desire which man has to assume control over the intellect of his fellow-man, and to bend another to his own opinion. So much of their "best wisdom" having been thus accepted by the Society at large, "fresh guidings" were frequently volunteered, until at last common sense revolted, and reason in some degree resumed her sway.

Jacob had succeeded in convincing the Meeting, that to go "to any place of common worship," to "wear mourning for a deceased relative or friend," to "allow a musical instrument inside the door," &c. &c., were sins of such enormity, as required that the offender should immediately be disowned. He now wished to go farther, and set an example for their imitation.

Blue had long been a forbidden colour for Friends to wear. Jacob declared, that "the simplicity of godliness required that all men and women should array themselves in white. With untanned shoes, unbleached stockings, flannel-coloured knee-breeches, coat and waist-coat, and a light drab broad-brimmed hat, he appeared in the Meeting, accompanied by his wife, who was clad from head to foot in coarse, unbleached calico. He would not allow anything to be in his house, except it were white. His walls were white-washed, and his doors painted white. His wife united heart and hand in his "guiding." One morning she collected every article of china and earthenware in her house, on which was any colour, or even gilding. She opened her hall-door, and on the door steps smashed them all to pieces. Her husband applauded her "noble deed" as he called it; delighted at such praise from him, she continued the work of demolition; her looking-glasses were brought out next and destroyed with a large stone which she picked up in the street; for this he called her "a noble-minded woman." His mahogany and rosewood furniture were replaced with common white wood; and even the patchwork quilt was banished from his white abode.

The majority of the Friends stoutly resisted these "leadings and guidings." Ministers, elders, and overseers, had all united in his opinions, so long as they personally were not subjected, or likely to be so, to any restriction. They could never be tempted to go "to a place of common worship" or "to put on mourning," &c., &c., therefore they fully united in his wishes to shackle "the body." Not one iota would they yield when it concerned their own dear selves.

A person not well versed in the mysteries of Quakerism, might imagine that there was quite as much sense, and religion also, in obliging every one to dress in white, as there is in forbidding any one to wear black, but the leaders and heads of the Society discovered so very important a difference, that whilst they rejected the one, they retained the other, and keep it enrolled amongst those rules of which they say —"May the evidence which it (the Book of Discipline) exhibits of the concern of the Society, from time to time, to maintain the profession of the truth in its primitive purity, and to observe the precepts and practices taught and exemplified by the Lord Jesus Christ and his Apostles, commend themselves to the consciences and willing acceptance of all our members."

Jacob and his disciples, who altogether numbered more than one hundred, finding they were not allowed to have the entire governing of the Society, separated from it, and incorporated themselves into a sect called White Quakers. The original Friends, now denominated Black Quakers, in contra-distinction, disowned the White Quakers, and they, in return, disowned them.

Friends never engage in controversy, whether it is that they consider their standing as a religious body so very high as to be above the test of Scripture, reason, and intellect; or whether an innate feeling that their doctrines and peculiarities will not bear examination, prevents them, so it is. The White Quakers challenged them in vain. Month after month they published a large tract, entitled "The truth as it is in Jesus," and therein asserted, and attempted to prove, that they, and they only, were the true followers of George Fox. The Friends took no notice of the publication, and it soon dropped to the ground.

Following out their theory, that they were, or rather that their leader was, "inspired," in all his vagaries, they implicitly obeyed his "guidings." The White Quakers had amongst them people of wealth, good family, education as good as Friends generally have; and it is impossible to believe that so large a number could all have been mad, each performing the strangest acts, and submitting to the most unheard of privations, as Jacob directed them. Property was in common amongst them, and Jacob was the cash-keeper. Many thousand pounds passed into his hands in this way. The widowed mother of some young children was one of his followers, and she gave up not only her own money, but also that to which her children were entitled on coming of age. The relatives of the children instituted an action against Jacob to oblige him to give up their property, but in vain; he suffered imprisonment for two or three years on account of it; but gained his point in defiance of the law. I do not know how it was managed, but he did not refund the money, and he obtained his liberty.

One time he would command an elderly lady, who had been all her life accustomed to the luxuries of wealth, to go early of a cold winter's morning, in her scanty white calico raiment, without shoes or stockings, carrying in her hand a wooden bowl full of coarse stirabout, and eat it with an iron spoon, sitting on the steps of the Bank of Ireland, "for a sign unto the people." Another delicate young woman was ordered to wash for the whole establishment; unused to such hardship, she soon fell a victim to it, and died untended and uncomforted.

The White Quakers had Meeting-houses in several different towns. The police were often called on to restrain them. They went into the "steeple houses," as George Fox had done, to disturb the congregations, and "to testify against men wearing white shirts," (surplices.)

They also went into Friends' Meeting to denounce them.

Three White Friends, one man and two women, walked up the aisle of the Meeting-house on the Sabbath morning, about half an hour after the assembly had been seated in silence; they stood quiet for a few minutes, and then exclaimed in very loud voices—"Woe, woe, to this bloody house, and to this bloody people," and then quietly went away again. On other occasions they tried to break up the Meetings; and when Friends tried to turn them out, threw themselves down on their backs, and kicked, and screamed, and yelled, blaspheming and cursing in the most awfully wicked and outrageous manner.

They professed to be religious people, and quoted Scripture for every thing—with, of course, their own interpretation attached to it.

One very favourite text was—"To the pure all things are pure." On the adaptation of this to themselves, whom they considered as "the pure," they indulged in the most monstrous indelicacy and licentiousness. Half a dozen of them attempted to parade the streets in Waterford, arm in arm, men and women without a vestige of clothing. The same text was Jacob's warrant for changing his wives, whenever he inclined to honour any of his female followers with a temporary preference. And even now, whilst I write, this scandalous sect exists, and continues to perpetrate enormities which are a disgrace to civilization.

When it was ascertained that morality was held in light esteem amongst them, some of the Friends, whose wives had adopted the White Quaker tenets, became alarmed; and with the assistance, readily granted, of the police, they stormed the abode of Jacob, and forcibly took each man his wife, away from the den of iniquity.

The distress which this schism caused among the

Friends, who are very much connected by intermarriages with one another, was very great. Some were induced to look into the root from which such gross error sprung; and finding that there was indeed the germ of fanaticism in the doctrine of inspiration (as held by the Society) apart from the authority of the Holy Scriptures, have safely and happily enshrined themselves in that comprehensive and most rational Article of the Established Church—"Holy Scripture containeth all things necessary to salvation; so that whatever is not read therein, nor may be proved thereby, is not to be required of any man that it should be believed as an article of faith, or be thought requisite or necessary to salvation." Others, alas! have been disgusted at the exhibition; and trusting to their own common sense, natural good feeling, and moral propriety, look on religion as only useful for fools or knaves.

There is still very much of the leaven of the White Quaker theory in the Society of Friends. There is great need to watch its developments. It does assume a more plausible form, but is constantly to be seen peeping out. A religious system which is built upon insulated texts of Scripture, is ever liable to lead its votaries astray. Truth may even become error, when separated from its attendant truth; and it appears to me, that all sectarianism has sprung from this exaltation of one accepted truth over another, which being less palatable, is placed in comparative abeyance at first, and afterwards entirely banished, as inconvenient and of less importance. Thus Friends approve of, and often quote—"There is neither male nor female, but ye are all one in the Lord;" whilst—"I suffer not a woman to preach," is never heard amongst them. Again: "Work out your own salvation with fear and trembling," is an approved doctrine; whilst, "Believe on the Lord Jesus Christ, and thou shalt be saved," is called a dangerous text, and so of many other texts.

About four years ago, an English Friend waited on me, to request me to enter my name as a subscriber to an edition of the Bible, which a Committee of Friends were intending to publish. The printed prospectus stated, that the work was designed to be one suited for daily perusal in Friends' families; that from it would be carefully excluded every passage that was indelicate and unfit for reading aloud; and also those portions which might be called dangerous, which it was possible the unlearned and unstable might wrest to their own destruction. Seven shillings and sixpence was to be the price of the book. Whether or not it was completed I never heard, as I declined subscribing, and entreated the messenger to read the last chapter of Revelation, before he made himself any further a party to so wicked a scheme.

One more episode in my own story brought my connection with the Society of Friends to a termination. According to the rules, my children continue to be members until they attain their majority. Some kindly disposed Friends wished me to place one of our boys at the Friend's school at Sidcot. We had heard much said in favour of that establishment, of the kind care taken of the lads, who are all under fourteen years of age, and of the excellent instruction they received from masters aud tutors, who were selected for their piety, as well as for their ability and superior education. The Committee of management were Friends of the highest respectability and standing in the Society, whose wealth and influence combined to raise the school to perfection. I felt very unwilling indeed to intrust my darling boy to the care of any "Friends;" but that was "prejudice." I had never heard one word derogatory of the system the school was conducted on, and reluctantly consented to let him go, satisfying myself with the hope, that if any religious instruction was given to him, it would be good so far as it went.

The preliminaries were all satisfactorily arranged, and he sailed for Bristol accompanied by his father. They travelled on, and arrived in safety at Sidcot School, Somersetshire. They found the house and grounds spacious, comfortable and commodious; just as it had been described to us. When the time arrived for the father to leave, a violent thunder-storm came on; he was politely invited to remain until the following morn; and as the rain was tremendously heavy he consented to do so. In the evening it cleared up, and a Quaker lady who resided near, sent them an invitation to go take tea with her. They went. The kind Quaker lady, to whom we owe a debt of gratitude which can never be repaid, had a long and private conference with the master of the school. Nothing then transpired. They returned to the school, and father and son were accommodated with an excellent bed. The parting was to be at ten o'clock, to meet the train. At breakfast the master looked anxious and distressed; a note from the lady, at whose house they had taken tea the evening before, was put into his hands, and then he hastily, and as if overruled, requested a private interview with the father. He then told what this good women had charged him to communicatc—that the whole school was infected with the most abominable sin—all were polluted. Ten minutes sufficed to repack his trunks; and my son was saved by the gracious interposition of Providence, from the contamination of such iniquity.

On returning to Bristol, and requesting the school Committee there, to refund the money which had been paid, of course the reason was given for taking the child home again, and horror and indignation were expressed at the crime, and the neglect which was perilling the souls and bodies of so many poor children, who had been confidingly entrusted to their care.

The "Friends" took it all very coolly. They were very sorry indeed that the circumstance had been discovered; but they hoped, as our son was not remaining there, we "would see the propriety of not allowing it to transpire." One said, "It was not worth talking about. He would send his own son there without hesitation." And there it remains to the present moment. Can it be, that Friends believe that God will call every man to account for all his words, and thoughts, and deeds, and continue to disregard his laws, and to despise his instructions? Honoured and respected by the world—esteemed for their industry and benevolence—remarkable for their quiet and peaceable lives, as much as for their peculiar garb—the separation in which they live from their fellow-creatures, has enveloped the Society in a mantle of obscurity; and, by lulling them to rest so satisfied with themselves, and with the fame they have acquired, has conduced to their present degeneracy. Like the Laodiceans, they are "rich and increased with goods, and have need of nothing;" and they know not that they "are wretched, and miserable, and poor, and blind, and naked;" or, in the words of our blessed Saviour, "Ye also outwardly appear righteous unto men, but within ye are full of hypocrisy and iniquity."

The current of man's disposition naturally tends towards evil. If a garden be not dug and planted, the weeds will spring up; and the richer and better the soil, the more abundant will be the crop of them. So with the heart of a child—the evil is natural, the good must be planted. Three times every year, and three times only, Friends hold what they call Youths' Meetings, from ten till about half-past eleven generally on a third-day morning. About half that time is spent in silence; the remainder is occupied in reading some portion of the Book of Discipline, or the death-bed scene of some unnaturally perfect youth, or advices on the peculiarities of the Society. That is the only religious instruction the Friends give to their youth; the parents may or may not give further. Sunday Schools are not approved of; and if a mother, feeling her own incapacity to impart sound scriptural education, and aware of the need of it for the souls of her children, dares to send them to the Church School, she is sure to be visited by the overseers, and obliged either to give up her connection with the Friends, or to withdraw her children from the Scriptural School. I have known repeated instances of this, and have admired and availed myself of the kind condescension of more than one clergyman, who held his school on the week-day, affording the Quaker mother an opportunity of entrusting her darlings to his teaching, unknown to the overseers.

The indifference with which the Friends regarded the scandalous state of Sidcot School, severed the last link of the chain which the remembrance of Quakerism, as I had seen it in my father's life, had bound me in.

Nobody, unless they have passed through the ordeal, can conceive how very painful it is to feel one's-self cast off from all earthly communion with the Church —branded as unfit to worship God in the society of those who were one's fellows,—disowned by them, as one guilty of crime which mortals might not forgive —slighted in public, and repulsed in private—banished from their company on earth, and clearly given to understand, that into that heaven which is prepared for Friends, I had no chance of being received. I sought for admission into the Church of England and Ireland; and there, with all my family about me, found a ready entrance. Six children, husband and wife, were all baptized together—eight persons. We entered "into the ark of Christ's Church, in faith and hope, there to pass through the waves of this troublesome world, that finally we may come to the land of everlasting life."

I had my Quaker doubts of the necessity of water Baptism to the very hour in which I submitted to it. But although it might be non-essential to salvation, I could not see that there was any thing wrong in the act itself, even Friends' writings do not condemn it as sinful; only as a substitute for the baptism of the Holy Ghost, they reject it; consequently, I felt quite willing to submit my own judgment in a non-essential matter, to the superior wisdom of the enlightened Church Divines. On the doctrines of Baptism, as well as on that of the Lord's supper, I have personally experienced the truthfulness of that gracious promise, —"If any man will do his will, he shall know of the doctrine whether it be of God." It seemed to me an ungracious thing to refuse to do anything, which by any possibility might be considered as well pleasing to the Almighty, becauee the omission of it would not deprive me altogether of His salvation. I therefore resolved to do it as his will, and I now know assuredly that those doctrines are from God.

As I conceive it is utterly impossible that Quakerism can survive this generation—that the enlightened intellect of the young people, will submit to the dictation of "blind leaders" much longer—and that common sense will continue to yield to the puerilities which have supplanted the restraints imposed upon us by the Law of the Lord; so I would hope that the inestimable value of the soul, and the awful certainty, that when this short period of probation is over and gone, we must enter either the realms of everlasting glory, or the gloomy dungeons of misery and despair, may induce the great and intelligent mass of the Society to reject the fanaticism which has already perilled their souls; and to fly for safety from the wrath to come, to where alone it is to be found, "in the blood of the Lord Jesus Christ, which cleanseth us from all sin."

It is now-a-days considered a very improper thing to speak of hell; and a most uncharitable man is he deemed, who ventures to intimate that any body is in danger of being committed to its burning chambers. God who is all love, had told us there is a hell reserved for the ungodly, as surely as there is a heaven prepared for the righteous. "The devil rejoices when Christians are silent about hell." The Society of Friends have fallen into that snare; and from ceasing to speak of it, have alas! ceased to fear it.

"Do you believe the Bible? Then depend upon it,

hell will be intense and unutterable woe. It is vain to talk of all the expressions about it being only figures of speech. The pit, the prison, the worm, the fire, the thirst, the blackness, the darkness, the weeping, the gnashing of teeth, the second death—all these may be figures of speech, if you please. But Bible figures mean something beyond all question; and here they mean something which man's mind can never fully conceive. Oh! reader, the miseries of mind and conscience are far worse than those of the body. The whole extent of hell, the present suffering, the bitter recollection of the past, the hopeless prospect of the future, will never be thoroughly known, except by those who go there."

The ministers of the Society of Friends never speak of these things—they are to them as though they were not; but the great fact remains true as the Scriptures which reveal it to us, and awful as it is true.

There are imperfections and infirmities of some kind in every communion on earth. "Infallibility is not for this dispensation; for if the preaching of Christ which was indeed infallible, did not bow the hearts of all his hearers—if the eloquence and inspiration of Saint Paul failed to subdue his auditors—if the Holy Scriptures, the infallible word of the living God, has not been able to banish error from men's minds, how shall the potsherds of the earth presume to teach of their puny wisdom as infallible?" But the Bible is an unerring guide to salvation, and the "wayfaring men, though fools, shall not err therein." If any man is willing to be saved, the Lord is willing to save him. A light streaming from the pearl gates of heaven, illumines the straight and narrow way which leads to the mansions of rest, and Jesus, the Angel of the Covenant, stands with outstretched hand, to welcome the weary pilgrim home, with the gracious words, "Come unto me, all ye that labour and are heavy laden, and I will give you rest."

In narrating my experience of what Quakerism is, I have endeavoured to draw a distinct line between the body of the sect, and the officers who, in the name of the body, carry on its operations.

Many things are done in the name of the Society, which the individuals who compose the Society would shrink from participating in, were they aware of what is done ostensibly in their behalf. Whilst the present practice continues, the overseers of each Meeting—perhaps four or six individuals—do just what they like, and are irresponsible; whilst the odium of their bigotry and injustice falls on the whole Society. I would therefore in parting from my kind Quaker readers, suggest the propriety of requiring all letters addressed to the Monthly Meetings, to be read aloud in them, instead of, as now, allowing two people—who perhaps have interest in keeping the communication secret—to take letters out of the Meeting-room—read them by themselves, and then dispose of them, either by a select Committee, or by handing them over to the overseers. I wrote to the Monthly Meeting three times; and am fully persuaded, that had my letters been read aloud there, the injustice done to me would not have been sanctioned. I complained of the falsity of the overseers, and the overseers themselves were appointed to do me justice. Whilst letters are thus suppressed, this state of things will most naturally continue. Ministers, elders, and overseers, are subject to like passions and feelings with other men and women, and are quite as little likely to expose their own order to censure.

Is it not as unmanly as it is unreasonable, blindly to allow some half-dozen individuals to decide, in the name of the whole Meeting, on any point, without allowing the assembly to hear and judge for themselves? When it is resolved to disown any member, would it not be fair and just to allow the accused to appear before the Meeting, and either to speak or to write in his own defence? The vilest criminal is allowed, in courts of law, to say what he can, openly and publicly, for himself; and shall the Society of Friends, in the nineteenth century, continue to award their verdict at the instigation of some half-dozen, or more, individuals, without allowing the accused to be heard, and without the Meeting itself being even made aware of any of the circumstances of the case, but such as these half-dozen individuals think fit to bring before them?

I am persuaded that all the evils which now abound in the Society have arisen from the neglect of the Holy Scriptures.

In banishing his Word from the public assemblies,

God was dishonoured and despised; and he has said, "Them that honour me I will honour, and they that despise me shall be lightly esteemed." Banished from public worship, the Bible has been neglected in private. The casual reading of a chapter, or a psalm, perhaps once a day, is a mere form, and leaves the mind untaught in the Word of God, and, consequently, exposed and without defence, to the attacks of our great arch-enemy, who is ever watching to seize on every undefended avenue to man's heart. St. Peter, in his catalogue of those eight Christian virtues which are required to make "our calling and election sure," places "knowledge" the third highest on the list; and it is because the ministers, elders, and overseers have not that "knowledge," and because they despise "knowledge," that they speak and act as they now do. Therefore, my good reader, if you are a Quaker, insist, I pray you, on your preachers especially, being well versed in the Bible; and be assured, if they have it in their heads and in their hearts, they will not object to have it in their hands also, but, on the contrary, they will never dare to stand up in your galleries without holding it up as their warrant for addressing you.

And, my good reader, if you are a member of the Established Church of England and Ireland, and feel pity for the ignorance which has led to the results I have described, remember, I pray you, that whilst Satan has lulled so many into a fatal disregard of the knowledge of God's laws, you have had the Holy

Scriptures openly taught in your Churches, and have basked in the beams of the Sun of Righteousness.

The Quaker has a soul to be saved as well as another man, and the clergyman who has Quakers in his parish, will, I hope, when he knows how ignorant they are of the true Christian faith, include them in his labours of love.

And, oh! may the Lord Jesus Christ, whose aid I have invoked in writing every page of this volume, condescend to bless it, and make it instrumental in his cause. When a garden is overgrown with weeds, even a feeble old woman is sometimes usefully employed in plucking them up; so my desire has been to pluck up those weeds which I saw overruning the good ground in this corner of the garden of the Lord; and thus help—all roughly though it be—to prepare it for the reception of that good seed of the kingdom, which the well-skilled husbandman may plant, and which, watered with the dew of heaven, may yet bring forth fruit to the honour and glory of God.

THE END.

A CATALOGUE

OF

VALUABLE AND IMPORTANT WORKS,

PUBLISHED AND FOR SALE BY

J. W. MOORE,

BOOKSELLER, PUBLISHER, AND IMPORTER,

193 CHESTNUT STREET, OPPOSITE THE STATE-HOUSE,

PHILADELPHIA.

THE WORKS OF MICHAEL DE MONTAIGNE, comprising his Essays, Letters, a Journey through Germany and Italy; with notes from all the Commentators, Biographical and Bibliographical Notices, &c., &c., &c. By WILLIAM HAZLITT. 1 vol. 8vo., pp. 686, cloth, $2 50; half calf and half morocco, $3 50.

"This is a truly valuable publication, and embodies much that may be ead with profit."—*Inquirer.*

"This work is too well known, and too highly appreciated by the literary world, to require eulogy.—*North American.*

"So long as an unaffected style and good nature shall charm—so long as the lovers of desultory and cheerful conversation shall be more numerous than those who prefer a lecture or a sermon — so long as reading is sought by the many as an amusement in idleness, or a resource in pain — so long will Montaigne be among the favourite authors of mankind."—*Hallam.*

BURTON'S ANATOMY OF MELANCHOLY. What it is, with all the kinds, causes, symptoms, prognostics, and several cures of it. In three partitions: with their several sections, members, and subsections, philosophically, medically, and historically opened and cut up. A new edition, corrected and enriched by translations of the numerous classical extracts. To which is prefixed an account of the author. From the last London edition. 1 vol. 8vo., cloth, $2 50; half calf and half morocco, $3 50.

"The book is an inexhaustible fountain, where every mind, no matter what may be its peculiar organization, or the nature of its momentary needs, can draw at will nourishment and strength; such perfect mingling of immense erudition, profound thought, sparkling humour, and exuberant fancy, exists no where else out of Shakspeare."—*City Item.*

WEISS ON WATER CURE. The Hand Book of Hydropathy, for Professional and Domestic use: with an Appendix, on the best mode of forming Hydropathic establishments. Being the result of twelve years' experience at Grafenberg and Freywaldau. By Dr. J. WEISS. 12mo., cloth, $1 00.

"The intention of the author in this work, is to render himself intelligible to the non-professional reader, so that the treatment by water may be safely introduced into domestic use, and exert its influence where medical assistance is not to be obtained."—*Messenger.*

BIBLIA HEBRAICA. Secundum Editiones. Jos. Athiae, Joannis Leusden, Jo. Simonis Aliorumque, inprimis Everardi Van Der Hooght, D. Henrici Opitii, et Wolfii Heidenheim, cum additionibus Clavique Masoretica et Rabbinica, Augusti Hahn. Nunc denuo recognita et emendata ab Isaaco Leeser, V. D. M., et Josepho Jaquett, V. D. M. The above is stereotyped from the last Leipsic edition, and beautifully half bound in the German style, thick 8vo., price reduced to $2 25.

"Its typography is beautiful, and it is justly admired by Hebrew scholars who have examined it. Its superior accuracy, it is believed, will be acknowledged, on a comparison with any Bible extant. One thing which gives elegance and excellence to the work, should be particularly noticed by all who desire a Bible that can be easily read, all the vowel points and accents are in their right places, which cannot be said of all former editions—and therefore the student can never be in doubt respecting the letters to which they belong."—*Christian Observer.*

THE FAMILY SHAKSPEARE, in one volume; in which nothing is added to the original text; but those words and expressions are omitted which cannot with propriety be read aloud in a family. By THOMAS BOWDLER, Esq. From the sixth London edition, royal 8vo., cloth, $3.

"The nature and object of this work are too well known to require explanation, and many a family will feel obliged to Mr. Moore for furnishing an edition of the immortal dramatist; garbled, indeed, because expurgated—but in many respects less garbled than some of the separate plays as prepared for the stage—which can be recommended to parents and guardians, and introduced into the mixed domestic circle without hesitation or fear."—*North American.*

PARTNERS FOR LIFE: A Christmas Story. By CAMILLA TOULMIN. With illustrations by John Absolon. 12mo., cloth, 75 cents; gilt, $1; paper covers, 38 cents.

"Another Christmas book by a lady! and by one whose short tales and graceful and tender poetry are carrying her name into every household, and will extend her influence, both abroad and home; for it is always exercised for good."—*Art Union.*

THE FOREST MINSTREL. A Collection of Original Poems, by Mrs. LYDIA JANE PIERSON. Edited by the Rev. B. S. Schenck. 1 vol. 12mo., cloth, 75 cents; fancy, $1.

TRAVELS OVER THE TABLE LANDS AND CORDILLERAS OF MEXICO; with observations upon the *Religion, Political Institutions, Commerce, Agriculture and Civilization* in Mexico; embracing accounts of the manner of mining and coining silver in that country. With an Appendix, comprising biographies of Emperor Don Augustin Iturbide and the Ex-President General Don Antonio Lopez De Santa Anna. By ALBERT M. GILLIAM, late U. S. Consul at California, Mexico. With Maps and Plates. 1 vol. 8vo., cloth, $2.

THE MEMOIRS OF MRS. ELIZABETH FRY, Edited by two of her daughters. 2 vols. 8vo., cloth, with portrait, $3 50; half morocco, $5.

The record of the life and experience of such a labourer in the field of genuine philanthropy and benevolence, is an invaluable memoir, and will doubtless be so regarded by the Christian community.

"If the work could meet with a circulation equal to its deserving, it would find eager welcome in every family in Christendom. It affords a beautiful exemplification of Christian character. Each page breathes fervent piety. Charity, the most Godlike of virtues, animates every word. The Memoir possesses peculiar value from the fact that it is prepared by two daughters of the deceased, who have taken great care, and manifested good judgment in their labour of love."—*City Item.*

TAYLOR (R. C.) STATISTICS OF COAL. The Geographical and Geological distribution of Mineral Combustibles or Fossil Fuel, including, also, Notices and Localities of the various Mineral Bituminous Substances employed in Arts and Manufactures; with maps, elegantly coloured, and diagrams; embracing, from official reports of the great coal-producing countries, the respective amounts of their production, consumption, and commercial distribution in all parts of the world, together with their prices, tariffs, duties, and international regulations. Accompanied by nearly four hundred statistical tables, and eleven hundred analyses of mineral combustibles, with incidental statements of the statistics of Iron manufactures, derived from authentic authorities. Prepared by RICHARD COWLING TAYLOR, Fellow of the Geological Society of London, member of the American Philosophical Society, &c. &c. Royal 8vo., cloth, $5 00.

"It is a most invaluable work—a monument of industrious and careful research—a treasury—a very encyclopedia of coal, extending to all associated branches of information, worthy to rank with the most complete and thorough economic manuals with which the world is yet acquainted. There is no such work, in fact, on the subject of coal, in any language; it is a mine of instruction, and a whole library of reference, which not coal and iron miners only, but statisticians and statesmen, will find worthy of their attention."—*North American.*

"It is indeed one of the most remarkable books of the day; exhibiting a vast amount of scientific knowledge and statistical information, and a laborious patience that is as praiseworthy as it is rare."—*Pittsburg Commercial.*

MYSTERIES OF CITY LIFE; or, Stray Leaves from the World's Book. Being a series of Tales, Sketches, Incidents, and Sermons, founded upon the Notes of a Home Missionary. By JAMES REES, author of "The Philadelphia Locksmith," "The Night Hawk Papers," &c. 12mo., paper, 75 cents; cloth, $1 00.

"The book is original in its conception and execution; its details carry such evidence of reality with them, that the reader can scarcely take them for fiction, and we much doubt if they are; at the same time, the incidents are often so startling, and so vividly and painfully represented to the mind's eye, that we could wish they were not facts—or rather, we could wish there were no such facts really existing in the darker vistas of human life. The work is of that class which irresistibly captivates the attention; and when the reader has once begun, he must go through it, impatient of all interruption. But the best remains to be said: the book is unexceptionably moral, and altogether decorous. This, in the present state of literature, is a very rare kind of excellence, and the praise it calls forth, is the most valuable tribute that an author can receive."—*Pennsylvanian.*

MEMOIRS OF THE PRETENDERS AND THEIR ADHERENTS. By J. H. JESSE. (Moore's Select Library, Nos. 1 and 2.) 2 vols. 18mo., paper, 75 cents; cloth, $1 25.

A SUMMER'S JAUNT ACROSS THE WATER; including Visits to England, Ireland, Scotland, France, Switzerland, Germany, Belgium, &c. By J. JAY SMITH. (Moore's Select Library, Nos. 4 and 5.) 2 vols. 18mo., paper, $1 00; cloth, $1 50.

MY OWN HOME AND FIRESIDE; being Illustrations of the Speculations of Martin Chuzzlewit & Co., among the "Wenom of the Walley of Eden." By SYR. Second Edition. 1 vol. 12mo., paper, 50 cents; cloth, 75 cents.

"From the mere glimpse we have taken of this book, it seems a strange, powerfully written work, and has sufficiently arrested our attention to lay it aside for an attentive and careful perusal."—*North American.*

"It abounds in incident, wit, humour, and pathos, and will be remarkable among the many works now issuing from the press."—*Inquirer.*

GRAY'S ELEGY WRITTEN IN A COUNTRY CHURCHYARD. Embellished with thirty-three spirited Illustrations, by R. S. GILBERT. 8vo., embossed cloth, gilt, $1 50; Turkey morocco, $3 00; coloured plates, embossed cloth, gilt, $2 00; coloured plates, Turkey morocco, $3 75.

"It is got up with a degree of excellence most creditable to the enterprise of the publisher, and which the celebrated poem well deserves. It is superbly printed, on the very best paper, and each leaf contains a verse of the poem, illustrated by a wood-cut in the highest style of the art, engraved by Gilbert, from designs by the most eminent English artists."—*Pennsylvanian.*

"The poem itself is one of the most elegant English compositions now extant, and the style in which it is now offered to its admirers is highly creditable to the artists and publisher."—*Morning Post.*

SCENES AND ADVENTURES IN SPAIN, from 1835 to 1840. By Poco Mas. (Moore's Select Library, No. 3.) 1 vol. 18mo., paper, 38 cents; cloth, 63 cents.

THE PROSE WORKS OF JOHN MILTON, with a Biographical Introduction by R. W. Griswold. 2 vols. 8vo., cloth, $4 00.

FIRST LESSONS IN FRENCH, by Miss Colman, illustrated with beautiful engravings. Square 16mo., embossed muslin, 50 cents.

CHILD'S FIRST PRAYER BOOK. With ten splendid Plates, beautifully printed in colours. Second Edition. 1 vol., 18mo., 75 cents.

"It is by far the most attractive book of the kind for children that we have seen. Every page differs in the style of printing and illustration. Different coloured inks, gold, &c., will please the eye of the young and lead them to look to the substance of the volume through its agreeable illustrations."—*North American.*

CHILD'S DRAWING BOOK OF OBJECTS: Studies from Still Life, for young pupils and drawing classes; containing two hundred and eighty-eight objects. 4to., cloth, $2 00.

SMITH'S JUVENILE DRAWING BOOK, containing the rudiments of the Art, in a series of Progressive Lessons, 24 plates of subjects, easily copied. Small 4to., cloth, 88 cents.

HOUSEHOLD VERSES. By Bernard Barton. Embellished with a Vignette Title Page and Frontispiece. 12mo. Illuminated covers, new edition, 50 cents; cloth, gilt, 75 cents.

"A very pretty edition of the eighth, and, we believe, last volume, the death-gift of the estimable Quaker Poet, a writer always a favourite with the public, 'from whom,' as he said himself, 'he never met with aught but courtesy and kindness.'"—*North American.*

"The poems of so sweet a minstrel, should have a place in every well-selected Library."—*Inquirer.*

REMAINS OF WILLIAM S. GRAHAM; With a Memoir. Edited by George Allen, Professor of Languages in the University of Pennsylvania. 1 vol. 12mo., with Portrait, boards, 75 cents; cloth, gilt, $1 00.

"This is a most attractive book in outward form, and the interest of its contents, in our esteem, does justice to its external appearance. It is the fresh wreath which love and friendship have intertwined to hang over the early grave of genius. It is not the mere record of a bright and sparkling mind, whose light has expired, but it is the memorial also of a warm heart, earnest in its devotion to the service of God and the good of man."—*Banner of the Cross.*

BUNYAN'S MISCELLANEOUS WORKS. 1 vol. 12mo., cloth, 63 cents.

AN AUTOBIOGRAPHY, AND LETTERS OF CAROLINE FRY, the author of "The Listener," "Christ our Law," &c. 12mo., cloth, 75 cents.

"It is a work that any religious parent might wish to place in the hands of his daughters, one that could scarce fail to leave a good and serious impression on the mind of a reader."—*Pittsburg Saturday Visitor.*

"This work, as the title imports, is an Autobiography of Mrs. Caroline Fry, a lady distinguished for her piety. As such it will be interesting to the Christian world, as it should be to every one."—*Savannah Daily Republican.*

COMMERCE OF THE PRAIRIES; or, the Journal of a Santa Fe Trader during Eight Expeditions across the Western Prairies, and a Residence of nearly nine years in Northern Mexico. By JOSIAH GREGG. 2 vols. 12mo., Maps and Plates, $1 50.

"The volumes are illustrated with maps and engravings and are full of interest and information. A more agreeable or readable book has not been issued from the American press for years. The way-side incidents are quite exciting, while the reflections are sensible and sound."—*Inquirer.*

"The popularity of these sketches may be inferred from the fact that the title page bears the imprint of the fourth edition. It is very unassuming in style, and at the same time graphic, exhibiting a phase of life peculiar to the regions it has undertaken to describe."—*Neal's Gazette.*

WEEK AT GLENVILLE. By a Philadelphia lady. With numerous illustrations. Cloth, plain plates, 50 cents; cloth, coloured plates, 63 cents; cloth, gilt edge, plain plates, 63 cents; cloth, gilt edge, coloured plates, 75 cents.

"This little work will be a favourite with children, for whose especial benefit it was written. The lady authoress has succeeded in writing a book which must interest the youthful mind, and instil into it the elements of pure morality."—*Inquirer.*

CHRISTIANITY: AND ITS RELATIONS TO POETRY AND PHILOSOPHY. 12mo., cloth, 50 cents.

COE'S DRAWING-BOOK OF AMERICAN SCENERY With 34 Views from Nature, with instructions for beginners in Landscape. 4to., cloth, $1 25.

"This is an excellent work, and greatly calculated to assist young people."—*Inquirer.*

FOWNE'S PRIZE ESSAY ON CHEMISTRY, as exemplifying the wisdom and beneficence of God. 12mo., cloth 50 cents.

AGRICULTURAL BOTANY; an Enumeration and Description of useful Plants and Weeds, which merit the notice, or require the attention, of American Agriculturists. By WILLIAM DARLINGTON, M. D. 1 vol. 12mo., cloth, $1.00

"The volume is evidently the result of much labour and research, as well as of a very intimate acquaintance with the subject considered. It will be found of interest to the general reader, and invaluable to the young farmers of the United States."—*Inquirer.*

THE BOOK OF COMMON PRAYER. Standard Edition. 18mo., morocco, extra, $2.50; morocco extra, bevelled boards, $3.50; with velvet, clasps, and full mountings, various sizes and prices.

JUST PUBLISHED,

THE YOUNG MAN'S WAY TO HONOUR, INTELLIGENCE, AND USEFULNESS. By the Rev. A. ATWOOD. 1 vol. 12mo., cloth, 50 cents.

"A work which should be placed in the hands of every youth, before he has passed his 'chrysalis state.'"—*Drawing Room Journal.*

ELLEN SEYMOUR; or, the Bud and the Flower. A Tale. By Mrs. SAVILE SHEPHERD, (formerly Anne Houlditch.) 1 vol. 12mo., cloth, 88 cents.

"An admirably told tale. The interest continually increases as you advance, till it becomes wellnigh impossible to lay the volume down."—*Cincinnati Herald.*

THE THEORY OF EFFECT; embracing the Contrast of Light and Shade, of Colour and Harmony. By an Artist. With fifteen illustrations by Hinckley. 12mo., cloth, 50 cents.

"The author writes clearly, felicitously, and with a complete mastery of his subject."—*Philadelphia Advertiser.*

IN PRESS,

CHAMBERS'S PAPERS FOR THE PEOPLE. 12 vols., fancy boards.

THE SPECTATOR. New edition. 4 vols. 12mo., cloth.

IMPORTATION OF FOREIGN BOOKS.

J. W. MOORE continues to import either old or new books in the different departments of Literature, by the single copy or in quantities, (on the most favourable terms, and with the greatest despatch,) for the Trade, Colleges, and Literary and Professional Gentlemen. If by steamer, in about thirty days; if by packet, at a less expense, in about fifty or sixty days.

Through his agent in London he is able to give the most careful attention to all orders from private individuals, Booksellers, and Public Institutions. An order for a single volume will always receive the same attention as larger orders.

ORDERS FORWARDED BY EVERY STEAMER,

And if the books can be readily procured, they will be received by return steamer.

FOREIGN PERIODICALS AND NEWSPAPERS.

All the leading Periodicals and Newspapers of the Continent supplied with punctuality and on the most reasonable terms. Subscribers at a distance will have their copies regularly mailed to their address.

BOOKS IMPORTED TO ORDER FROM LONDON, LEIPSIC, AND PARIS.

A CATALOGUE

OF A VERY EXTENSIVE COLLECTION OF

STANDARD WORKS,

IN EVERY DEPARTMENT OF LITERATURE, SCIENCE, AND ART,

MOSTLY ENGLISH EDITIONS,

NOW IN PRESS.

It will be sent gratis on application, POST PAID.

Country Booksellers supplied with all Foreign and American Publications at a small commission on cost, and all orders executed with despatch.

www.ingramcontent.com/pod-product-compliance
Lightning Source LLC
La Vergne TN
LVHW010154110826
845151LV00002B/517

9781425536510